Research Series on Responsible Enterprise Ecosystems

This book series focuses on sustainability, governance, and diversity in SMEs, small businesses, and startups. The series aims to unlock the potential of sustainability, governance, and diversity within SMEs, fostering a new era of responsible and inclusive entrepreneurship.

Delving into the challenges and opportunities of sustainable practices and governance in these organizations, it provides a platform for scholars, researchers, and practitioners to share their valuable insights and experiences. The series encourages and features innovative approaches, best practices, and real-life case studies, showcasing successful integration of sustainability, governance, and diversity principles. This diverse collection of knowledge will resonate with readers from various backgrounds, including law, management, accounting, CSR practices, and more, encouraging a cross-disciplinary dialogue. From circular economy models to gender diversity initiatives, the books offer pragmatic solutions for sustainable corporate governance. As the world navigates socio-economic and environmental crises, the series also emphasizes the resilience of SMEs in regenerating societies. By championing ethical conduct and inclusiveness, the series envisions SMEs as powerful drivers of positive change.

With each volume maintaining a coherent pedagogy and content style, the series is a must-have resource for educators, managers, entrepreneurs, and scholars alike.

Kouafilann A. Sory

Banking the Missing Middle

Risk, Distance, and SME Credit in the West African Monetary Union

Springer

Kouafilann A. Sory
Fidelis Finance Group
Ouagadougou, Burkina Faso

ISSN 3004-8834 ISSN 3004-8842 (electronic)
Research Series on Responsible Enterprise Ecosystems
ISBN 978-3-032-34581-3 ISBN 978-3-032-34582-0 (eBook)
https://doi.org/10.1007/978-3-032-34582-0

This Springer imprint is published by the registered company Springer Nature Switzerland AG
The registered company address is: Gewerbestrasse 11, 6330 Cham, Switzerland

This book is dedicated to:

In cherished memory of my mother, Katianicia Minata, and father, Tiemoko Sianhoua, whose faith, courage, and example continue to guide me, reminding me of the power of perseverance and the enduring importance of discipline, ethics, humility, and lifelong self-improvement.

Foreword

Few questions are more important to the future of African private-sector development than how to broaden access to productive finance for small and medium-sized enterprises. Across the continent, SMEs sustain commercial life, support employment, and serve as a bridge between microenterprises and larger formal firms. Yet many of them continue to face persistent barriers in formal credit markets.

This book addresses that challenge through the revealing case of Burkina Faso. In doing so, Dr. Kouafilann A. Sory makes a valuable contribution to a wider debate in banking and development finance. Rather than reducing the SME financing gap to a simple question of banker caution, he asks a more useful and more practical question: how do institutional structures, branch geography, information frictions, and lending practices shape the place of smaller firms within formal banking?

That shift in emphasis is one of the book's major strengths. It moves the discussion beyond abstract statements about risk and toward the real architecture of credit decisions. Banks do not lend in the abstract. They lend through procedures, information systems, approval chains, branch networks, and monitoring practices. When smaller firms are difficult to document, classify, or assess, access to finance becomes structurally constrained. This book shows why that institutional reality matters.

Its contribution is also important because it is grounded in original evidence and close attention to the banking environment in Burkina Faso. That national focus gives the study both specificity and wider relevance. The issues examined here—borrower opacity, relationship lending, local presence, and the challenge of financing the "missing middle"—extend well beyond one country. They are central to the effort to build more inclusive, more resilient, and more development-oriented financial systems across Africa.

For financial institutions, regulators, policymakers, and development practitioners, the message is timely. Expanding SME finance is not simply a matter of urging banks to lend more. It requires stronger information ecosystems, better borrower documentation, improved integration between branch-level knowledge and central approval processes, and lending approaches adapted to the realities of smaller firms while preserving sound risk management.

This is, therefore, a useful and policy-relevant book. It speaks not only to scholars of banking, finance, and development, but also to practitioners concerned with the practical challenge of widening access to credit without weakening prudential discipline. For that reason, it deserves careful attention.

Aboubakar Nacanabo

Minister of Economy and Finance
of Burkina Faso

President of the Council of the Ministers of Finance
of the West African Economic
and Monetary Union(WAEMU)

Chairman of the Board of Governors
of the Islamic Development Bank (IsDB)
Ouagadougou, Burkina Faso

Preamble

This book is a revised and expanded version of my PhD thesis, *Risk Aversion Behaviors in the Bank-SMEs Relationship: Predictors of Credit in Burkina Faso* (Franklin Hudson International School of Management, 2021). While the thesis provided the empirical foundation, this book has been substantially reframed for a broader scholarly and professional readership concerned with banking, development finance, regulation, and private-sector growth in West Africa. Its empirical core remains Burkina Faso. Its analytical and policy horizon, however, is the wider monetary and banking space of the *Union Monétaire Ouest Africaine* (UMOA).

That broader framing reflects both institutional logic and practical experience. The original study was conducted in Burkina Faso, using archival bank information and survey evidence from officers and managers directly involved in SME lending. Those data anchor the book's empirical claims. At the same time, the problems examined here are not unique to one national market. Over 25 years of executive practice in SME finance in Burkina Faso, and over the past decade in Côte d'Ivoire, alongside exposure to operations linked to Mali, Togo, and Benin, I have repeatedly encountered the same underlying tensions: weak borrower legibility, costly information production, branch-to-head-office frictions, collateral shortfalls, and a recurring gap between the economic importance of SMEs and their place in formal bank portfolios.

The regional extension of the book is therefore deliberate but disciplined. It does not claim to offer pooled statistical proof for all UMOA member states. It argues instead that evidence from Burkina Faso speaks to a broader banking space because the Union shares a common monetary authority, currency, and prudential architecture, as well as many of the same cross-border banking groups. In that setting, mechanisms can travel even when outcomes differ. The institutional question is not whether every market is identical. It is whether a common supervisory and banking environment reproduces comparable obstacles in the financing of smaller firms. This book answers that question cautiously but firmly in the affirmative.

Its central argument is that the scarcity of SME finance is explained inadequately by the language of abstract risk aversion alone. The deeper issue is institutional. Smaller firms are often economically important but administratively difficult to read. Where accounting records are thin, collateral is imperfect, and soft information remains trapped at the branch level, banks tend to retreat toward larger, more standardized, and easier-to-monitor clients. The missing middle in finance is therefore produced not only by prudence, but by the organization of prudence.

My hope is that this book will speak to more than one audience at once. It is written for scholars of banking, finance, and development, as well as for commercial bankers, regulators, central bankers, development finance practitioners, and policymakers working to widen access to productive credit without weakening discipline. If the book succeeds, it will do so by showing that better SME finance in West Africa does not begin with exhortation. It begins with better information, better organizational design, and a more realistic understanding of how banks decide.

Fidelis Finance Group
Ouagadougou, Burkina Faso

Kouafilann A. Sory

Acknowledgments This book has benefited from the generosity, encouragement, and support of some key persons.

My deepest thanks go to my family. I am especially grateful to my wife, Kady, for her unwavering support, and to my daughters, Katianicia and Yadia, whose love, assistance, and encouragement sustained me throughout the long journey from research to the publication of this book.

I express my deep gratitude to Professors Tobie de Coning and Cesar Baena for their guidance, intellectual generosity, and valuable advice during the formative stage of my PhD thesis.

I would also like to express my sincere appreciation to Dr. Brahim Anane for carefully reading the manuscript and for the wise and generous counsel he shared, drawn from his decades of proven experience as a bank CEO and his rich, diversified practice in SME lending spanning more than four decades. I am equally grateful to Dr. Adama Coulibaly, Minister of Economy, Finance and Budget of Côte d'Ivoire and a former UNDP Country Director, and to Christian Adovelande, former President of BOAD and EBID, for the richness of the insights they shared, drawn from their extensive and proven experience as policymakers in the field of economy and finance. Their comments and pragmatically grounded suggestions strengthened this book's practical and policy relevance.

My sincere thanks also go to the chief executive officers, managers, and bank officers in Burkina Faso who generously shared their time, data, and professional insights. I am especially grateful to the Board Directors and Managers of Fidelis Finance for their support and the practical perspectives they contributed to this work.

Finally, I wish to thank the administration, faculty, and fellow doctoral colleagues at the Franklin Hudson International School of Management for the stimulating academic environment in which this research first took shape.

Any remaining errors or omissions are my responsibility.

Competing Interests The author has no competing interests to declare that are relevant to the content of this manuscript.

Contents

1 **General Introduction** ... 1
1.1 From a Burkina Faso Dataset to a WAMU Argument ... 3
References ... 6

2 **The Economic Stakes of SME Finance in Burkina Faso and WAMU** ... 7
2.1 SMEs, Employment, and Structural Change ... 9
2.2 Innovation, Competitiveness, and Financing Capacity ... 12
2.3 Family Firms, Continuity, and Growth ... 15
2.4 Survival, Failure, and Financial Fragility ... 18
2.5 Bank Relationships and Enterprise Resilience ... 22
2.6 Managerial Capacity and the Productive Use of SME Finance ... 25
2.7 Synthesis ... 26
References ... 27

3 **Risk, Distance, and Information in a Shared Banking Space** ... 33
3.1 Psychological and Strategic Dimensions of Risk ... 36
3.2 Agency Theory and the Principal-Agent Problem ... 37
3.3 Risk Theory, Behavioral Finance, and Decision-Making under Uncertainty ... 41
3.4 Information Asymmetry in Banking ... 45
3.5 Information Asymmetry and Small and Medium-Sized Enterprises ... 50
3.6 Synthesis ... 53
References ... 54

4 **Banks, Branches, and Borrowers in Burkina Faso and the WAMU Banking Space** ... 59
4.1 A Resilient Economy Inside a Shared Monetary Union ... 59
4.2 Productive Strengths, Resources, and Demographic Potential ... 60
4.3 A Banking Sector that Is Broader, Stronger, and More Innovative than Older Accounts Imply ... 62

4.4 Fidelis Finance as a Practitioner Vignette: Product Innovation and SME Finance in Burkina Faso . . . 65
4.5 Burkina-Based Banking Brands and Their Weight in the WAMU Financial Space . . . 68
4.6 Digital Modernization and Regional Connectivity . . . 71
4.7 Why Burkina Faso Is a Revealing Case for This Book . . . 72
4.8 Synthesis . . . 73
References. . . 73

5 How Banks Decide in the WAMU Banking Space . . . 75
5.1 Technology in Lending Decisions . . . 77
5.2 Beyond Conventional Loans: Leasing, Factoring, Guarantees, and Risk-Capital Channels. . . 82
5.3 Information Technology and the Infrastructure of Credit Assessment. . . 83
5.4 Small and Medium Enterprise-Side Factors in Lending Decisions . . . 86
5.5 Managerial Capability and Borrower Legibility . . . 90
5.6 Bank-Side Factors, Lender Discretion, and Trust . . . 91
5.7 Emotional Intelligence, Soft Information, and Officer Behavior. . . 95
5.8 Behavioral Finance and Other Factors Related to Lending Decisions . . . 98
5.9 AI, Alternative Data, and the Future of SME Credit Decisions. . . 99
5.10 Synthesis . . . 100
References. . . 101

6 Data, Measurement, and Empirical Strategy: Burkina Faso Evidence, WAMU Relevance. . . 105
6.1 Research Philosophy and Methodological Choice . . . 107
6.2 Research Design. . . 109
6.3 Population, Sampling, and Fieldwork . . . 110
6.4 Instrumentation and Variable Construction . . . 111
6.5 Data Collection, Analysis, and Model Specification . . . 111
6.6 Reliability, Validity, and Research Ethics . . . 113
6.7 Synthesis . . . 115
References. . . 115

7 What Drives SME Lending? Evidence from Burkina Faso and Lessons for WAMU . . . 117
7.1 The Architecture of the Evidence . . . 119
7.2 Sample Composition and the Structure of Bank Involvement. . . 120
7.3 Geospatial Relationship. . . 122
7.4 Information Asymmetry. . . 126
7.5 Demographic Characteristics. . . 129
7.6 Bank Perception of SMEs . . . 130
7.7 Regional Lessons for WAMU . . . 131
Reference . . . 133

8 From Burkina Faso to WAMU: What Travels, What Varies 135
8.1 The Future of the Missing Middle: From Credit Rationing to Intelligent Credit Infrastructure 138
8.2 Final Synthesis: Takeaway Value and Contributions 139

Appendix A: Supplementary Diagnostics and Figures 143

Appendix B: SME Product Selection Logic 149

About the Author

Dr. Kouafilann A. Sory is a West African finance leader, entrepreneur, and institution builder whose career has been devoted to expanding access to capital and supporting enterprise growth across the region.

With more than thirty years of experience in banking, finance, investment, and development advisory, he is widely recognized for his strategic insight, his commitment to SME financing, and his role in promoting innovative financial instruments such as leasing, factoring, and private equity. For over two and a half decades, he has led Fidelis Finance, guiding its regional expansion and establishing it as a reference institution for business financing in the WAMU zone. He is also Chairman of AfriCapital Partners, a pan-African investment company he co-founded to back high-potential businesses and mobilize the capital required for their transformation.

Dr. Sory holds a PhD in International Business Administration, with a specialization in Behavioral Finance, from the Franklin Hudson International School of Management. His professional path includes senior responsibilities at the Central Bank of West African States (BCEAO), where he contributed to banking supervision and financial sector reform, as well as advisory assignments for leading international institutions, including the IFC (World Bank Group) and FMO Netherlands.

Beyond finance, he has held major leadership positions in regional and international bodies, including President of the WAEMU Regional Chamber of Commerce, First Vice-President of APBEF Burkina, member of the Institute of Directors in London, Senator of Junior Chamber International, and Charter President of the Saphir Lions Club of Ouagadougou. His outstanding contribution to economic development has earned him numerous national and international distinctions, among them the rank of Grand Officer of the Order of the Stallion of Burkina Faso.

List of Abbreviations

ATM	Automated teller machine
BCEAO	Central Bank of West African States (Banque Centrale des États de l'Afrique de l'Ouest)
BOAD	West African Development Bank (Banque Ouest Africaine de Développement)
EBID/BIDC	ECOWAS Bank for Investment and Development/Banque d'Investissement et de Développement de la CEDEAO
CFA	African Financial Community (Communauté Financière Africaine) The CFA franc (XOF) has a fixed exchange rate to Euro : €1= XOF 655.957
ECOWAS / CEDEAO	Economic Community Of West African States/ Communauté Économique des États de l'Afrique de l'Ouest
EBIS	Domestic systemically important banks / Établissements Bancaires d'Importance Systémique
EI	Emotional intelligence
GDP	Gross domestic product
IFC	International Finance Corporation
IMF	International Monetary Fund
MLR	Multiple linear regression
SME/SMEs	Small and medium-sized enterprise(s)
TBF	Theory of behavioral finance
UNDP	United Nations Development Programme
WAEMU/UEMOA	West African Economic and Monetary Union / Union Économique et Monétaire Ouest Africaine
WAMU/UMOA	West African Monetary Union (Union Monétaire Ouest Africaine)
VIF	Variance inflation factor

List of Figures

Fig. 2.1 Why SME finance matters: the economic transmission chain. Source: Author's conceptual synthesis . . . 25

Fig. 3.1 Burkina Faso's resilient productive base, shared WAMU architecture, and selective banking depth make it an empirical core for disciplined regional lessons. Source: Author's conceptual synthesis. . . . 35

Fig. 3.2 Agency theory and the principal-agent problem in SME lending. Legend: Agency theory explains SME lending as a delegated decision problem shaped by information asymmetry, adverse selection, moral hazard, and the institutional costs of controlling borrower behavior under uncertainty. Source: Author's conceptual synthesis based on agency theory, principal-agent theory, information asymmetry, and the discussion developed in Sect. 3.2. . . . 41

Fig. 3.3 Risk theory, behavioral finance, and decision-making under uncertainty. Legend: Bank risk appraisal combines measurable credit risk, perceived risk, behavioral interpretation, and institutional filters; SME exclusion may occur when these dimensions reinforce one another. Source: Author's conceptual synthesis based on risk theory, behavioral finance, decision-making under uncertainty, and the discussion developed in Sect. 3.3. . . . 44

Fig. 3.4 Information asymmetry in banking. Legend: Information asymmetry shapes banking decisions through adverse selection, moral hazard, and the institutional mechanisms used to transform borrower information into usable credit evidence. Source: Author's conceptual synthesis based on Sect. 3.4 and the banking literature on information asymmetry, adverse selection, and moral hazard. . . . 49

Fig. 3.5 The missing middle is not a simple funding gap. It emerges where risk, distance, and information combine to limit borrower legibility. Source: Author's conceptual synthesis based on Sect. 3.5, Information Asymmetry and Small and Medium-Sized Enterprises . . . 53

Fig. 4.1 Burkina Faso as a revealing banking case within WAMU. *Source: author's conceptual synthesis based on this section, a banking sector that is broader, stronger, and more innovative than older accounts imply* 65
Fig. 4.2 Cross-border banking footprint of Burkina-linked brands in WAMU. *Source: Author's conceptual synthesis based on this section, Burkina-based banking brands and their weight in the WAMU financial space* 71
Fig. 5.1 Banking missing middle: soft information, hard information, and lending technologies. *Author's conceptual synthesis based on Sect. 5.1* 80
Fig. 5.2 SME financing products and conditions of use. *Source: Author's synthesis based on his experience* 81
Fig. 5.3 The SME credit decision chain. *Source: author's conceptual synthesis based on this section, Information technology and the infrastructure of credit assessment* 83
Fig. 6.1 From Burkina Faso evidence to WAMU relevance: the architecture of inference. *Source: author's conceptual synthesis* 107
Fig. 7.1 What drives SME lending? A ranked architecture of explanations. *Source: author's conceptual synthesis based on this section, the architecture of the evidence* 120
Fig. 7.2 From Burkina Faso findings to WAMU lessons: what travels and what varies. Source: Author's conceptual synthesis based on Sect. 7.7 132
Fig. 8.1 How this book creates value for key stakeholders 140
Fig. A.1 Normal P-P plot of regression for geospatial relationship variables 145
Fig. A.2 Normal P-P plot of regression for information asymmetry variables 146
Fig. A.3 Normal P-P plot of regression for demographic variables 147
Fig. A.4 Normal P-P plot of regression for bank perception of small and medium enterprises 148
Fig. B.1 SME product selection logic under risk, distance, information, and collateral constraints. Source: Author's conceptual synthesis 149

List of Tables

Table 4.1 Country coverage of the 13 Burkina-present cross-border brands in WAMU, end-2024 . . . 68
Table 4.2 Union-wide footprint of the 11 banking groups present in Burkina Faso, end-2024. . . . 69
Table 4.3 Union-wide footprint of the two nonbank financial brands present in Burkina Faso, end-2024. . . . 69
Table 4.4 Consolidated weight of the 13 Burkina-present cross-border brands in WAMU, end-2024 . . . 70
Table 4.5 Banking-only weight of the 11 banking groups in WAMU, end-2024 . . . 70
Table 5.1 A practical reading of emotional intelligence in SME lending. . . . 97
Table 7.1 Institutional composition of the sample. . . . 121
Table 7.2 Branch network distribution by location . . . 123
Table 7.3 Criteria used to define and target SME clients. . . . 123
Table 7.4 Location of key loan-processing functions. . . . 124
Table 7.5 Reported drivers of bank involvement in SME finance . . . 125
Table 7.6 Additional geospatial indicators used in the analysis. . . . 125
Table 7.7 Geospatial model of SME lending intensity. . . . 125
Table 7.8 Information conditions in SME credit assessment . . . 127
Table 7.9 Reported sources of reliable borrower information . . . 127
Table 7.10 Perceived relevance of rating and information systems . . . 128
Table 7.11 Information-asymmetry model of SME lending intensity . . . 128
Table 7.12 Professional profile of lending staff in the sample. . . . 129
Table 7.13 Reported importance of competencies and emotional intelligence . . . 130
Table 7.14 Demographic model of SME lending intensity . . . 130
Table 7.15 Bank-level and officer-level perceptions of SMEs. . . . 131
Table 7.16 Perception model of SME lending intensity. . . . 131

Table A.1 Collinearity diagnostics for the geospatial model 143
Table A.2 Collinearity diagnostics for the information-asymmetry model 144
Table A.3 Collinearity diagnostics for the demographic model 144
Table A.4 Collinearity diagnostics for the perception model 144

Chapter 1
General Introduction

Across the West African Monetary Union (WAMU), hundreds of thousands of firms remain too large for microfinance yet too small, distant, or opaque for conventional bank lending. Commonly referred to as small and medium-sized enterprises (SMEs), they occupy the missing middle. However, defining an SME remains problematic: definitions vary not only across WAMU member states but also from one bank to another. In the absence of a unanimously accepted definition, several thresholds are nevertheless widely shared: total assets of up to XOF 1 billion, annual turnover of up to XOF 3 billion, and up to 250 employees. This book uses these thresholds only as indicative reference points. These firms are central to employment, trade, and local production networks and often represent the most dynamic layer of domestic private initiative. Yet their access to formal bank credit remains persistently constrained. This contradiction forms the starting point of the present book. The issue is no longer whether SMEs matter to the region's economies; their importance is beyond dispute. The real question is why firms so essential to jobs, commerce, and economic diversification continue to stand at the margins of the formal banking system. The central question is not whether SMEs need finance, but how banks and specialized financial institutions can transform SME activity into credible, monitorable, and financeable information.

This book examines that problem through the empirical case of Burkina Faso and interprets it within the wider banking and monetary space of WAMU. That formulation is deliberate. The statistical evidence presented here comes solely from Burkina Faso. The research draws on archival bank information and survey evidence from officers and managers directly involved in SME lending in Ouagadougou and Bobo-Dioulasso. The study, therefore, does not claim to estimate credit allocation patterns across all member states of the Union. What it does claim is that the mechanisms identified in Burkina Faso—organizational distance, information frictions, branch geography, screening constraints, and the unequal conversion of soft information into formal approval—are plausibly relevant across a regional banking space governed by common institutions and populated by many of the same cross-border banking groups.

K. A. Sory, *Banking the Missing Middle*, Research Series on Responsible Enterprise Ecosystems, https://doi.org/10.1007/978-3-032-34582-0_1

That distinction is central to the method and to the ambition of the book. A weak version of regionalization would simply universalize a national case and assume away variation. This book does not take that route. Instead, it treats Burkina Faso as an analytically revealing case within a common monetary and supervisory architecture. WAMU is not a metaphorical region stitched together after the fact. It is an institutional space structured by a shared central bank, a shared currency, and a shared banking supervision framework. Those common arrangements do not erase national differences in market depth, sectoral composition, legal enforcement, security conditions, or the pace of financial deepening. But they do create a sufficiently integrated environment to justify a regional conversation about how banks encounter, classify, and ration credit to smaller firms.

The central argument is straightforward. SME credit scarcity is explained inadequately by the familiar language of banker caution alone. Banks do not lend or refuse in the abstract. They lend through routines, branch networks, approval hierarchies, documentation requirements, internal data systems, and repeated judgments under uncertainty. Small firms are often not excluded because they are unproductive in principle, but because they are expensive to know. They leave weaker documentary traces, offer less standardized collateral, and require more effort to interpret. Under those conditions, the financing gap appears not simply as a shortage of appetite, but as a failure of institutional legibility. The missing middle in finance arises when economically important firms cannot be translated into decision-quality banking information at an acceptable cost.

This institutional reading matters for three reasons. First, it alters the diagnosis. If the main obstacle were only the subjective psychology of loan officers, reform would center on attitudes. If the obstacle lies more deeply in how banks gather, process, and transmit information, then the relevant reforms concern organization, measurement, delegation, and monitoring. Second, it alters the scale of the debate. SME finance ceases to be a narrow product question and becomes a problem of market architecture: who can be seen, who can be scored, who can be monitored, and on what terms. Third, it alters the argument's regional relevance. Once the problem is framed as one of institutional design, the fact that WAMU member states share supervisory and monetary structures becomes analytically significant, even where national lending outcomes remain uneven.

Burkina Faso offers an especially useful empirical core for this argument. It combines a strong economic dependence on smaller firms with a banking system in which formal credit remains selective. The original study on which this book is based gathered evidence from 127 officers and managers and combined it with bank-level archival data. One of its key descriptive findings was that SME lending represented roughly one-third of the observed lending totals over the period examined. This is an important point. The book is not about total exclusion. SMEs are present in formal portfolios. The problem is that their presence remains limited, unevenly distributed, and highly contingent on banks' management of uncertainty.

The empirical findings yield a clear hierarchy of explanations. The strongest results concern bank organization and branch geography. Bank classification and local branch presence are far more powerful predictors of SME lending intensity than the demographic profile of loan officers. Information frictions matter as well, but more selectively. Perceptions of SMEs matter too, but not in a way that displaces the primacy of organizational structure. The implication is that the financing problem is not best understood as a story about bankers' personal conservatism. It is better understood as a problem of organizational capacity, informational infrastructure, and the uneven distribution of proximity between banks and firms.

That conclusion travels beyond one country, but it must travel carefully. WAMU member states share the same monetary authority and a common prudential and supervisory space, yet they do not share identical banking outcomes. Credit concentration, financial depth, sectoral specialization, digital uptake, competition, and enforcement costs vary. For that reason, this book does not collapse the Union into a single empirical market. It advances a more precise claim: The mechanisms documented in Burkina Faso are likely to recur across WAMU because the same broad institutional architecture shapes interactions among banks, documentation, and smaller firms. The book, therefore, offers regional lessons rather than pooled regional estimates.

The regional perspective is also strengthened by practice. The author's professional experience in SME finance across Burkina Faso and Côte d'Ivoire, as well as exposure to operations linked to Mali, Togo, and Benin, repeatedly reveals the same practical tensions that the Burkina Faso data bring into analytic focus. These include the mistrust between lenders and borrowers, the weakness of standardized SME accounting information, the difficulty of reconciling branch-level knowledge with head-office approval systems, and the tendency of prudentially sound banks to favor firms that are easier to classify rather than firms that are merely economically important. This experience is not presented here as substitute evidence. It is used as regional banking intelligence to help explain why the empirical case resonates beyond its place of collection.

The book contributes to three overlapping conversations. It contributes to the literature on SME finance by showing that the missing middle problem is not simply a demand-side funding gap, but a bank-side problem of information processing and organizational design. It contributes to the literature on relationship lending by demonstrating that proximity is not merely interpersonal; it is spatial, institutional, and procedural. And it contributes to African banking and development finance by grounding these debates in original evidence from Burkina Faso while placing them within the wider WAMU space, where banking supervision, the monetary authority, and many banking groups already operate regionally.

1.1 From a Burkina Faso Dataset to a WAMU Argument

The answer is not that all member states are the same. They are not. The answer is that the book's regional claim operates at the level of mechanisms and institutional lessons rather than at the level of pooled coefficients. Because the Union shares a common monetary authority, a common currency, and a common banking supervision framework, banks across the space confront SMEs through related prudential logics and broadly comparable informational constraints. Where firms remain hard to document, where branch knowledge is difficult to escalate, and where approval systems privilege standardized evidence, the same kinds of exclusionary outcomes can emerge even if their magnitude differs by country.

This is why the book deliberately separates three levels of argument. The empirical core is Burkina Faso. The analytical frame is WAMU. The policy horizon is regional. Once those levels are distinguished, the contribution becomes both more modest and more useful. It does not pretend to have proven identical outcomes across West Africa. Instead, it shows how a national case can illuminate a common regional challenge in the financing of productive enterprise.

The contribution is also methodological. A recurring weakness in discussions of regional SME finance is the temptation either to remain trapped within isolated national cases or to generalize far beyond the evidence. This book tries to avoid both errors. It remains explicit about its empirical boundaries, but it also treats institutional commonality as analytically meaningful. The argument does not claim that Burkina Faso statistically represents all eight member states. It says that a rigorously specified case can illuminate a shared regional problem when the mechanisms under study are embedded in common institutions.

From that perspective, the normative stakes become clear. Better SME finance in WAMU will not come from exhorting banks to abandon prudence. Nor will it come from romanticizing small firms or assuming that all rejected borrowers are viable. The task is more demanding. It is to improve the systems through which banks learn about, verify, monitor, and decide on smaller firms. That requires stronger borrower documentation, better internal data systems, more credible use of credit information infrastructures, better integration between branch-level knowledge and head-office approval processes, and lending technologies adapted to firms that are economically central but administratively thin.

One further implication follows from this framing. The book is concerned with the quality of financial intermediation, not only with its volume. A banking system may grow quickly in assets, deposits, and digital reach, yet still leave a large part of the productive middle class weakly served. That possibility is central to the West African story. The policy challenge is therefore not only to make finance larger, but to make it more capable of recognizing viable firms before they become either too distressed or too large to need relationship-based support. The missing middle is a problem of timing as much as one of access: Many firms need finance at the stage when they are emerging, formalizing, and building credibility, precisely when conventional systems tend to find them hardest to read.

That distinction also matters because the "missing middle" is not simply a problem of too little money in the system. Across the Union, banks have accumulated deposits, strengthened prudential ratios, expanded branch networks, and increasingly participated in cross-border groups. Yet many SMEs remain outside the range of borrowers who can be comfortably classified within standardized lending routines. The book, therefore, asks a more demanding question than whether banks are liquid enough to lend. It asks how a banking system that is deeper, more formalized, and more regionally integrated still produces a persistent gap between economically important firms and the kinds of borrowers that formal finance finds easiest to serve (Abraham & Schmukler, 2017).

Seen in that light, the contribution of the book is threefold. Empirically, it is anchored in original evidence drawn from Burkina Faso's principal banking centers, where loan officers, managers, and institutional records reveal how SME lending is screened, structured, and constrained. Conceptually, it shifts the center of gravity away from a narrow language of banker psychology and toward a broader account of organizational prudence, branch geography, information frictions, and the internal architecture of credit approval. Practically, it speaks to a wide audience—commercial banks, regulators, central bankers, development finance institutions, and SME-support ecosystems—by asking what would have to change for more firms to become prudently financeable rather than rhetorically celebrated but institutionally excluded (Berger & Udell, 2006; Brixiová et al., 2020).

The regional framing follows from WAMU's institutional structure. The Union combines a common monetary authority, shared prudential rules, and the growing presence of the same banking groups across national markets. This does not erase national variation. Credit depth, competitive intensity, borrower structure, and digital maturity differ across member states. But it does mean that the mechanisms examined here are not idiosyncratic. They travel across a common banking space in which distance, legibility, collateral quality, and information-processing capacity continue to shape who receives credit and under what terms. The result is a book that remains disciplined about what the Burkina Faso evidence proves, while remaining ambitious about what that evidence helps us understand regionally.

For that reason, the book should not be read as a plea for indiscriminate credit expansion. Its argument is more exacting. The objective is not to weaken prudential discipline, but to improve the institutions through which prudence is exercised. If banks can generate more credible information on smaller borrowers, if branch knowledge can travel upward without being lost, and if credit technologies can better accommodate firms that are viable but administratively thin, then the domain of financeable enterprise can widen without abandoning sound banking principles. In that sense, the book is about how to make prudence more intelligent rather than less demanding (Berger & Udell, 2002; Angori et al., 2019).

The chapters that follow develop this argument in sequence. Chapter 2 explains why SME finance is a structural economic issue rather than a niche banking issue. Chapter 3 lays out the conceptual framework, centered on agency theory, information asymmetry, and relationship lending. Chapter 4 situates the discussion within Burkina Faso's banking landscape and the wider WAMU setting. Chapter 5 examines how banks decide, with special attention to lending technologies, hard and soft information, and institutional judgment under uncertainty. Chapter 6 explains the architecture of the evidence and clarifies the scope of inference. Chapter 7 presents the empirical results and ranks the main explanations. Chapter 8 returns to the book's regional horizon, asking what Burkina Faso's evidence can legitimately teach us about financing the missing middle across WAMU.

References

Abraham, F., & Schmukler, S. L. (2017). *Addressing the SME finance problem*. World Bank Research and Policy Briefs. http://documents1.worldbank.org/curated/en/809191507620842321/pdf/Addressing-the-SME-finance-problem.pdf

Angori, G., Aristei, D., & Gallo, M. (2019). Lending technologies, banking relationships, and firms' access to credit in Italy: The role of firm size. *Applied Economics, 51*(58), 6139–6170. https://doi.org/10.1080/00036846.2019.1613503

Berger, A. N., & Udell, G. N. (2002). Small business credit availability and relationship lending: The importance of bank organization structure. *The Economic Journal, 112*(477), 32–53. https://doi.org/10.1111/1468-0297.00682

Berger, A. N., & Udell, G. N. (2006). A more complete conceptual framework for SME finance. *Journal of Banking & Finance, 30*(11), 2945–2966. https://doi.org/10.1016/j.jbankfin.2006.05.008

Brixiová, Z., Kangoye, T., & Yogo, T. U. (2020). Access to finance among small and medium-sized enterprises and job creation in Africa. *Structural Change and Economic Dynamics, 55*, 177–189. https://doi.org/10.1016/j.strueco.2020.08.008

Chapter 2
The Economic Stakes of SME Finance in Burkina Faso and WAMU

Small and medium-sized enterprises (SMEs) matter in Burkina Faso, and for many of the same reasons they matter across the West African Monetary Union (WAMU): They occupy the space between subsistence activity and large-scale capital, generate employment, sustain local commerce, and often serve as the first institutional form through which entrepreneurship becomes economically visible. Burkina Faso is the empirical core of this book, but the economic stakes considered in this chapter extend beyond a single country, as smaller firms play a similar intermediary role across the Union's monetary and banking space.

This chapter argues that SME finance is economically important not simply because small firms are numerous, but because credit constraints alter the trajectory of the entire sector. When SMEs lack reliable access to finance, they do not merely grow more slowly. They invest less, hire less, modernize less, and become more vulnerable to interruption, competition, and failure. In this sense, the problem of SME finance is not a narrow banking issue. It is a question about the organization of growth.

The chapter, therefore, operates on two levels at once. At the level of evidence, it remains anchored in Burkina Faso. At the level of interpretation, it asks why SME underfinancing matters for economies in which a relatively narrow layer of large firms coexists with a wide base of small businesses that remain structurally underbanked. That broader lens is essential if the Burkina Faso case is to yield disciplined regional lessons rather than merely local description.

The economic role of SMEs is usually first observed through employment. Small firms absorb labor, create entry points into formal and semiformal business activity, and widen the productive base beyond a limited circle of large clients. Their contribution is especially important in economies where wage employment is scarce and where large firms alone cannot generate broad-based opportunities (Ayandibu & Houghton, 2017; Brixiová et al., 2020). Yet the value of SMEs extends beyond job creation. They also contribute to market dynamism. They bring new products, new services, and new forms of commercial adaptation into local economies. In settings

K. A. Sory, *Banking the Missing Middle*, Research Series on Responsible Enterprise Ecosystems, https://doi.org/10.1007/978-3-032-34582-0_2

characterized by structural constraints, they often serve as the most flexible component of the productive system.

That flexibility, however, should not be romanticized. Smaller firms are also fragile. Their margins are thinner, their reserves smaller, and their ability to absorb shocks more limited. For that reason, the question of finance is central. A large firm may survive a period of weak sales by drawing on accumulated capital, established collateral, or long-standing lender confidence. A smaller firm often cannot. The same downturn that is manageable for a large borrower may become existential for a small one.

This is why access to credit matters so much. Credit is not only a source of expansion capital. For SMEs, it can also be working capital, liquidity insurance, a bridge through volatility, or the difference between temporary difficulty and permanent closure. The absence of finance, therefore, has cumulative effects. It delays investment, weakens productivity, discourages technology adoption, narrows strategic choices, and reduces the firm's ability to respond to competition. Where formal lending is difficult to obtain, firms may remain trapped in a low-investment equilibrium: too small to generate the documentation banks prefer, and too underfinanced to become the kind of business banks are willing to support.

Seen from this perspective, the relationship between finance and innovation becomes clearer. Innovation in small firms should not be treated as a separate heroic narrative of entrepreneurship. It is often conditional on financing capacity. Firms adopt new technologies, improve processes, professionalize management, and enter new markets when they possess the financial resources to do so. Where financing is scarce, innovation becomes selective, delayed, or impossible. The relevant issue, therefore, is not whether SMEs can be innovative in principle. It is whether the financial environment allows innovation to move from aspiration to practice.

The same applies to organizational form. Many SMEs are family-managed or built around tight interpersonal networks. In some cases, that can enhance continuity, trust, and strategic flexibility. But it does not remove the financing problem. If anything, it often intensifies the overlap between business reputation, personal wealth, informal governance, and borrowing capacity. For banks, this means that the boundary between the firm and the owner may appear blurred. For the firm, access to formal finance may depend heavily on the legibility of its accounts, the credibility of its owner, and the quality of its relationship with lenders.

This leads directly to the question of survival. SMEs fail for many reasons, but financial fragility is one of the most consequential. Smaller firms are exposed to multiple pressures at once: competition, thin capitalization, operational volatility, limited managerial slack, and weak buffers against economic shocks. When access to finance is added to this list, the effects are magnified. A firm that cannot secure liquidity when revenues fall, cannot finance inventory when demand returns, or cannot refinance short-term strain may not survive long enough to become efficient.

Failure, in other words, is not just a business outcome. It is also an informational outcome. Where firms cannot produce the kinds of records banks trust, or where banks cannot collect enough reliable information to distinguish promising firms from risky ones, caution becomes systematic. Under those conditions, small firms do not face isolated refusals; they face an environment in which financing is structurally harder to obtain. That environment does not merely sort firms into good and bad. It can also penalize potentially viable firms that remain opaque to lenders.

This is why bank relationships matter. For SMEs, relationships with banks are not peripheral. They are often among the few mechanisms by which uncertainty can be reduced over time. Repeated interactions allow lenders to observe repayment behavior, managerial discipline, and business continuity. They enable the production of soft information that rarely appears in formal statements. In difficult times, these relationships can become even more important. Firms with stronger ties to lenders may be better positioned to negotiate, explain temporary difficulties, or maintain access to credit when conditions deteriorate (Iwanicz-Drozdowska et al., 2018; Berger & Udell, 2002).

The question is particularly important in Burkina Faso. The existing literature says much about the economic importance of SMEs in general, but far less about how SME survival, financing constraints, and bank relationships interact in this specific national setting. That gap matters. Burkina Faso is not just another instance of a generic SME problem. It is a case in which small firms operate within a banking environment marked by selective credit allocation, informational frictions, and uneven access to formal finance.

The central implication of this chapter is straightforward. The economic significance of SMEs is inseparable from the financial conditions under which they operate. Where credit is scarce, expensive, opaque, or relationally restricted, the developmental contribution of SMEs is narrowed. Where banks can process uncertainty more effectively, smaller firms are better able to survive, invest, and contribute to the economy beyond subsistence. The problem of SME finance is therefore not secondary to development. It is one of its institutional foundations.

2.1 SMEs, Employment, and Structural Change

SMEs are an important part of the economy. Researchers have noted the important role of SMEs in increasing job creation and gross domestic product (GDP) shares (Kersten et al., 2017; Mandl & Patrini, 2018). Kumar (2017) reported that SMEs accounted for at least 50% of jobs in various developing countries. The author noted that SMEs facilitated job creation, especially of better and more inclusive jobs (Kumar, 2017). As such, Kumar highlighted the need to support this sector, given SMEs' significant contribution to broader economic development. In addition, Pichler noted the key role of SMEs in job creation.

Viewing this topic from a socioeconomic perspective, Pichler described the significant role of SMEs in job creation and economic dynamics. A review of both theoretical and empirical literature on SMEs and their roles in business settings shows that SMEs are driving forces of structural change and a "stabilizing factor for safeguarding a given economic setting with its institutional framework in the dynamics of change." Pichler further noted the need to highlight the current role of

SMEs in the labor market and welfare. Similarly, Yazdanfar and Öhman underscored findings on the vital role of SMEs in firm-level growth and job creation, drawing on Swedish SME data. The authors examined the link between firm sales growth and employment levels as a proxy for SME job creation. Gathering data from 2009 to 2012, the authors analyzed information on 13,548 Swedish SMEs across four industry sectors.

Their findings showed that successful SMEs created the most jobs across all industries. The findings showed that growth, as measured by revenue, was a competitive advantage among SMEs and was positively and significantly associated with the number of employees hired by the sampled Swedish SMEs. In addition to growth, as measured by revenue, factors of age and size were also found to be positively and significantly associated with the number of employees hired by the sampled SMEs (Yazdanfar & Öhman, 2018).

Similarly, Brixiová et al. (2020) noted the impact of SMEs on job creation in sub-Saharan Africa. The authors examined SME-level data from 42 African countries. Their findings showed that SMEs' ability to create jobs increased with available funding and firm size. Thus, Brixiová et al. proposed increased access to funding for SMEs in Africa, especially because SMEs in African countries were constrained from creating more jobs due to a lack of formal financing. Jang (2018) added to these findings and noted that, in addition to increased funding for SMEs, governments also needed to support SMEs through policies. The author focused on Korea's manufacturing sector. Specifically, Jang examined the association of SME and government policy factors with the creation of new employment.

Jang gathered and analyzed survey data from 2828 SME manufacturing firms in Korea from 2013 to 2015. The findings showed that, aside from financial factors, the Korean government's policies significantly contributed to job creation by SMEs. This body of findings provided significant information on SMEs' contributions to job creation across countries (Brixiová et al., 2020; Jang, 2018). These findings highlighted the need for increased support and financing options targeted at SMEs, which could propel economies in developing countries, such as those in Africa.

SMEs may be small compared to corporations, but they have significant value due to employment creation (Nure et al., 2020). As such, Nure et al. further added to the findings of Brixiová et al. and Yazdanfar and Öhman. Nure et al. examined tourism SMEs and found that these businesses can help address labor deficits in their respective countries. Similarly, Nure et al. underscored the need for bank managers to provide more support to the SME sector, as increased financing would maximize job creation and enhance productivity within tourism SMEs. This body of findings highlighted the importance of SMEs to the economy, especially their role in driving growth through job creation. This vital knowledge showed that SMEs could be used as a strategy to improve the socioeconomic standing of various countries, which could be highly beneficial during economic crises (Kersten et al., 2017; Mandl & Patrini, 2018).

More research has shown the impact of SMEs on employment rates, especially in economic crisis settings. According to the literature, increases in the number of SMEs have resulted in higher employment levels. Hlahane (2018) reported similar findings in his study, which investigated the economic impact of SMEs on Johannesburg's local economy, where socioeconomic issues prevail.

The author concluded that SMEs need government support, as the SME sector helps meet citizens' needs by providing employment opportunities (Hlahane, 2018). Kersten et al. reported similar findings in a systematic review of the effectiveness of SME finance. The authors also conducted a multivariate meta-analysis. The results showed a positive and significant association between SME finance and capital investment, firm performance, and employment rates. SMEs significantly contributed to economic development, especially in low- and middle-income countries. Ayandibu and Houghton explained this phenomenon when exploring the role and impact of SMEs in local economic development. Ayandibu and Houghton, like previous authors, concluded that SMEs employed more labor-intensive production processes than corporations (Hlahane, 2018; Kersten et al., 2017).

Hence, SMEs tended to have larger workforces than other businesses (Ayandibu & Houghton, 2017). This body of knowledge showed how the SME sector contributed to workforce growth and job creation, thereby accelerating economic development. According to Yazdanfar and Öhman, various firm-level factors can affect job creation in SMEs. In addition to sales growth, size, and SME age, Fakieh et al. and Liu et al. added that technology within SMEs impacted job creation. For instance, Liu et al. examined Korean SMEs to explore the association between organizational capabilities and job creation. The authors collected survey data from 414 SMEs and found that technological and manufacturing capabilities significantly increased firms' export growth, thereby increasing job creation (Liu et al., 2019). Additionally, other work concluded similar findings when examining the impact of SMEs and cloud computing on the national economy and global competitiveness.

Fakieh et al. noted that the use of cloud-based services and technologies significantly improved business innovation, thereby increasing SMEs' competitive advantages. The authors examined SMEs in Australia that had adopted cloud computing, noting increased job creation following its adoption (Fakieh et al., 2016). These findings showed that technology is a key driver of job creation within SMEs. The development and implementation of innovative technologies could increase job creation rates within SMEs, yielding positive results for economic development.

The employment significance of SMEs should be understood in both structural and numerical terms. Smaller firms do not merely add jobs at the margin; they enlarge the kinds of economic participation available in an economy. They create spaces for apprenticeship, self-employment, trading intermediation, local service provision, processing, logistics, and early-stage formalization. In countries where the number of large firms remains limited, this layered employment function is economically decisive. It widens access to income, creates managerial learning, and helps distribute the gains of growth beyond a narrow cluster of capital-intensive firms. For Burkina Faso and similar WAMU markets, the labor-market importance of SMEs is therefore inseparable from questions of domestic diversification and social inclusion (Ayandibu & Houghton, 2017; Brixiová et al., 2020).

Employment effects also explain SME finance's macroeconomic relevance. A firm that secures working capital can stabilize payroll, maintain inventories, and continue purchasing from suppliers. A firm that fails to secure it may shed labor long before it formally exits the market. In that sense, access to finance changes the quality and durability of employment, not just the volume of loans on bank balance sheets. The missing middle in finance is thus also a missing middle in employment formation: Too many firms are large enough to matter for jobs, but too small or opaque to fit the lending templates most banks prefer (Abraham & Schmukler, 2017; Kumar, 2017).

2.2 Innovation, Competitiveness, and Financing Capacity

Innovation in SMEs is a key driver of firm growth. Scholars have underscored the role of innovation in driving SME growth (Colclough et al., 2019; Genc et al., 2019). Colclough et al. explored this topic in their investigation of Norwegian export SMEs and SME innovation. Using a quantitative approach, Colclough et al. found that SMEs' innovation orientation was significantly associated with SME performance. Their results also revealed that ambidextrous SMEs had the strongest innovation performance, leading to increased market growth and advantages. The authors further underscored the importance of ambition and entrepreneurial capability within SMEs, as these characteristics positively enhance innovation. Hughes et al. concurred with these findings in their examination of young technology-based SME firms in incubators. Similarly, Hughes et al. underscored the importance of enhancing innovation ambidexterity within firms to develop strategic success. This body of findings showed the impact of innovation within SME firms; SME innovation might lead to positive performance results. Furthermore, these findings showed that SME innovation was driven most strongly by entrepreneurial ability and ambition (Colclough et al., 2019; Hughes et al., 2020).

Technological innovation is a vital aspect of SME innovation; SME firms can improve performance both internally and externally (Chege & Wang, 2020; Kallmuenzer & Scholl-Grissemann, 2017). For instance, Chege and Wang conducted a literature review on this topic, examining information technology innovation and its impact on job creation by SMEs in developing countries (Chege & Wang, 2020).

Using the seven-step approach, Chege and Wang (2020) gathered and synthesized relevant data on this topic. Their findings showed that technology innovations significantly impacted job creation rates in SMEs. The authors identified technology innovation as a driving force for economic development within SMEs. Technology innovation increases SME competitiveness, including access to international markets. Kallmuenzer and Scholl-Grissemann also conducted a study on this topic, identifying two categories of SME innovation: technological and managerial. The authors employed a knowledge-based perspective and examined the impacts of these types of firm innovations on performance. The authors gathered data from 152 manufacturing family SMEs based in Germany, Austria, and Switzerland. Their findings showed that family firm innovation had a key role in SME growth and opportunities. The authors also found that only through technological innovation could SME managers capitalize on product and process innovation (Kallmuenzer & Scholl-Grissemann, 2017). This body of literature has shown the importance of innovation within SMEs in driving growth and expansion opportunities. Technological innovation needs to be a focus for SME firms to drive significant growth and performance improvements.

Innovation is a key driver for SME performance. According to the literature, the extent of firms' innovation is significantly correlated to their business performance. Prange and Pinho (2017) examined this topic further among SME firms, presenting their international performance and the factors and drivers of that performance. The authors took a resource-based view of 120 selected SME exporting firms based in Portugal. Their findings showed a significant effect of innovation on organizational performance. Makri et al. concurred, reporting similar findings and highlighting the importance of fostering innovation in SMEs. Similarly, Makri et al. examined the antecedents and performance outcomes of export innovativeness. The authors gathered and analyzed data from 168 SME direct exporters. Their findings revealed that firm innovativeness was significantly and positively associated with export performance (Makri et al., 2017), which was consistent with Prange and Pinho's findings. Makri et al. added to this finding by outlining the following factors that affected the degree of innovativeness among SME firms: decentralization in decision-making, export market orientation, information exchange, and export market dynamism. This body of findings showed a significant positive link between firm innovativeness and performance, particularly among exporting SMEs. More research is needed on the associations among these factors in African SMEs.

Given the importance of innovation in SMEs, SME owners face financial constraints that significantly affect their ability to develop innovative processes and products. According to the literature, various SMEs face financial constraints that deter their innovation efforts. The authors underscored the importance of supporting SMEs facing financing constraints, as SME innovations during economic crises are vital (Madrid-Guijarro et al., 2016). The authors conducted an in-depth analysis of the factors affecting innovation to provide insight into the types of financing constraints that limited innovation in SMEs. The authors conducted a literature review, gathering and analyzing prior research on innovation, financial constraints, and SME characteristics. The authors then employed a quantitative approach, gathering survey data from 267 SMEs based in Spain. The results revealed that financial constraints had a significant negative effect on innovation within SMEs, especially during economic crises. The authors proposed developing long-term banking relationships, which might mitigate SMEs' financial constraints and enhance their capacity for innovation (Madrid-Guijarro et al., 2016).

Lööf and Nabavi (2016) noted similarly in their examination of evidence from Swedish exporting firms. The authors also focused on innovation and financial constraints in SMEs, using data from only 8300 exporting SMEs in Sweden. The findings showed that financial or credit constraints negatively affected innovation within firms, including cash holdings, cash flow, and debt in SMEs (Lööf & Nabavi, 2016). Similarly, Lööf and Nabavi underscored the significant role of innovation in SMEs, especially during economic crises. Lööf and Nabavi found that innovation within SMEs, particularly in high-technology sectors, may offset the negative impact of financial shocks during economic crises. This body of knowledge highlighted the importance of innovation in SME firms, which may be hindered by financial constraints. This potential hindrance to innovation needs to be addressed, as innovation within SMEs can offset the negative effects of economic downturns.

Researchers have also underscored the need to enhance innovation performance within SMEs, specifically by strengthening financial capacity in this sector. For one, Božić and Rajh (2016) found that financial constraints are a barrier to innovation for SMEs. The authors examined this topic, focusing on the factors constraining the innovation performance of 94 SMEs in Croatia. The authors gathered data from the selected firms via an online survey, and their findings showed that the firms were constrained by three major external factors. Analyzing the results, the authors found that two of the three major external factors were associated with a high intensity of financial constraints on SME firms' internal innovation activities. Božić and Rajh also identified organizational constraints as a barrier to the SME firms' innovation. Maldonado-Guzmán et al. concurred with these findings, employing evidence from SMEs based in Mexico. The authors of the study, like Božić and Rajh, explored the barriers to innovation in SMEs. Maldonado-Guzmán et al. gathered and analyzed 308 responses from service SMEs in the state of Aguascalientes, Mexico, using a researcher-developed instrument adapted from the literature. The findings showed three major barriers to innovation in SMEs in Mexico: external/environmental, financial, and human barriers (Maldonado-Guzmán et al., 2017). These findings provided additional empirical evidence on barriers to innovation in SMEs. Various barriers limit innovation within SMEs; however, financial constraints consistently pose a major hindrance.

To sum up, innovation in the SME segment should not be reduced to frontier technology or patentable inventions. For many firms in West Africa, innovation is more practical and cumulative: better inventory management, improved transport coordination, digitized payments, new sourcing relationships, revised packaging, or the gradual professionalization of accounting and customer management. These forms of innovation may look modest compared with large firms' capital expenditure, but they are often the mechanisms through which smaller firms raise productivity, improve margins, and survive competition. Their diffusion matters because they shape whether domestic firms remain trapped in low-capital routines or begin to scale into more durable enterprises (Addae-Boateng & Dzisi, 2016; Chege & Wang, 2020).

Yet these innovations are rarely self-financing. They require time, working capital, modest investment, and enough organizational slack for experimentation. Where firms operate permanently at the edge of liquidity, they innovate defensively rather than strategically. They patch, postpone, and improvise rather than upgrade. This is why credit conditions matter for competitiveness. Short maturities, excessive collateral demands, or recurrent refusals do not merely reduce the amount borrowed. They alter the horizon within which the firm can act, often forcing entrepreneurs to prioritize immediate survival over investments that would make the business more productive, more visible, and, eventually, more bankable (Belas et al., 2017; Abraham & Schmukler, 2017).

2.3 Family Firms, Continuity, and Growth

Various SMEs are run by families. According to the literature, there are many advantages of family involvement in SMEs. Breckova (2016) examined this topic in the context of family businesses in the Czech Republic. The author captured respondents' perceptions of the barriers facing family businesses and of the advantages associated with family-owned SMEs. Breckova conducted quantitative surveys among 505 respondents based in the Czech Republic. The findings showed that 69% of respondents reported a significant advantage for family-run businesses, specifically due to their flexibility. For example, 82% of the respondents cited flexibility as the major advantage of family-run businesses. Only 6% of the chosen sample reported a negative view of the family business. Additionally, respondents in the study cited other advantages of family businesses: company stability, a positive company atmosphere, and a positive attitude toward employees (Breckova, 2016).

However, Breckova (2016) identified one major disadvantage of family businesses: limited access to financing, a problem commonly found among SMEs. González-Cruz and Cruz-Ros also noted the advantages of SME family businesses and examined family involvement and its impact on performance. The authors noted high performance as one of the main advantages of SME family businesses; this was found to be true in cases in which the SME family business had a family chief executive officer and a board composed of nonfamily directors. Additionally, González-Cruz and Cruz-Ros linked first-generation SME family businesses without family governance structures and with low ownership concentration to high performance outcomes. These findings showed the various advantages of family involvement in SMEs, such as performance, company stability, a positive company atmosphere, and a positive attitude toward employees (Breckova, 2016; González-Cruz & Cruz-Ros, 2016).

Other researchers have examined the performance impact of family-run businesses on firms (Lwango et al., 2017; Mokhber et al., 2017). For one, Lwango et al. examined family influence and its impact on SME performance across firm size and age. The authors gathered data on 4240 family-run firms in the United States using a quantitative approach. Their findings showed that active family ownership was positively associated with SME profitability. However, Lwango et al. noted that this association between SME family ownership and profitability was negatively moderated by firm size and age. Mokhber et al. similarly examined family business performance in SMEs, administering surveys to 50 family business successors in Malaysian SMEs. The authors also employed a quantitative approach to examine the effects of family succession-planning factors on the performance of family businesses within SMEs. The findings revealed that the preparation level of heirs and family members as business members was significantly linked to positive performance outcomes within the SME firm. Randolph et al. built on these findings and sought to explain the improved performance of family-owned SMEs. The authors employed a goal-systems approach to examine this topic and noted that, compared with nonfamily SMEs, family-owned SMEs have noneconomic objectives that significantly and positively influence performance. Such noneconomic goals included family and community objectives that positively impacted the family-owned SME's performance (Randolph et al., 2019).

Consistent with earlier work, Bokhari et al. (2020) noted the importance of succession planning in family-owned SMEs. In the more recent study, Bokhari et al. examined the impact of succession planning (cognitive, structural, and relational ties), strategic flexibility, and organizational improvisation on business sustainability. The authors utilized the triple bottom line as the study's framework. Their findings revealed that cognitive, structural, and relational ties had significant positive impacts on the business sustainability of family-owned SMEs. Their findings also revealed a positive and significant relationship among succession planning, strategic flexibility, organizational improvisation, and business sustainability. These findings showed the importance of succession planning for cognitive, structural, and relational ties, as well as strategic flexibility, to ensure the growth and business sustainability of family-owned SMEs. More research was needed to examine whether this association could also be generalized to other countries, such as those in Africa, which justified the current study. Nonetheless, this body of knowledge highlighted the importance of SME family businesses, the role of family members as business successors, and their impact on SME performance, all of which remain crucial to the growth and sustainability of family-owned SMEs (Bokhari et al., 2020; Lwango et al., 2017).

There are other factors to consider in the success of high-growth family SMEs, aside from having family members as business successors. According to the literature, financial indicators, including the liquidity ratio, solvency ratio, firm age, cash flow, and working capital, are the most vital factors for ensuring SME growth. This conclusion was drawn from an examination of 45,000 family business SMEs in Italy (Megaravalli & Sampagnaro, 2019). Their quantitative analyses indicated that, in addition to having family members as business successors, SME family business owners should also consider financial indicators (liquidity ratio, solvency ratio, firm age, cash flow, and working capital) identified as predictors of firm growth. This significant information showed that SMEs were commonly low in credit financing, as previously found by Breckova. Saridakis et al. added to these findings when examining the impact of the family effect on the growth of SMEs in the United Kingdom. The authors first compared the growth rates of family- and nonfamily-owned SMEs and then examined the growth behaviors of family-run SMEs against those of nonfamily-run SMEs. The findings showed that financial indicators were significant in ensuring the growth of family-owned SMEs. In addition to financial indicators, the authors highlighted the importance of ensuring managerial competence in family-owned SMEs, which was just as vital in nonfamily-owned SMEs. This body of knowledge identified factors in financial indicators and managerial competence that ensure the growth and success of family-owned SMEs, which were also crucial for nonfamily-owned SMEs (Megaravalli & Sampagnaro, 2019; Saridakis et al., 2018).

Innovation is also a vital aspect to consider in the growth of family SMEs. Researchers have noted that family-owned SMEs are more likely to be innovative than nonfamily-owned SMEs (Németh & Dőry, 2019). For one, Németh and Dőry examined this topic using empirical research on the factors influencing innovation performance in family firms. The authors found that family SMEs introduced more innovations than other companies (Németh & Dőry, 2019).

However, other researchers have noted that innovativeness in family-owned SMEs is lower than in nonfamily-owned SMEs (Steeger & Hoffmann, 2016; Zulfiqar et al., 2020), which contrasts with the conflicting findings reported by Németh and Dőry. For one, Zulfiqar et al. examined family-owned SMEs and their propensity to adopt lean innovation strategies in the emerging economy. The authors collected data over 10 years, extracting it from the China Stock Market and Accounting Research (CSMAR) database. The authors employed descriptive statistics, correlations, and panel data analysis techniques to analyze the data. The findings showed that family firms were unmotivated to pursue and introduce lean innovation strategies. However, Zulfiqar et al. found that lean innovation strategies might be employed by managers of family-owned SMEs through increases in executives' compensation and wages. Steeger and Hoffmann also examined this phenomenon, specifically studying German SMEs. The authors selected a large cross-sectional sample of German SMEs, drawing on agency theory as the study's theoretical framework. The findings showed that family firms were less innovative than nonfamily firms, indicating the need to further analyze the factors driving innovation within family-owned SMEs (Steeger & Hoffmann, 2016).

Given the conflicting findings regarding the level of innovation within family-owned SMEs, more research is needed to examine innovativeness in these firms and the key drivers of innovation (Addae-Boateng & Dzisi, 2016; Randolph et al., 2019). According to the literature, various factors need to be considered and evaluated by SMEs to determine whether to pursue innovation or not: "uniqueness of the idea, its market potential, cost, expert advice, the impact of both current and future environmental forces, availability of raw materials and supplies, and the idea's future appeal" (p. 388). These factors need to be examined further in the context of family-owned SMEs to determine whether they can drive and enhance innovation in these firms.

Many SMEs in Burkina Faso and the wider Union are family-managed or embedded in dense interpersonal networks. That characteristic often brings strengths that formal analysis underestimates: continuity of commitment, reputation effects, flexible labor contributions, and strong owner oversight. In environments where external enforcement is uneven and shocks are frequent, family and kinship structures may provide the trust and resilience that help keep smaller firms operating. These features are part of the real productive economy of WAMU and should not be dismissed as mere informality. They often sustain firms through the early and most fragile stages of growth.

At the same time, these same strengths can create difficulties in the transition to formal bankability. When ownership, management, household cash flow, and enterprise accounts are closely intertwined, the firm may appear less legible to external lenders. Governance that is internally coherent may still look insufficiently documented from the standpoint of a credit committee. The challenge, then, is not to oppose family firms to "modern" firms, but to ask how enterprises can preserve the relational strengths that support continuity while producing the records, separations, and governance signals that formal banks require. The financing gap often opens precisely at that transition from a socially credible business to an administratively credible borrower.

2.4 Survival, Failure, and Financial Fragility

SME survival depends on various factors that are key to SME growth and sustainability. According to the literature, SMEs face various challenges that threaten their growth and existence, such as limited access to funding, a lack of a market to serve, a lack of a one-stop office, and the unwillingness of service providers, such as banks and agencies, to enter into contracts with SMEs. Sitharam and Hoque (2016) added to this finding, noting that crime and corruption also threatened the existence and sustainability of SMEs in South Africa. Further to this finding, SMEs need to be aware of and prepare for competition, both locally and internationally, to protect their market shares and positions (Sitharam & Hoque, 2016).

Also, Prasanna et al. (2019) added to these assertions by Sitharam and Hoque and Rankhumise and Masilo, noting that SMEs needed to acknowledge and identify technological threats and challenges in the face of competition. The authors examined the sustainability of SMEs in a competitive environment by conducting a systematic review of the challenges they face and their performance. The authors noted three major competitive challenges faced by SMEs: the sustainability challenge, the global challenge, and the technological challenge. The researchers further outlined the factors that SMEs should consider to ensure technological progress amid competition, including social capital, links with multinational and transnational corporations, innovation, sharing and networking, information technology, and the adoption of productivity-enhancing technology. Furthermore, the authors noted the importance of a skilled technology workforce and of SMEs' ability to identify new opportunities for advanced technologies in the market. This body of knowledge highlighted the challenges faced by SMEs as vital to address for their survival and sustainability. These challenges included competition, lack of funding, technological advancement, and even corruption in some settings, such as in Africa (Prasanna et al., 2019; Rankhumise & Masilo, 2017).

One of the major challenges SME firms face is a lack of funding. Various researchers have noted that SMEs face funding challenges, especially in their early stages of operation (Bertrand, 2016; Kraima et al., 2018). Tjano (2019) examined this topic, when analyzing the early-stage formal SME funding challenges in

Windhoek, Namibia. The author reported that the SME failure rate was at 75% during the early stage. Employing a descriptive approach, the author gathered data from 120 randomly selected registered SME operators in Windhoek using the Statistical Package for the Social Sciences. The findings showed that various factors negatively affected SMEs' success rates in the early stages: inadequate funding, limited government assistance, and numerous requirements. Thus, Tjano concluded that more support is needed for SMEs, especially during these early stages. This support includes extending programs and support policies that provide funding without collateral requirements, providing ample training for SMEs on maintaining financial records and preparing financial statements, establishing different forms of government assistance for SMEs, and creating a strong SME funding agency. Abbasi et al. noted a similar pattern in their examination of the financial struggles of SMEs. The authors noted that SMEs often faced limitations and hurdles while accessing finance from financial institutions. This factor undermined the sustainability of SMEs, underscoring the need for government support, particularly through business enterprise financing and access to alternative financing options. This body of knowledge highlighted the funding challenges SMEs commonly faced, hindering their expansion and growth. This problem needs to be acknowledged and addressed because SMEs support economies, significantly contributing to a country's growth and development (Abbasi et al., 2017).

According to the literature, SMEs also face financing challenges in other contexts, not just during their earliest stages of operation, due to factors related to race/ethnicity and social capital (Bertrand, 2016; Howell, 2019). Kraima et al. examined this topic in their study of bank financing of SMEs in Tunisia. The authors employed 50 SME business owners in Southwestern Tunisia. The findings showed that social capital was significantly and positively correlated with financial access and resources. This finding is vital information because research has shown that race/ethnicity and social capital may be linked (Bertrand, 2016; Howell, 2019).

Similarly, Bertrand (2016) and W. Lee and Black examined this topic when focusing on SME lending challenges for minority owners. Bertrand first found that minority SME owners were more likely to need to provide additional collateral to obtain credit. The findings also showed that Asians, African Americans, and Hispanics were the minorities that experienced the most challenges and discrimination in the SME credit market. However, less discrimination might be experienced when bank relationships were lengthened, according to Bertrand. W. Lee and Black concurred with these findings in their examination of immigrant SME owners and their access to credit. The authors noted that immigrant business owners commonly experienced challenges obtaining credit from financial institutions, such as banks. Some reasons for such barriers to credit access included language barriers and a lack of trust toward immigrant groups. This body of findings revealed the apparent barriers to accessing credit that minority groups and immigrant SME owners commonly experience. Financial institution managers need to provide additional loan options or improve communication to enhance access to credit for this population (Lee & Black, 2017).

According to the literature, ethnic minorities face greater financial constraints when running their businesses, especially in the initial stages. Howell (2019) examined the relationships among ethnicity, finance, and entrepreneurship in China. The author found that within China, certain subgroups were more likely to obtain initial formal financing to start their SMEs. As a result, these subgroups had more success in running their businesses than other subgroups without access to initial formal financing. More interestingly, the results showed that the business performance gap narrowed when all minority-operated businesses had equal access to initial formal financing, underscoring the need to provide equal financing opportunities for all minorities and subgroups. Rahman et al. (2018) likewise examined the challenges faced by ethnic minority SME owners. The authors conducted one-on-one interviews with 25 ethnic minority business owners based in Scotland. The findings showed that a major issue was the lack of access to formal financing, along with strict immigration rules that threatened the continuity of one's stay in the country. Overall, these past findings showed that the SME credit system was not fully accessible to ethnic minority SME owners, thereby limiting the growth and sustainability of these SMEs. SMEs have been reported to have high failure rates in various contexts. According to the literature, SMEs in developing countries, such as those in Africa, experience failure before their first year of operation. Leboea (2017) added to this finding, noting that most SMEs would not move beyond their first growth phase. Most SMEs in countries such as South Africa do not even experience and tackle the survival, success, growth, maturity, and resource maturity stages. In Malaysia, Ambad et al. (2020) reported a staggering failure rate for SMEs: 60% of new SMEs fail within the first 5 years of establishment. The authors noted financial limitations, human resource problems, ineffective marketing strategies, and a lack of facilities as major contributors to SME failure rates in Malaysia. This high failure rate among SMEs is a critical issue to address, given SMEs' significant contribution to economic development and job creation (Kersten et al., 2017; Pichler, 2018).

Due to the high failure rates among SMEs, researchers have examined the determinants of SME failure (Makropoulos et al., 2020a, 2020b). Poor financial performance is a key factor contributing to failure rates among SMEs. According to the literature, SMEs often fail due to excessive financial debt. These financial limitations faced by SMEs are also exacerbated by national or global events, such as financial crises and the COVID-19 pandemic. Gourinchas et al. concurred, noting that SME failure rates had significantly increased due to the COVID-19 crisis. The authors examined this topic and reported that the failure rate of SMEs was estimated to increase by 9% points due to the COVID-19 pandemic (Gourinchas et al., 2020).

Cressy and Bonnet (2018) and Chowdhury and Alam added that funding constraints during economic difficulties were among the top reasons for SME failure. Cressy and Bonnet examined the impact of bank credit constraints on SMEs, noting that these constraints led to a 64–70% increase in the risk of SME failure. The findings showed that financial limitations and risk played major roles in SME failure, which also limited SMEs' abilities to survive and grow their start-up businesses. Chowdhury and Alam also reported similar findings in their examination of the factors affecting SMEs' access to finance in Bangladesh. The authors engaged 86

SMEs, conducted interviews with these firms, and administered questionnaires. Their findings showed various financial limitations faced by SMEs in Bangladesh, specifically from a lack of access to loans from financial institutions. The SME managers also reported a lack of collateral required by banks, corruption within banks, and significantly high interest rates as factors that hindered their access to bank loans. Overall, these factors are vital to consider because a lack of financing leads to SME failures in Bangladesh, which are already numerous. These findings identified financial limitations as one of the major reasons for SME failure (Chowdhury & Alam, 2017; Cressy & Bonnet, 2018). More support needs to be provided to SMEs, especially by banking institutions, to expand financing options that fund their survival and sustainability.

Various factors are linked to SME failure, including weak director characteristics, the economic environment, and the extent of firm growth (Makropoulos et al., 2020a, 2020b). Makropoulos et al. examined this topic when analyzing the determinants of failure processes in SMEs based in the United Kingdom. In addition to financial indicators, the authors focused on nonfinancial indicators as determinants of SME failure. Using a sample of failed UK SMEs, the authors collected data on financial ratios, board characteristics, the macroeconomic environment, sectoral information, and regional data. The findings showed that director characteristics, such as director age and gender composition, were significant factors in the failure processes of UK SMEs (Makropoulos et al., 2020b). As such, one should consider not only financial metrics but also nonfinancial indicators when determining the reasons behind SMEs' failure rates.

Other researchers have highlighted factors related to predicting SME failure. According to the literature, SMEs' financial health and the country's bankruptcy policies are significant predictors of SME failure. Using hazard models, Gupta et al. (2018) found that SME firms' financial health alone did not determine or predict SME failure. Nikolić et al. added to these findings when investigating the factors influencing SME failure. Using a qualitative approach, the authors administered a questionnaire to entrepreneurs on this topic and employed quantitative techniques to analyze the findings. The findings showed that the SMEs' level of recovery, firm life cycle phase, and sector were significant factors that both influenced and predicted SME failure (Nikolić et al., 2018).

Thus, the authors proposed that more support be provided to aid the growth and development of SMEs (Nikolić et al., 2018). This body of findings provided deeper insight into the factors that significantly impacted SME failure, which were vital to this area of the topic. These findings could be used by banking institution decision-makers to guide the development of effective ways to support and manage SMEs (Gupta et al., 2018; Nikolić et al., 2018).

Survival is often treated as an entrepreneurial quality, but for smaller firms, it is also a condition of financing. Many enterprises do not fail because demand permanently disappears or because the owner lacks initiative. They fail because temporary cash-flow stress becomes impossible to bridge. Delayed customer payments, a weak harvest, higher transport costs, or a brief interruption in trading conditions can become existential for a firm lacking access to stabilizing liquidity. In such contexts, credit is not only expansion capital. It is also the difference between volatility that can be absorbed and volatility that becomes terminal (Cressy & Bonnet, 2018).

This is why the financial fragility of SMEs must be understood in dynamic terms. A firm with weak reserves cannot wait for long administrative processes, repeatedly renegotiate supplier terms, or finance a long period of informal self-insurance. Once liquidity tightens, the business often underinvests, reduces stock levels, defers maintenance, and loses market position, which in turn makes it appear riskier to lenders. The vicious circle is clear: Weak access to finance raises fragility, and greater fragility later justifies further caution by lenders. Breaking that circle requires a banking system capable of distinguishing between structural unviability and temporary opacity or strain (Abraham & Schmukler, 2017; Akinsola & Ikhide, 2019).

2.5 Bank Relationships and Enterprise Resilience

Bank relationships are crucial to SME survival. Authors have underscored this finding and noted the need to further explore SME-bank relationships in different contexts (Iwanicz-Drozdowska et al., 2018; Wang et al., 2019). According to the literature, good relationships with banks are key to SME success and growth. The authors examined the effects of local banks on the future of challenged SMEs in Poland, using data from 2006 to 2015. The findings showed that local banks were key to assisting troubled SMEs, especially during economic crises. Wang et al. (2019) noted a similar pattern when examining SME-bank relationships across 19 selected European countries.

The authors also explored the impact of bank market power on SME survival (Wang et al., 2019). The findings revealed that bankers were more likely to lend to SMEs with whom they had a long-term relationship. Bank managers were more likely to engage in long-term SME lending to foster healthy relationships with such SME firms (Wang et al., 2019). This body of knowledge showed the role of bank relationships in SME survival. These findings could be used by SME firm managers to highlight the importance of developing and focusing on relationships with local banks to increase the chances of SME lending.

Bank credit decision-makers prioritize SME firms with good character, as this knowledge indicates healthy client relationships (Wasiuzzaman et al., 2019). This finding differs from the usual 5C framework for lending credit: character, capital, capacity, conditions, and collateral. Boulanouar et al. found this finding when examining banking relationships in New Zealand. The authors conducted a qualitative study, gathering data through interviews with bank representatives (Boulanouar et al., 2020).

The findings showed that New Zealand bank managers paid attention to healthy client relationships, prioritizing three credit criteria: financials, security, and character (Boulanouar et al., 2020). New Zealand bankers underscored the importance of maintaining good relations with borrowers and conducting adequate character evaluations. In a more recent study, Saputra et al. noted similar outcomes when examining the impact of character, capacity, capital, collateral, and conditions on bank loans. The authors focused on borrowers' viewpoints by collecting questionnaire data from 105 participants. The findings showed that character, capacity, and conditions had significant impacts on bank financing to borrowers. In addition to these findings, capital and collateral had no significant impact on SME loans (Saputra et al., 2020). This body of knowledge highlighted the importance of character as a determinant of SME loan approval by banks.

Lack of creditworthiness is also a key factor hindering SMEs' access to bank loans and other forms of financial capital (Wasiuzzaman et al., 2019). Njue and Mbogo explained this finding while examining the factors that hindered SMEs' access to bank credit. The authors examined qualitative and quantitative data gathered from 17 banks in Kenya. The results showed that creditworthiness information was a significant factor hindering SMEs' access to bank loans and services. Aside from the usual financial factors of assets and the capital standing of SMEs, the SME owner's honesty, character, and trustworthiness were identified as vital factors that significantly and negatively affected SMEs' access to finance from Kenyan banks (Njue & Mbogo, 2017).

Wasiuzzaman et al. (2019) concurred with Njue and Mbogo's assertions by investigating creditworthiness and access to finance among a sample of selected manufacturing SMEs in Malaysia. The authors surveyed 158 SMEs and collected questionnaire responses on their SME characteristics, credit access, and creditworthiness. The results indicated that the SME owner's character had a significant impact on whether banks would grant loans to the SME. Aside from character, creditworthiness was a significant positive determinant of access to bank credit. In addition, the ability to provide collateral was significant for SMEs' access to formal financing. Wasiuzzaman et al. concurred with the findings of Njue and Mbogo. Wasiuzzaman et al. added that creditworthiness was significant for SMEs' access to formal financing, regardless of whether the SMEs had social ties to large firms. Therefore, creditworthiness is more vital than having links, relationships, or alliances with large firms (Wasiuzzaman et al., 2019).

This body of knowledge further justified the importance of a high-quality bank-SME relationship, which should be fortified by the SME owner's character (Njue & Mbogo, 2017; Wasiuzzaman et al., 2019). This significant knowledge can help SME managers secure formal financing from banks. More researchers have noted the importance of character as a factor for SME bank lending. These authors have noted the value of nonfinancial indicators, such as character, in improving the SME lending process and relationships with banks. Boushnak et al. (2018) examined this topic in their case study, studying factors influencing credit decisions for lending to SMEs.

The authors used questionnaires to gather responses from 313 credit risk and marketing employees from a selected Egyptian bank (Boushnak et al., 2018). The findings showed that SME owners' character was a vital factor in determining whether bank managers would lend credit to SMEs. In addition to this finding, their results showed that SME capacity and capital size were vital factors influencing banks' decision-making processes for lending to SMEs. Brighi et al. noted similar findings when examining 9898 SMEs and the funding decisions made by bank managers. The authors employed an intertemporal framework and showed that having a durable bank relationship could help shift the loan decision process in favor of SMEs. In a more recent case study, Ramadhan noted similar findings when examining the determinants of SMEs' loan defaults in selected banks in Tanzania. The author employed a mixed-method approach in the study, using questionnaires and observation techniques to gather data from 150 participants. The findings showed that the character of an SME owner was a significant determinant of SME loans. The author concluded that banks need to develop relationships with SMEs to properly evaluate the character of the SME owner/manager. Wu et al. concurred with Ramadhan's findings and noted that a strong bank-SME relationship would increase the likelihood of access to credit and grants for SME firms. Hence, there was a need to develop bank-SME relationships, specifically in China, where productive SME-bank relationships were lacking, as identified by Wu et al. Therefore, more research is needed to determine SME-bank relationships in African countries, such as Burkina Faso. This body of literature highlighted the vital importance of SME owners' character in increasing their chances of obtaining bank loans and credit (Ramadhan, 2020; Wu et al., 2018). Having a strong character could help SME owners build healthy relationships with their banks, increasing the chances of growth and success.

Social and political connections are also significant in SMEs' access to bank financing. According to several authors, SME owners should focus on building and fortifying connections to access long-term capital and financial grants from banks (Hasan et al., 2017; Jackowicz & Kozłowski, 2019). Hasan et al. (2017) delved further into this topic, exploring the local context of the bank-SME relationship in Poland.

The authors found that political ties and recent connections were vital to increasing the chances of SME bank financing (Hasan et al., 2017). This association was found to be stronger during financial crises. Jackowicz and Kozłowski noted similarly in their examination of the social ties between SME managers and bank employees. The authors determined the impact of bank-SME ties using a dataset from Poland. Their findings showed that social ties significantly increased the likelihood that SMEs obtained bank financing. This association was found to be stronger when social ties were between bank decision-makers, such as managers, and SME owners. This body of knowledge demonstrated an in-depth empirical understanding of the dynamics of the bank-SME relationship; political ties, recent connections, and relations with bank decision-makers were shown to be vital to SME survival. Small firms would have a better chance of accessing long-term capital and financial grants from banks based on such information (Hasan et al., 2017; Jackowicz & Kozłowski, 2019).

Relationship lending matters because it allows banks to learn what documents alone cannot fully reveal. Repeated contact, branch visits, repayment history, and accumulated local knowledge can reveal whether a borrower's difficulties are chronic or temporary, whether the entrepreneur has discipline, and whether the firm

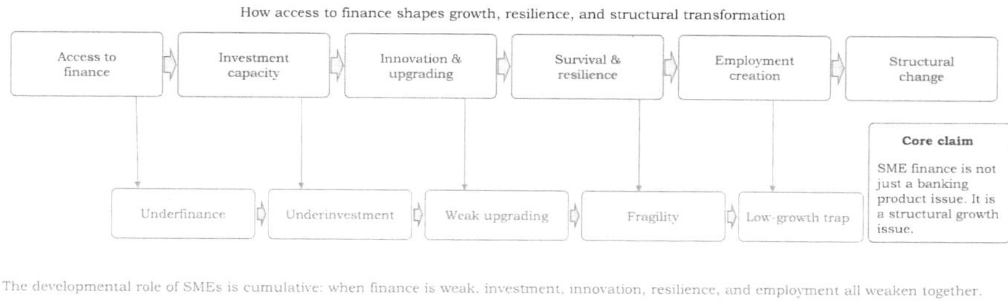

Fig. 2.1 Why SME finance matters: the economic transmission chain. Source: Author's conceptual synthesis

occupies a stable niche in its market. That knowledge is especially valuable where audited accounts are rare or incomplete. In that setting, the bank-firm relationship serves as a mechanism for converting soft information into prudent judgment, reducing the extent to which smaller firms are excluded simply because they do not appear to be large corporate borrowers on paper (Berger & Udell, 2002; Angori et al., 2019).

But relationships are only economically useful when they can be institutionalized. If they depend exclusively on personal ties, they remain fragile, uneven, and difficult to scale. If they are ignored by head office approval routines, local information never becomes credit. The most productive form of relationship lending is therefore not informal favoritism. It is a disciplined method of integrating local knowledge, borrower history, and contextual judgment into formal approval systems. The real challenge is to build credit processes in which relationship-based information deepens prudence rather than replacing it (Iwanicz-Drozdowska et al., 2018; Berger & Udell, 2006).

The argument developed in this chapter can be read as a cumulative chain of transmission. SMEs matter not only because they are numerous but also because constraints on their financing simultaneously alter investment, innovation, resilience, and employment. Figure 2.1 condenses that cumulative logic by showing how SME finance affects the wider economy through successive stages rather than through a single channel.

The figure clarifies why SME finance should be treated as a structural development issue rather than a narrow banking topic. When finance is weak, firms do not merely postpone borrowing. They invest less, upgrade less, become more fragile, and contribute less to employment and structural change. This cumulative perspective helps explain why the missing middle matters well beyond the credit market itself.

2.6 Managerial Capacity and the Productive Use of SME Finance

SME finance does not automatically produce development outcomes. Credit becomes economically meaningful only when it is transformed into productive investment, working capital stability, market expansion, improved processes, or resilience to shocks. This transformation depends not only on the availability of external finance but also on the SME manager's capacity to identify the appropriate financial solution and use it coherently within the firm's business model.

This point is important because SME finance is often discussed as if the central issue were simply whether a bank says "yes" or "no" to a loan request. In practice, the quality of managerial decision-making strongly shapes the usefulness of any financing obtained. A loan used to cover structural losses may worsen fragility; a leasing facility used to acquire productive equipment may improve capacity; factoring may ease working capital pressure where reliable invoices exist; and a guarantee-backed facility may allow a viable firm to overcome collateral constraints. The manager's role is therefore not peripheral to SME credit. It is part of the mechanism through which finance becomes growth.

For banks, this has a direct implication. The manager is not only the person requesting credit; the manager is also a source of information about the firm's discipline, adaptability, planning capacity, and willingness to formalize. Where financial statements are thin, the manager's credibility becomes part of the credit file. Where collateral is limited, managerial competence may influence whether the bank believes that projected cash flows are plausible. Where the firm operates in uncertain markets, the manager's ability to anticipate risk, negotiate with customers, and adjust costs becomes part of the lender's perception of repayment capacity.

This does not mean that good managers should replace good documentation. Rather, it means that managerial capacity should be understood as one channel through which soft information can become bankable information. A bankable SME is not only a firm with assets. It is also a firm whose management can explain its activities, document its cash flows, justify its financing needs, and choose the most appropriate instrument for the problem at hand. In this sense, SME finance is inseparable from managerial quality.

African evidence supports the importance of this broader view. Studies on SME finance in Africa suggest that access to finance is associated with firm performance and that credit constraints can hinder firm growth. In West Africa, research on the Economic Community of West African States (ECOWAS) countries also identifies the top manager's experience, firm size, legal rights, credit information depth, and export orientation as factors associated with access to finance (Fowowe, 2017; Quartey et al., 2017).

This managerial dimension reinforces the chapter's synthesis. SME finance matters because it supports investment, employment, innovation, and resilience. But it matters most when the financing instrument, the firm's managerial capacity, and the bank's information requirements are aligned.

2.7 Synthesis

Taken together, the literature reviewed in this chapter suggests that the developmental significance of SMEs cannot be reduced to a simple count of firms. Their economic importance lies in what they mediate: the transition from subsistence activity to accumulation, from household enterprise to more durable business organization, and from localized commerce to wider market participation. Where this segment remains underfinanced, the economy loses more than individual projects. It loses a mechanism of diversification and upward mobility.

That is why SME finance matters as a structural question. Employment creation, innovation, family continuity, survival under competition, and resilience in periods of stress are all shaped by access to finance. The link between these dimensions is cumulative. Firms that cannot finance inventory, equipment, process improvements, or temporary working capital gaps are less likely to survive long enough to professionalize. The financing problem, therefore, becomes a selection problem for the economy itself: which firms grow, which remain small, and which disappear before their potential is tested.

For Burkina Faso, the implication is immediate. For WAMU more broadly, the analytic lesson is the same even when national magnitudes differ: A policy language that celebrates entrepreneurship while leaving the institutional conditions for SME finance unresolved will underperform in growth, resilience, and inclusion. The missing middle is therefore not only a national financing gap; it is a regional development problem expressed through different country settings.

References

Abbasi, W. A., Wang, Z., & Abbasi, D. A. (2017). Potential sources of financing for small and medium enterprises (SMEs) and role of government in supporting SMEs. *Journal of Small Business and Entrepreneurship Development, 5*(2), 39–47. https://doi.org/10.15640/jsbed.v5n2a4

Abraham, F., & Schmukler, S. L. (2017). *Addressing the SME finance problem*. World Bank Research and Policy Briefs. http://documents1.worldbank.org/curated/en/809191507620842321/pdf/Addressing-the-SME-finance-problem.pdf

Addae-Boateng, S., & Dzisi, S. G. (2016). Innovation enhancement in family business SMEs in Ghana. *International Journal of Innovation Science, 8*(4), 388–403. https://doi.org/10.1108/IJIS-07-2016-0014

Akinsola, F., & Ikhide, S. (2019). Bank lending to small and medium scale enterprises (SMEs) and business cycle in South Africa after the global financial crisis. *The Journal of Developing Areas, 53*(1), 78. https://doi.org/10.1353/jda.2019.0005

Ambad, S. N. A., Andrew, J. V., & Awang Amit, D. H. D. (2020). Growth challenges of SMEs: Empirical evidence in Sabah, Malaysia. *ASEAN Entrepreneurship Journal, 6*(1), 8–14.

Angori, G., Aristei, D., & Gallo, M. (2019). Lending technologies, banking relationships, and firms' access to credit in Italy: The role of firm size. *Applied Economics, 51*(58), 6139–6170. https://doi.org/10.1080/00036846.2019.1613503

Ayandibu, A. O., & Houghton, J. (2017). The role of small and medium scale enterprise in local economic development (LED). *Journal of Business and Retail Management Research, 11*(2), 133–139. https://www.jbrmr.com/

Belas, J., Rahman, A., Rahman, M. T., & Schonfeld, J. (2017). Financial constraints on innovative SMEs: Empirical evidence from the Visegrad countries. *Engineering Economics, 28*(5), 552–563. https://doi.org/10.5755/j01.ee.28.5.18204

Berger, A. N., & Udell, G. N. (2002). Small business credit availability and relationship lending: The importance of bank organization structure. *The Economic Journal, 112*(477), 32–53. https://doi.org/10.1111/1468-0297.00682

Berger, A. N., & Udell, G. N. (2006). A more complete conceptual framework for SME finance. *Journal of Banking & Finance, 30*(11), 2945–2966. https://doi.org/10.1016/j.jbankfin.2006.05.008

Bertrand, J. (2016). Borrowing challenges for minorities: How lending technologies affect discrimination in the SME credit market. *SSRN*. https://doi.org/10.2139/ssrn.2864491

Bokhari, I. H., Muhammad, A. B., & Zakaria, N. (2020). Succession planning, strategic flexibility as predictors of business sustainability in family-owned SMEs: Moderating role of organization improvisation. *Pakistan Journal of Commerce and Social Sciences, 14*(1), 368–387. https://www.econstor.eu/handle/10419/216875

Boulanouar, Z., Locke, S., & Holmes, M. (2020). An analysis of the SME–bank match made in heaven: The case of New Zealand main banks and their relationship-managed SMEs. *Qualitative Research in Financial Markets, 12*(4), 391–411. https://doi.org/10.1108/QRFM-12-2018-0139

Boushnak, E., Rageb, M. A., Ragab, A. A., & Sakr, A. M. (2018). Factors influencing credit decision for lending SMEs: A case study on national bank of Egypt. *Open Access Library Journal, 5*(11), 1–17. https://doi.org/10.4236/oalib.1104996

Božić, L., & Rajh, E. (2016). The factors constraining innovation performance of SMEs in Croatia. *Economic Research-Ekonomska Istraživanja, 29*(1), 314–324. https://doi.org/10.1080/1331677X.2016.1168040

Breckova, P. (2016). Family business in the Czech Republic. *European Research Studies Journal, 19*(4), 3–16. https://www.um.edu.mt/library/oar/handle/123456789/29508

Brixiová, Z., Kangoye, T., & Yogo, T. U. (2020). Access to finance among small and medium-sized enterprises and job creation in Africa. *Structural Change and Economic Dynamics, 55*, 177–189. https://doi.org/10.1016/j.strueco.2020.08.008

Chege, S. M., & Wang, D. (2020). Information technology innovation and its impact on job creation by SMEs in developing countries: An analysis of the literature review. *Technology Analysis & Strategic Management, 32*(3), 256–271. https://doi.org/10.1080/09537325.2019.1651263

Chowdhury, M., & Alam, Z. (2017). Factors affecting access to finance of small and medium enterprises (SMEs) of Bangladesh. *USV Annals of Economics and Public Administration, 2*(26), 55. https://touroscholar.touro.edu/gsb_pubs/12/

Colclough, S. N., Moen, Ø., Hovd, N. S., & Chan, A. (2019). SME innovation orientation: Evidence from Norwegian exporting SMEs. *International Small Business Journal, 37*(8), 780–803. https://doi.org/10.1177/0266242619870731

Cressy, R., & Bonnet, J. (2018). *The long-run impact of bank lending constraints and other economically important factors on SME failure (No. halshs-01910293)*. https://halshs.archives-ouvertes.fr/halshs-01910293

Fakieh, B., Blount, Y., & Busch, P. (2016). SMEs and cloud computing: The benefits to the national economy and global competitiveness. In *Proceedings of the 13th European, Mediterranean and Middle Eastern Conference on Information Systems (EMCIS 2016)* (pp. 39–52)

Fowowe, B. (2017). Access to finance and firm performance: Evidence from African countries. *Review of Development Finance, 7*(1), 6–17. https://doi.org/10.1016/j.rdf.2017.01.006

Genc, E., Dayan, M., & Genc, O. F. (2019). The impact of SME internationalization on innovation: The mediating role of market and entrepreneurial orientation. *Industrial Marketing Management, 82*, 253–264. https://doi.org/10.1016/j.indmarman.2019.01.008

González-Cruz, T. F., & Cruz-Ros, S. (2016). When does family involvement produce superior performance in SME family business? *Journal of Business Research, 69*(4), 1452–1457. https://doi.org/10.1016/j.jbusres.2015.10.124

Gourinchas, P. O., Kalemli-Özcan, Ș., Penciakova, V., & Sander, N. (2020). *COVID-19 and SME failures (No. w27877)*. National Bureau of Economic Research. https://www.nber.org/papers/w27877.

Gupta, J., Gregoriou, A., & Ebrahimi, T. (2018). Empirical comparison of hazard models in predicting SMEs failure. *Quantitative Finance, 18*(3), 437–466. https://doi.org/10.1080/14697688.2017.1307514

Hasan, I., Jackowicz, K., Kowalewski, O., & Kozłowski, Ł. (2017). Politically connected firms in Poland and their access to bank financing. *Communist and Post-Communist Studies, 50*(4), 245–261. https://doi.org/10.1016/j.postcomstud.2017.10.003

Hlahane, M. M. (2018). *The economic impact of small and medium enterprises on the local economy of Johannesburg* [Doctoral dissertation, University of Johannesburg]. University of Johannesburg Repository.

Howell, A. (2019). Ethnic entrepreneurship, initial financing, and business performance in China. *Small Business Economics, 52*(3), 697–712. https://doi.org/10.1007/s11187-017-9980-5

Hughes, M., Hughes, P., Morgan, R. E., Hodgkinson, I. R., & Lee, Y. (2020). Strategic entrepreneurship behaviour and the innovation ambidexterity of young technology-based firms in incubators. *International Small Business Journal: Researching Entrepreneurship*. https://doi.org/10.1177/0266242620943776

Iwanicz-Drozdowska, M., Jackowicz, K., & Kozłowski, Ł. (2018). SMEs' near-death experiences. Do local banks extend a helping hand? *Emerging Markets Review, 37*, 47–65. https://doi.org/10.1016/j.ememar.2018.05.004

Jackowicz, K., & Kozłowski, Ł. (2019). Social ties between SME managers and bank employees: Financial consequences vs. SME managers' perceptions. *Emerging Markets Review, 40*, 100619. https://doi.org/10.1016/j.ememar.2019.05.004

Jang, H. (2018). Association of SME and government policy factors with the creation of new employment: Manufacturing industry in Korea. *Social Sciences, 7*(6), 100. https://doi.org/10.3390/socsci7060100

Kallmuenzer, A., & Scholl-Grissemann, U. (2017). Disentangling antecedents and performance effects of family SME innovation: A knowledge-based perspective. *International Entrepreneurship and Management Journal, 13*(4), 1117–1138. https://doi.org/10.1007/s11365-017-0443-x

Kersten, R., Harms, J., Liket, K., & Maas, K. (2017). Small firms, large impact? A systematic review of the SME finance literature. *World Development, 97*, 330–348. https://doi.org/10.1016/j.worlddev.2017.04.012

Kraima, M. T., Mighri, Z., & Sghaier, A. (2018). The financing of SME in the south-west of Tunisia: Between the current potential and the challenges to be overcome. *Journal of Academic Research in Economics, 10*(1), 176–195. http://www.jare-sh.com/

Kumar, R. (2017). *Targeted SME financing and employment effects: What do we know and what can we do differently?* World Bank. https://doi.org/10.1596/27477

Leboea, S. T. (2017). *The factors influencing SME failure in South Africa* [Master's dissertation, University of Cape Town].

Lee, W., & Black, S. L. (2017). Small business development: Immigrants' access to loan capital. *Journal of Small Business & Entrepreneurship, 29*(3), 193–209. https://doi.org/10.1080/08276331.2017.1297106

Liu, F., Park, K., & Whang, U. (2019). Organizational capabilities, export growth and job creation: An investigation of Korean SMEs. *Sustainability, 11*(14), 3986. https://doi.org/10.3390/su11143986

Lööf, H., & Nabavi, P. (2016). Innovation and credit constraints: Evidence from Swedish exporting firms. *Economics of Innovation and New Technology, 25*(3), 269–282. https://doi.org/10.1080/10438599.2015.1076196

Lwango, A., Coeurderoy, R., & Roche, G. A. G. (2017). Family influence and SME performance under conditions of firm size and age. *Journal of Small Business and Enterprise Development, 24*(3), 629–648. https://doi.org/10.1108/JSBED-11-2016-0174

Madrid-Guijarro, A., García-Pérez-de-Lema, D., & Van Auken, H. (2016). Financing constraints and SME innovation during economic crises. *Academia Revista Latinoamericana de Administración, 29*(1), 84–106. https://doi.org/10.1108/ARLA-04-2015-0067

Makri, K., Theodosiou, M., & Katsikea, E. (2017). An empirical investigation of the antecedents and performance outcomes of export innovativeness. *International Business Review, 26*(4), 628–639. https://doi.org/10.1016/j.ibusrev.2016.12.004

Makropoulos, A., Weir, C., & Zhang, X. (2020a). Stages and determinants of European Union small and medium sized firms' failure process. *International Journal of Computational Economics and Econometrics, 10*(3), 242–263. https://doi.org/10.1504/IJCEE.2020.108389

Makropoulos, A., Weir, C., & Zhang, X. (2020b). An analysis of the determinants of failure processes in UK SMEs. *Journal of Small Business and Enterprise Development, 27*(3), 405–426. https://doi.org/10.1108/JSBED-07-2019-0223

Maldonado-Guzmán, G., Garza-Reyes, J. A., Pinzón-Castro, S. Y., & Kumar, V. (2017). Barriers to innovation in service SMEs: Evidence from Mexico. *Industrial Management & Data Systems, 117*(8), 1669–1686. https://doi.org/10.1108/IMDS-08-2016-0339

Mandl, I., & Patrini, V. (2018). *European born globals: Job creation in young international businesses*. Routledge.

Megaravalli, A. V., & Sampagnaro, G. (2019). Predicting the growth of high-growth SMEs: Evidence from family business firms. *Journal of Family Business Management, 9*(1), 98–109. https://doi.org/10.1108/JFBM-09-2017-0029

Mokhber, M., Gi, T. G., Rasid, S. Z. A., Vakilbashi, A., Zamil, N. M., & Seng, Y. W. (2017). Succession planning and family business performance in SMEs. *Journal of Management Development, 36*(3), 330–347. https://doi.org/10.1108/JMD-12-2015-0171

Németh, K., & Dőry, T. (2019). Influencing factors of innovation performance in family firms–based on an empirical research. *Vezetéstudomány-Budapest Management Review, 50*(5), 58–71. https://doi.org/10.14267/VEZTUD.2019.05.06

Nikolić, N., Jovanović, I., Nikolić, Đ., Mihajlović, I., & Schulte, P. (2018). Investigation of the factors influencing SME failure as a function of its prevention and fast recovery after failure. *Entrepreneurship Research Journal, 9*(3). https://doi.org/10.1515/erj-2017-0030

Njue, M. N., & Mbogo, M. (2017). Factors hindering SMEs from accessing the financial products offered by banks. *International Journal of Finance, 2*(3), 67–85. https://carijournals.org

Nure, G., Bazini, E., & Madani, F. (2020). SME: Apparently small but of great derivative value! Literature review of tourism SMEs to create employment and access to finance. *Business and Economic Research, 10*(2), 1–25. https://www.berjournal.com

Pichler, J. H. (2018). In quest of SME-conducive policy formulation. *Entrepreneurial Business and Economics Review, 6*(1), 105–113. https://www.ceeol.com/search/article-detail?id=722324

Prange, C., & Pinho, J. C. (2017). How personal and organizational drivers impact on SME international performance: The mediating role of organizational innovation. *International Business Review, 26*(6), 1114–1123. https://doi.org/10.1016/j.ibusrev.2017.04.004

Prasanna, R. P. I. R., Jayasundara, J. M. S. B., Naradda Gamage, S. K., Ekanayake, E. M. S., Rajapakshe, P. S. K., & Abeyrathne, G. A. K. N. J. (2019). Sustainability of SMEs in the competition: A systemic review on technological challenges and SME performance. *Journal of Open Innovation: Technology, Market, and Complexity, 5*(4), 100. https://doi.org/10.3390/joitmc5040100

Quartey, P., Turkson, E., Abor, J. Y., & Iddrisu, A. M. (2017). Financing the growth of SMEs in Africa: What are the constraints to SME financing within ECOWAS? *Review of Development Finance, 7*(1), 18–28. https://doi.org/10.1016/j.rdf.2017.03.001

Rahman, M. Z., Ullah, F., & Thompson, P. (2018). Challenges and issues facing ethnic minority small business owners: The Scottish experience. *The International Journal of Entrepreneurship and Innovation, 19*(3), 177–193. https://doi.org/10.1177/1465750317753932

Ramadhan, M. (2020). *Determinants of SMEs loan defaults in commercial banks in Tanzania: A case study of CRDB bank* [Doctoral dissertation, Mzumbe University]. Mzumbe University Repository.

Randolph, R. V., Alexander, B. N., Debicki, B. J., & Zajkowski, R. (2019). Untangling non-economic objectives in family & non-family SMEs: A goal systems approach. *Journal of Business Research, 98*, 317–327. https://doi.org/10.1016/j.jbusres.2019.02.017

Rankhumise, E. M., & Masilo, K. H. (2017). The effect of government support on the success of small and medium enterprises: A comparative study between South Africa and China. *Journal of Economics and Behavioral Studies, 9*(6), 166–173. https://doi.org/10.22610/jebs.v9i6(J).2013

Saputra, E., Resmi, S., Nurweni, H., & Prasetyo, T. U. (2020). Do character, capacity, capital, collateral, and conditions as affect on bad loans. *Journal of Accounting and Finance Management, 1*(2), 100–110. https://doi.org/10.38035/jafm.v1i2

Saridakis, G., Lai, Y., Torres, R. I. M., & Mohammed, A. M. (2018). Actual and intended growth in family firms and non-family-owned firms: Are they different? *Journal of Organizational Effectiveness: People and Performance, 5*(1), 2–21. https://doi.org/10.1108/JOEPP-04-2017-0033

Sitharam, S., & Hoque, M. (2016). Factors affecting the performance of small and medium enterprises in KwaZulu-Natal, South Africa. *Problems and Perspectives in Management, 14*(2–2), 277–288. https://doi.org/10.21511/ppm.14(2-2).2016.03

Steeger, J. H., & Hoffmann, M. (2016). Innovation and family firms: Ability and willingness and German SMEs. *Journal of Family Business Management, 6*(3), 251–269. https://doi.org/10.1108/JFBM-09-2015-0036

Tjano, C. (2019). An analysis of early stage formal SME funding challenges in Windhoek, Namibia [Master's thesis, University of Namibia]. http://hdl.handle.net/11070/2849

Wang, R., Lin, Z., & Luo, H. (2019). Blockchain, bank credit and SME financing. *Quality & Quantity, 53*(3), 1127–1140. https://doi.org/10.1007/s11135-018-0806-6

Wang, X., Han, L., & Huang, X. (2020). Bank market power and SME finance: Firm-bank evidence from European countries. *Journal of International Financial Markets, Institutions and Money, 64*, 101162. https://doi.org/10.1016/j.intfin.2019.101162

Wasiuzzaman, S., Nurdin, N., Abdullah, A. H., & Vinayan, G. (2019). Creditworthiness and access to finance: A study of SMEs in the Malaysian manufacturing industry. *Management Research Review, 43*(3), 293–310. https://doi.org/10.1108/MRR-05-2019-0221

Wu, J., Zhu, J., Gold, J., & Fang, H. (2018). Lending facilities versus banking service: Unbalanced bank lending to SMEs in China. *International Journal of Business and Globalisation, 20*(3), 328–353. https://doi.org/10.1504/IJBG.2018.091509

Yazdanfar, D., & Öhman, P. (2018). Growth and job creation at the firm level: Swedish SME data. *Management Research Review, 41*(3), 345–358. https://doi.org/10.1108/MRR-03-2017-0093

Zulfiqar, M., Yousaf, M. U., Islam, M. R., & Ghafoor, S. (2020). Family firms propensity to lean innovation in the emerging economy: A moderating role of executive's compensation. *Journal of Family Business Management.* https://doi.org/10.1108/JFBM-11-2018-0057

Chapter 3
Risk, Distance, and Information in a Shared Banking Space

Bank lending to small firms is often described as a problem of risk aversion. The phrase is useful, but too blunt. It suggests that small and medium-sized enterprise (SME) credit is constrained because bankers dislike risk more than they should. The argument of this book is different. Banks limit credit to SMEs chiefly when they cannot transform uncertainty into usable information. The decisive issue is not fear in the abstract, but the institutional capacity to know borrowers, compare them, price them, and monitor them over time.

Agency theory offers a first entry point. Every lending relationship contains a delegation problem. Before granting a loan, the bank cannot fully assess the borrower's quality or the project's reliability. After disbursement, it cannot monitor every decision the borrower makes. Hidden information produces adverse selection; hidden action produces moral hazard. These are not peripheral complications. They are at the heart of credit markets. Banks lend under conditions of incomplete information, and the structure of the loan contract reflects this (Ross, 1973; Bendickson et al., 2016).

Yet agency theory alone does not explain why some borrowers remain persistently outside formal credit. To understand SME finance, one must move from the abstract principal-agent problem to the concrete forms of information that banks can process. Large firms are often easier to evaluate because they leave documentary traces that fit standard lending procedures: audited accounts, stable statements, formal governance, registered assets, and longer operating histories. Smaller firms are different. Their records may be partial, their revenues volatile, their collateral difficult to verify, and their operations embedded in informal or semiformal business practices. The relevant problem is therefore one of informational opacity.

In this setting, information asymmetry should not be treated as a secondary variable. It is the central mechanism through which SMEs become either bankable or excluded. When information is thin, banks do not merely charge more for risk. They alter the whole structure of the credit relationship. They may reduce the loan size, shorten the maturity, require additional collateral, intensify monitoring, insist on

K. A. Sory, *Banking the Missing Middle*, Research Series on Responsible Enterprise Ecosystems, https://doi.org/10.1007/978-3-032-34582-0_3

more documentation, or refuse the application entirely. Credit rationing is not simply the absence of lending. It is the selective organization of lending under uncertainty (Stiglitz & Weiss, 1981; Berger & Udell, 2006).

This distinction matters because it shifts attention from attitudes to technologies of judgment. Banks do not lend with abstract preferences alone. They lend through routines: internal databases, credit committees, rating systems, collateral rules, delegated authority, branch reports, and follow-up mechanisms. The crucial question is not whether a banker says SMEs are risky. It is whether the bank possesses a workable method for converting incomplete information into a contract it is willing to sign.

At this point, the distinction between hard and soft information becomes essential. Hard information is standardized, verifiable, and easily transmitted across organizational levels. Financial statements, tax records, registered collateral, formal cash-flow documentation, and bureau data all fall into this category. Soft information is different. It is relational, contextual, and often difficult to encode in centralized systems. It may include knowledge of the owner's reputation, local market position, credibility of suppliers and clients, or repeated observations gathered through face-to-face contact. For smaller firms, soft information often serves as the bridge between opacity and trust (Campbell et al., 2019; Yosano & Nakaoka, 2019).

Once soft information becomes important, distance enters the analysis. Geographic proximity is not only a logistical variable. It is an informational one. Distance affects how often bankers and borrowers meet, how easily site visits can be carried out, how quickly problems are detected, and how much locally grounded judgment can be incorporated into the lending process. Branch networks matter for this reason. A branch is not merely a sales outlet; it is an information node. Where banks maintain meaningful local presence, they are better able to gather and update borrower knowledge that does not appear in formal files (Zhao & Jones-Evans, 2017; Zhao et al., 2020).

This also helps explain why bank organization matters as much as borrower quality. A centralized bank may possess more capital but be less capable of handling opaque, smaller clients if decision-making depends heavily on standardized documentation. A more locally embedded structure may be better positioned to support relationship lending, even if it has fewer resources overall. What matters is not size alone, but the interaction between organizational design and information-processing capacity. This book, therefore, treats bank scale, branch geography, and decision architecture as integral to SME credit rather than background conditions.

The same logic clarifies why personal psychology should not carry too much explanatory weight. Behavioral finance has correctly shown that decisions are not always reducible to strict utility maximization. But in the present context, the most important question is not whether individual officers are cautious by temperament. It is whether they operate inside systems that reward careful information production or systems that punish ambiguity by default. Loan officers matter, but they matter within institutional constraints.

A more useful way to think about SME credit, then, is as a problem of institutional legibility. Some firms are easy to classify and therefore easy to finance. Others

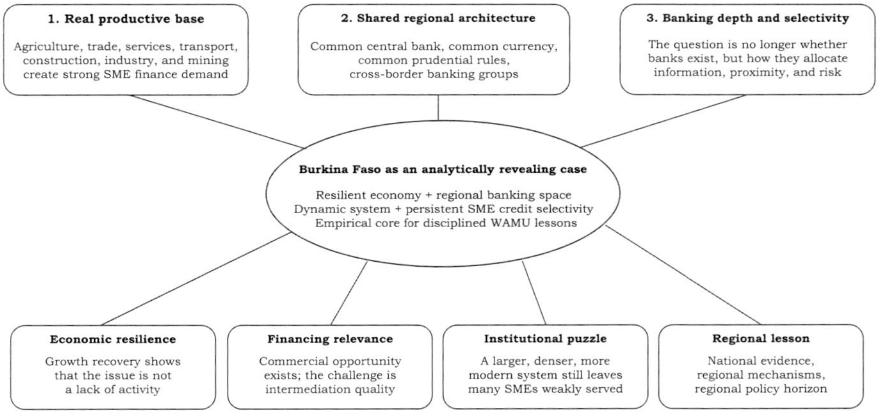

Fig. 3.1 Burkina Faso's resilient productive base, shared WAMU architecture, and selective banking depth make it an empirical core for disciplined regional lessons. Source: Author's conceptual synthesis

are economically active but administratively difficult to read. Where the costs of understanding a borrower are high, banks tend to retreat toward standardized clients, larger exposures, or sectors they know better. This is one reason why smaller firms can be central to employment and commerce yet remain peripheral to formal credit markets.

Four propositions guide the analysis that follows. First, information asymmetry is a structural feature of SME lending, not a marginal imperfection. Second, branch geography and repeated contact affect credit allocation by shaping the production of soft information. Third, credit outcomes depend as much on organizational lending technologies as on the characteristics of borrowers themselves. Fourth, the relevant outcome is not only whether credit is granted, but also on what terms, under what screening conditions, and with what intensity of bank involvement.

In a shared banking space such as WAMU, these mechanisms matter doubly. Banks operate under a common monetary authority and prudential expectations, and, in many cases, within cross-border groups whose lending practices span member states. The point is not that national outcomes are identical. It is that distance, branch reach, hard and soft information, delegated authority, and screening discipline are analytically portable mechanisms across the Union.

Seen in this way, the scarcity of SME finance is not simply a story of conservative banks facing needy firms. It is a story about how formal financial institutions decide which enterprises are sufficiently knowable to deserve capital. The issue is not merely that uncertainty exists. The issue is how banks manage it, where they manage it, and which firms can survive the process.

Figure 3.1 summarizes this argument and shows why Burkina Faso serves as an empirically grounded national case with disciplined regional relevance for West African Monetary Union (WAMU).

The figure summarizes the chapter's central proposition. Burkina Faso matters not simply because it is the site of the original fieldwork (Sory, 2021), but because it concentrates in one national setting the institutional and economic conditions that make the "missing middle" visible. The country's productive structure creates real financing demand, its banking system has expanded in scale and reach, and its membership in WAMU gives its lending patterns a broader regional significance. Yet this same setting still produces selective outcomes for SME credit.

The implication is important for the rest of the book. The SME finance problem cannot be explained only by weak demand, insufficient liquidity, or general banker caution. It must also be understood as a problem of how a regionally embedded banking system processes borrower legibility, organizational distance, and prudential uncertainty.

3.1 Psychological and Strategic Dimensions of Risk

In economics, finance, and banking, risk is not merely a technical matter of probabilities and expected losses. It is also a human, cultural, and psychological experience. Statistical models help estimate exposure, but they do not fully explain how decisions are made. Investors, bankers, and entrepreneurs confront uncertainty with memory, emotion, fear, ambition, and prior experience, not as perfectly rational calculators. For that reason, any serious account of risk must move beyond purely numerical models.

A useful starting point is the distinction between objective risk and perceived risk. Objective risk refers to exposure that can be described in measurable terms, such as default probabilities, volatility, collateral values, or expected losses. Perceived risk, by contrast, concerns how decision-makers interpret those exposures. Two situations may be statistically similar yet lead to different decisions because they are framed differently or carry different meanings. In this sense, emotion is not external to rational choice. It is part of the mechanism through which individuals assess danger, opportunity, and possible loss (Damasio, 1994). Risk, therefore, has a dual character: It signals not only the possibility of harm, but also the possibility of gain.

A risky choice is also relational rather than purely individual. In many settings, especially those described by game theory, decision-makers must act under uncertainty while anticipating others' likely responses. Strategic interdependence makes trust, incomplete information, and expectation part of the substance of risk rather than mere background conditions. The prisoner's dilemma remains a useful illustration because it shows how individually defensive reasoning can generate collectively inferior outcomes (Von Neumann & Morgenstern, 1944). This insight is especially relevant in lending relationships, where the bank must evaluate not only a borrower's project, but also the borrower's likely behavior after disbursement, the quality of disclosed information, and the credibility of future commitments.

Behavioral research adds a further layer by showing that gains and losses are not evaluated symmetrically. Prospect theory demonstrated that people tend to avoid risk when outcomes are framed as gains but become more willing to accept risk when equivalent outcomes are framed as losses (Kahneman & Tversky, 1979). This asymmetry helps explain why avoiding a certain loss may become more compelling than pursuing the highest expected value. In financial decision-making, the framing of uncertainty can therefore matter as much as the underlying numbers. Risk perception is shaped not only by outcomes themselves, but also by how those outcomes are presented, remembered, and anticipated.

The analysis of risk must also take account of adaptation. Individuals and organizations often do not seek absolute safety; instead, they regulate their exposure until they reach a level of risk they consider acceptable. This idea, associated with the literature on target risk and risk compensation, helps explain why safer systems do not always lead to proportionally safer behavior (Wilde, 1994). When actors feel more protected, they may compensate by taking greater risks elsewhere. In banking, this logic is important because regulatory safeguards, improved collateral arrangements, or stronger internal procedures do not automatically eliminate risky behavior. They may instead alter how risk is distributed, perceived, or managed.

Taken together, these perspectives suggest that risk operates at three interconnected levels. First, there is a technical level concerned with probabilities, exposures, and consequences. Second, there is a strategic level concerned with interdependence, anticipation, and other actors' behavior. Third, there is a psychological level concerned with framing, perception, emotion, and tolerance for uncertainty. A chapter that treats risk only as a statistical variable would therefore miss an essential part of the phenomenon. Risk is also a way of perceiving, interpreting, and negotiating action in uncertain conditions.

So, to conclude this topic, rather than reducing risk to the mere probability of loss, this book understands risk as a decision context structured by uncertain outcomes, objective or perceived probabilities, and anticipated utilities, in which action may generate both potential harm and potential benefit. Understanding risk in these broader terms is especially important for this book. The financing of the "*missing middle*" cannot be explained solely through solvency ratios, collateral coverage, or default probabilities. In the real world of bank-SME relations, lenders interpret uncertainty through organizational routines, strategic expectations, and psychological frames. Borrowers, likewise, respond to financial conditions through hope, caution, mistrust, and incomplete knowledge. Risk is therefore not simply measured; it is experienced, judged, and managed. Recognizing this broader risk structure helps explain why, in the West African Monetary Union, distance, information quality, and the bank-SME relationship shape credit allocation more strongly than purely statistical models would suggest.

3.2 Agency Theory and the Principal-Agent Problem

Agency theory was used as a theoretical foundation to explore factors influencing banks' risk aversion and willingness to lend to SMEs in Burkina Faso. Agency theory concerns the relationships between managers and stockholders (Hill & Jones,

1992; Ross, 1973). Proposing agency theory, Mitnick and Ross (1973) developed the institutional and economic theories of agency, respectively. S. A. Ross introduced the study of agency, focusing on compensation contracting. S. A. Ross defined agency, in essence, as an incentive dilemma.

Conversely, Mitnick (1973, 2019) proposed that institutions formed around agency, thus developing and advancing to deal with agency. Mitnick (2019) noted the significance of this issue due to imperfections in agency relationships: "Behavior does not occur as preferred by the principal because it does not pay to make it perfect. But society creates institutions that attend to these imperfections, managing or buffering them, adapting to them, or becoming chronically distorted by them" (p. 3). Therefore, there was a need to view the institutional structures and their incentives to understand agency fully.

Additionally, agency theory investigates and explains the nature of the implicit and explicit contractual relationships among a firm's stakeholders (Hill & Jones, 1992; Ross, 1973). In view of agency theory, stakeholders include managers, stockholders, employees, customers, suppliers, creditors, communities, and the public. Using agency theory, Hill and Jones developed a paradigm to explain specific aspects of a firm's strategic behavior, the structure of management-stakeholder contracts, the processes that influence them, and the institutional structures that monitor and affect them. The resulting model in Hill and Jones's (1992) research was a generalized theory of agency, focusing on stakeholder agency.

As such, agency has two different sides: the agent side and the principal side. These two different sides present the basic agent-principal problem. The agent side refers to the activities and issues of identifying and delivering services, while the principal side refers to the activities and issues of guiding and rectifying agent actions (Mitnick, 2019). Cavanagh et al. defined agency theory as explaining social relations within the context of delegated authority, which generally results in problems of control. As such, one of the principles of agency theory is that problems may arise when one party, the agent, acts for another, the principal. Every action and correction has a resulting cost; as such, the principal (or the agent) does not gain anything by insisting on or providing perfect agency. Panda and Leepsa (2017) further noted that issues such as conflicts of interest, agency costs, differing risk preferences, information asymmetry, and moral hazard arose from the separation of ownership from control.

Considering the principal-agent dynamics, researchers have identified two broad forms of agency problems: those arising from hidden information and those arising from hidden action (Mas-Colell et al., 1995; Rauchhaus, 2009). Hidden information is associated with adverse selection because the lender cannot fully observe borrower quality before the contract is signed. Hidden action generates moral hazard because, after the contract is in place, the lender cannot perfectly observe or control the borrower's subsequent behavior. This distinction matters for SME lending because different remedies are required at each stage: Screening and signaling are most relevant before lending, while monitoring, covenants, and incentives become more important after disbursement.

Heckerman (1975) was the first scholar to apply S. A. Ross's theory of agency, modeling a compensation contract to encourage managers to make investment decisions in the owner's interest. More recent scholars have since used agency theory to examine social relations and structures, extending it from business and economics into political science, sociology, and state policy implementation (Bendickson et al., 2016; Mitnick, 2019).

According to researchers, the agent-principal problem also applies to banking (Dias & Mroczkowski, 2012; Ismail, 2011). Pirolo explained this finding in their study, noting that one of the problems in the modern business and banking world was that most stakeholders were not involved in running their businesses. Thus, stakeholders lack adequate knowledge to evaluate the risk of banking transactions, such as loans and interest payments, which presents as an agent-principal problem. Ismail added that bank managers often operate in the presence of various agents and principals, which present problems in financing and banking systems. Ismail explained this finding by examining the Islamic banking system. Ismail noted the following: "[The] problem arises under conditions of incomplete and asymmetric information when, for example, a principal hires an agent, the problem may arise that the two may not have the same interests, while the principal is, presumably, hiring the agent to pursue the interests of the former" (p. 6). The principal-agent problem is also prevalent in the banking system, where the principal attempts to recompense an agent for actions that are beneficial to the principal and costly to the agent, and in cases where elements of performance are costly to observe. The principal-agent problem arises when the principal knows less than the agent about something vital; furthermore, both the principal and the agent have conflicting interests (Ismail, 2011; Pirolo, 2020).

Other researchers have employed an agency-theoretic perspective, given the prevalence of the principal-agent problem in banks (Dias & Mroczkowski, 2012; Karanja, 2018). Dias and Mroczkowski examined this topic when investigating the risk-taking of financial institutions, specifically banks. The authors employed agency theory in their study, examining the motivations for risk-taking or risk-aversion decisions within banks. Their findings showed that banks that employ credit default swaps for speculative/trading purposes indicate a risk-taking motivation. On the other hand, banks that employ credit default swaps for hedging purposes indicate a risk-aversion motive. Karanja further explained that when bank managers implement the agency banking model, they create a principal-agent relationship, which increases both benefits and risks. As such, Karanja underscored the prevalence of the principal-agent problem in banks, noting that the two parties in the agency relationship should collaborate to mitigate the risk of fraud and losses. This vital information shows that fraud is a major factor negatively affecting banks and both parties in the agency relationship (Karanja, 2018; Kiburi, 2016).

As an agency theory related to banks' risk aversion and willingness to lend money to SMEs in Burkina Faso, this theory provided additional insight from an agent-principal perspective (Karanja, 2018; Kiburi, 2016). As such, agency theory offers insights into the factors that influence banks' risk aversion and willingness to lend to SMEs in Burkina Faso. From a theoretical perspective, the primary aim of research is to broaden the levels of explanation and understanding of the agent-principal problem in Burkina Faso (Kiburi, 2016).

Agency theory remains useful because lending is built on delegation under incomplete information. Before a loan is granted, the lender cannot fully observe project quality, borrower discipline, or reliability of projected cash flows. After disbursement, it cannot monitor every decision that affects repayment. Hidden information and hidden action are therefore basic features of credit markets rather than exceptional disruptions.

In banking, the principal-agent problem is layered. Depositors delegate to banks, management delegates to loan officers, and banks contract with borrowers whose behavior cannot be perfectly observed. This means that what is often described loosely as "risk" is, more precisely, a chain of incomplete contracts. Agency theory helps identify where incentives can diverge, but it becomes genuinely useful only when connected to actual lending routines, documentation practices, and monitoring technologies.

The usefulness of agency theory becomes even clearer once one recognizes how many layers of delegation exist within a modern banking system. Depositors rely on banks; boards rely on management; management relies on branch managers and loan officers; and the institution then relies on borrowers whose incentives it cannot perfectly observe. The credit decision is therefore not a single principal-agent problem but a chain of them. This helps explain why formal documentation, committees, collateral rules, and reporting structures matter so much: They are not bureaucratic ornaments, but devices for coping with the fact that each stage of the lending chain depends on imperfectly observed behavior at another stage (Ross, 1973; Bendickson et al., 2016).

Agency theory provides the first major theoretical lens for understanding why SME lending becomes difficult under conditions of incomplete information. In the bank-SME relationship, the problem is not limited to whether the borrower needs credit or whether the bank has liquidity to lend. The deeper issue is that different actors possess different information, face different incentives, and bear different costs when making credit decisions. Bank managers and loan officers act within delegated authority, while SME borrowers possess private information about their projects, repayment capacity, business discipline, and future effort.

Figure 3.2 summarizes this agency structure. It shows how delegation, information asymmetry, hidden information, and hidden action create agency costs that banks attempt to manage through screening, collateral, covenants, incentives, monitoring, and relationship lending.

The figure clarifies why SME lending cannot be reduced to a simple question of borrower demand or bank willingness. Banks operate through delegated decision structures in which managers and loan officers must evaluate borrowers whose future behavior cannot be fully observed. Before lending, the bank faces hidden information: The borrower may know more about the project's quality, the reliability of cash flows, and the true use of funds. After lending, the bank faces hidden action: The borrower may change behavior, redirect funds, reduce effort, or take risks that are costly for the bank to monitor.

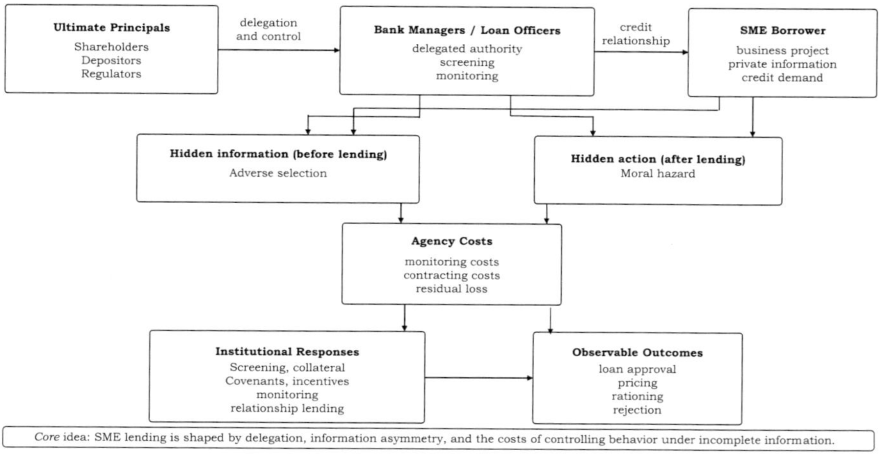

Fig. 3.2 Agency theory and the principal-agent problem in SME lending. Legend: Agency theory explains SME lending as a delegated decision problem shaped by information asymmetry, adverse selection, moral hazard, and the institutional costs of controlling borrower behavior under uncertainty. Source: Author's conceptual synthesis based on agency theory, principal-agent theory, information asymmetry, and the discussion developed in Sect. 3.2

These conditions generate agency costs. Banks, therefore, rely on institutional responses such as screening, collateral, covenants, relationship lending, monitoring, and internal approval procedures. For SMEs, however, these responses may also become exclusionary. When smaller firms lack standardized documentation, formal collateral, or a long credit history, the agency problem becomes more difficult to manage. The result may be higher pricing, tighter conditions, rationing, or rejection. This is one of the theoretical foundations of the missing middle: SMEs may be economically viable, yet remain difficult to finance because they are costly to evaluate and monitor.

3.3 Risk Theory, Behavioral Finance, and Decision-Making under Uncertainty

Agency theory explains why incomplete information and delegated authority create problems in the bank-SME relationship. Risk theory and behavioral finance then explain how banks interpret those problems when making lending decisions under uncertainty. The analysis, therefore, moves from the structure of the lending relationship to the psychology and institutional practice of credit judgment.

Risk theory is an amalgamation of different, more minor theorems. Its current iteration can be considered a subdiscipline of probability theory, focusing on how individuals make decisions under uncertainty or without complete information (Grandell, 2012). Risk theory has been applied to various fields, helping organizations in healthcare, insurance, and finance make reliable decisions and avoid unnecessary risk (Grandell, 2012).

According to the literature, there are four essential components in risk theory: risk, risk price, risk measure, and personal attitude to risk. In the finance sector, risk primarily refers to the possibility of loss, typically of capital or invested funds (Borch, 1967). Risk price refers to the potential depreciation of capital or investment earnings, often due to poor investment management, failure to diversify, or declining market prices. The third component, risk measures, comprises statistical measures such as variance, standard deviation, alpha, and beta. These values are based on historical risk measurements and quantify risk to investments. Finally, within risk theory, a personal attitude to risk is considered. Personal attitude to risk can be significant in decision-making and is often dependent on factors such as age, experience, goals, temperament, and the economic climate (Hillson & Murray-Webster, 2007).

When considered together, these components can indicate the amount and type of risks an investor is likely to encounter in a given situation (Borch, 1967). According to risk theory, an investor is apt to consider risk both affectively and analytically before making a decision. These facets of risk theory were instrumental in laying the foundation for behavioral finance, prospect theory, and regret theory (Dickason et al., 2017; Hammond, 2015).

The theory of behavioral finance (TBF) can be traced back to the 1980s, when it emerged as a component of behavioral economics (Amin & Pirzada, 2014). The development of behavioral finance is complex, as the fields of psychology and economics have increasingly focused on the decision-making of lenders, borrowers, and other stakeholders in the financial sector. The current iteration of TBF is credited to finance theorist Richard Thaler and psychologists Daniel Kahneman and Amos Tversky, who independently asserted that decision-making in the financial sector was not as straightforward as previously hypothesized. The TBF posits that financial decisions are not always based solely on utility and may also depend on the emotional reactions of those involved in financial decision-making (Dickason et al., 2017; Hammond, 2015).

Earlier theories that focused on decision-making and uncertainty, such as prospect theory and regret theory, form the framework for TBF (Kahneman & Tversky, 1979; Loomes & Sugden, 1982). Prospect theory, also developed, at least in part, by Kahneman and Tversky, states that financial decisions, especially those made by lenders, are contingent on the utility of the decision. If the risks were too high and the benefits too low, lenders were less apt to participate in loan creation (Amin & Pirzada, 2014; Hammond, 2015). Thus, the likelihood of participating in economic endeavors should be readily apparent when comparing risks and benefits.

Building on prospect theory, Loomes and Sugden (1982) argued that decision-making in scenarios with uncertain outcomes was not dependent on absolute utility. Instead, Loomes and Sugden hypothesized that decisions are made primarily by considering how much one would regret not participating in the endeavor should it be successful or by making the wrong choice.

Furthermore, this fear of being wrong may be irrational or exaggerated, leading to decision-making deficits (Zeelenberg, 2018).

The TBF and the prospect and regret theories that influence it each emphasize the importance of distinct facets of how human emotions affect financial decision-making (Amin & Pirzada, 2014; Hammond, 2015). This knowledge can be beneficial in times of uncertainty, which are common in financial markets (Amin & Pirzada, 2014; Hammond, 2015).

For the purposes of this book, these theories help explain why SME credit decisions are shaped by both measurable exposure and institutional interpretation. The point is not simply that bankers may be cautious, but that credit committees must justify decisions under uncertainty, often with incomplete information and asymmetric accountability for errors.

Behavioral approaches add an important qualification to purely mechanical accounts of lending. Decisions taken under uncertainty are not shaped by information alone. Loss aversion, salience, overreaction to recent defaults, and regret about future mistakes can all influence how ambiguous files are interpreted.

That said, the book does not treat psychology as a stand-alone explanation for the SME financing gap. Individual bias matters, but it is filtered through scoring systems, approval hierarchies, collateral rules, committee structures, and performance incentives. The relevant analytical question is therefore not whether judgment is behavioral, but how organizational design amplifies, disciplines, or redirects it.

Behavioral finance adds value here because real lending decisions are made by human beings operating under bounded attention, time pressure, and incomplete information. Recent defaults loom large. Sectoral shocks become salient. Ambiguous files invite caution. In committee settings, these tendencies can be amplified rather than neutralized, particularly when decision-makers know they will be judged more harshly for a bad loan than for a missed opportunity. That asymmetry pushes institutions toward borrowers who are easier to defend ex post, even if they are not always the borrowers with the highest developmental value. Behavioral finance is therefore not irrelevant to SME lending; it helps explain why uncertainty is often priced and managed asymmetrically (Amin & Pirzada, 2014; Bekerman & Zembylas, 2018).

Even so, the practical meaning of behavioral finance in this book remains limited and disciplined. Individual bias never appears in a vacuum. It is filtered through procedures, scoring tools, committee hierarchies, approval limits, and internal cultures of accountability. This is why a purely psychological account of SME exclusion is inadequate. Behavior matters, but it matters inside organizations whose structures determine which kinds of uncertainty are tolerated, escalated, or rejected. The more useful question is therefore not whether officers are risk averse in the abstract, but how institutions organize the way risk is perceived and processed.

Risk theory and behavioral finance extend the agency perspective by showing that lending decisions are shaped not only by information gaps but also by how uncertainty is measured, perceived, interpreted, and filtered inside banking institutions. Formal risk assessment focuses on measurable elements such as probability of default, collateral, repayment capacity, and expected loss. Behavioral finance adds that decision-makers do not process these elements neutrally. They interpret

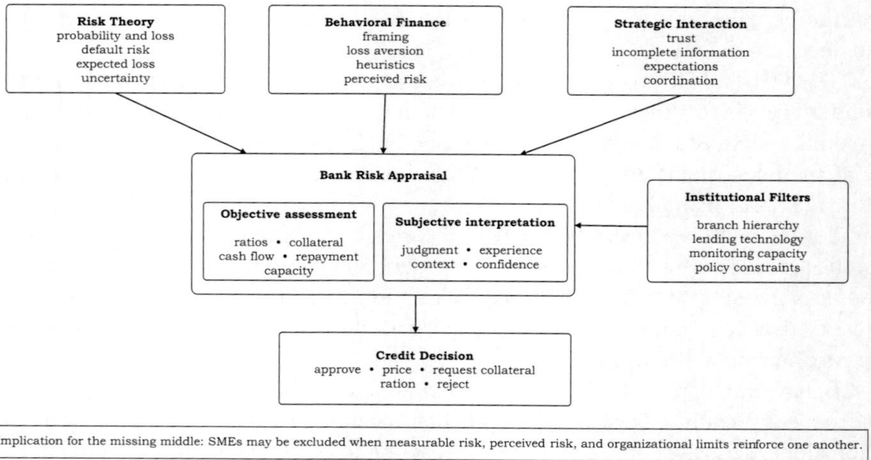

Fig. 3.3 Risk theory, behavioral finance, and decision-making under uncertainty. Legend: Bank risk appraisal combines measurable credit risk, perceived risk, behavioral interpretation, and institutional filters; SME exclusion may occur when these dimensions reinforce one another. Source: Author's conceptual synthesis based on risk theory, behavioral finance, decision-making under uncertainty, and the discussion developed in Sect. 3.3

risk through framing, loss aversion, prior experience, confidence, institutional routines, and expectations about borrower behavior.

Figure 3.3 brings these dimensions together. It shows how objective risk assessment, subjective interpretation, behavioral biases, and institutional filters interact before a bank reaches a credit decision.

The figure highlights the layered nature of risk in SME lending. At the first level, risk theory frames lending as a problem of probability, loss, default risk, and uncertainty. This is the technical dimension of credit appraisal. At the second level, behavioral finance shows that decision-makers interpret uncertainty through cognitive and psychological mechanisms such as framing, loss aversion, heuristics, and perceived risk. At the third level, strategic interaction reminds us that trust, incomplete information, expectations, and coordination shape the lending relationship itself.

These theoretical dimensions are then translated into bank risk appraisal. Some elements are objective and measurable: financial ratios, collateral, cash flow, and repayment capacity. Others are more subjective: officer judgment, experience, borrower credibility, local context, and confidence in the relationship. The final lending decision is also filtered through institutional constraints, including branch hierarchy, lending technology, monitoring capacity, internal policy, and prudential discipline.

This framework is important to the book's argument. It shows that the missing middle is not produced by risk alone, nor by banker caution alone. It emerges where measurable risk, perceived risk, behavioral interpretation, and organizational limits interact. SMEs may therefore be excluded not because they are necessarily unviable, but because the bank's risk appraisal system cannot convert imperfect and dispersed information into a defensible credit decision.

3.4 Information Asymmetry in Banking

Information asymmetry affects banking because credit decisions are made before the lender can fully observe the borrower's quality, incentives, and future behavior. Bergh et al. (2019) define information asymmetry as a "condition wherein one party in a relationship has more or better information than another" (p. 122). In banking, this concept is especially relevant because loan contracts are written under uncertainty and must anticipate both hidden information before lending and hidden action after disbursement.

According to the literature, five mainconceptual applications of information asymmetry are private information, different information, hidden information, lack of perfect information, and information impactedness. First, private information results when managers retain information about unobservable qualities (Bergh et al., 2019). Second, different information emerges when market intermediaries, such as analysts, use their expertise to interpret information gaps and promote their services. Third, hidden information arises when agents use non-observability to pursue their self-interest. Fourth, lack of perfect information arises when high-quality firm managers have incentives to signal their strong points to underinformed observers. Finally, information impactedness arises when transaction partners use provisions to shield against potential opportunistic behavior. The five main conceptual applications of information asymmetry can be found in investment banking, financial advisory roles, and business ventures. J. J. Lee underscored this finding when examining data on advisory relationships in U.S. mergers and acquisitions from 1981 to 2004. J. J. Lee's results showed that organizations that recurrently hired the same investment banks as financial advisors tended to overpay for acquisition targets. This finding was demonstrated by negative investor reactions, measured by cumulative abnormal returns (Lee, 2013). Furthermore, J. J. Lee found that the extent of overpayment for acquisition targets to the banks increased with the regularity of prior exchanges.

Similarly, other scholars noted the relevance of information asymmetry in banking. For instance, Patra (2019) and Tran et al. noted that information asymmetry in banking frequently involves opacity among insider managers. In banking, insider managers act as agents who control resources and make decisions over investments and retained earnings, whereas outside shareholders constitute the principal group (Patra, 2019, p. 6). Patra noted the relevance of information asymmetry in banking, examining the dividend signaling and smoothing by banking firms. The level of information asymmetry was examined among outsider principal groups. Lin et al. delved further into this topic, noting a significant positive relationship between dividend payouts and firm-level information asymmetry.

Tupangiu also noted the relevance of information asymmetry in banking, which occurs in relationships where one party, as the agent, holds information while the other party does not. Therefore, "to the extent that one of the parties to the financing agreement has information more or less accurate than another" (Tupangiu, 2017, p. 153), information asymmetry acts as a significant constraint in the financing of a project.

In their capacity as financial intermediaries, banks facilitate transfers of funds to agents or borrowers in need of funding or credit (Patra, 2019). Throughout this process, bank decision-makers should have thorough information to evaluate borrowers and their credit risks. During this process, information asymmetry and credit risk entail questioning and investigating the following facets: information issues between the bank and borrowers, the settlement of information issues, and bank decision-makers' activism in addressing information asymmetry (Tupangiu, 2017).

According to the literature, information asymmetry in banking may lead to or trigger financial crises. Despite the significant amount of information revealed to banks through credit applications, "the borrowers' advantage in the amount of information concerning their real creditworthiness impedes the effectiveness of the credit risk management process" (Pawłowska-Szawara, 2016, p. 471).

This finding is also viewed as prevailing information issues between the bank and the borrowers (Tupangiu, 2017). For one, consumers or borrowers may benefit from learning about unpaid consumer debts. This situation is an example of information asymmetry in banking, where clients have an advantage over banks (Nyoni, 2018; Pawłowska-Szawara, 2016).

In these cases, prevailing information asymmetry negatively impacts banking institutions. Nyoni (2018) highlighted the need to reduce information asymmetry in banking, as it can lead to bank closures, particularly in Zimbabwe. Nyoni examined this topic while investigating Zimbabwe's banking sector, which experienced the closure of several banks. The author found that several factors contributed to bank closures; however, information asymmetry was one of the most significant. Thus, Pawłowska-Szawara (2016) and Nyoni underscored the need for banks to reduce information asymmetry by adequately gathering and thoroughly analyzing information about borrowers and their respective credit standing.

Banks with varying levels of information asymmetry adopt different approaches and achieve different results in bank earnings management. Tran et al. (2019) noted this finding when examining discretionary loan-loss provision behavior in the U.S. banking industry. The authors gathered and analyzed data on U.S. public and private banks from 1986 (Q1) to 2013 (Q4). Their findings showed that discretionary loan-loss provisions were used as a proxy for conveying private information to investors. As a result, banks with relatively low earnings reported lower earnings when using discretionary loan-loss provisions (Tran et al., 2019).

Information asymmetry also impacts bank loan contracts. According to the literature, information asymmetry affects banks' risk assessment of enterprises, thereby influencing the terms of bank loan contracts. The authors used individual bank loan contract data to investigate the impact of corporate social responsibility information disclosure on information asymmetry in bank loan contracts (Zhigang et al., 2016). The findings showed that greater information disclosure led to more favorable bank loan contracts, characterized by lower interest rates, longer maturities, and higher loan amounts. The findings showed that the quality of corporate social responsibility information disclosure was significantly and positively related to loan terms and amounts (Zhigang et al., 2016). As such, information asymmetry impacts loan terms, rates, and amounts. Hence, voluntary information disclosure optimized the credit market environment and could serve as an empirical reference for the current study's assessment of banks' willingness to extend credit to SMEs in Burkina Faso.

Information sharing decreases bank credit risks and funding costs. Authors have noted the need to reduce information asymmetry and increase credit information sharing across African countries (Kusi et al., 2017; Kusi & Opoku-Mensah, 2018). Kusi and Opoku-Mensah examined this topic by investigating whether sharing credit information affected the funding costs of African banks. The authors gathered and analyzed data on credit information sharing and bank funding costs in Africa between 2006 and 2012, covering 233 banks across 17 African countries. The findings showed that the coverage by private credit bureaus significantly reduced banks' funding costs, highlighting the importance of providing credit information. The authors concluded that the presence, coverage, and quality of credit information sharing significantly decreased funding costs in Africa. Hence, establishing banking institutions that advocate for and practice credit information sharing is needed to reduce information asymmetry and decrease banks' funding costs in Africa. Kusi et al. noted similar findings when assessing the prevalence of bank credit risks, credit information sharing in Africa, and the impact of credit information-sharing institutions. The authors gathered and analyzed 548 bank observations from Africa between 2006 and 2012. Similarly, Kusi et al. found that credit information-sharing institutions reduced African banks' credit costs and risks. Therefore, the authors concluded that credit information-sharing policies were needed, particularly through private credit bureaus, to reduce banks' credit risks and funding costs (Kusi et al., 2017; Kusi & Opoku-Mensah, 2018).

Other researchers point in the same general direction, showing that information-sharing mechanisms work best when their coverage, data quality, and institutional use are strong. Asongu and Moulin (2016) examine how information and communication technologies can complement credit information institutions to reduce information asymmetry in access to finance in Africa. Boateng et al. (2018) examine information-sharing offices and market power in African banking, showing that the relationship is empirically important but institutionally nuanced.

This more cautious reading is important to the book's argument. Information-sharing offices, private credit bureaus, public registries, and digital data can improve credit assessment only when the information they provide is reliable, timely, and accepted within banks' decision systems. They reduce some frictions, but they do not eliminate the need for judgment, monitoring, and institutional accountability.

Information sharing and reduced information asymmetry may be beneficial in times of economic volatility, underscoring the value of credit bureaus. According to the literature, financial development, growth volatility, and information asymmetry are interrelated in the African banking system. The authors employed and analyzed data from 33 sub-Saharan African countries from 2004 to 2011, examining concepts of financial development and economic volatility (Ibrahim & Alagidede, 2017). The findings showed that private credit bureaus positively impacted financial development, highlighting the value of establishing information-sharing offices, considering economic volatility. Kusi et al. reported similar findings in their examination of information sharing across 25 Ghanaian banks. The authors evaluated the impact of information sharing on changes in banks' profits. Utilizing a Prais–Winsten panel regression analysis, the results showed that information sharing via authorized credit reference bureaus significantly increased banks' profitability. The findings further revealed that information sharing significantly reduced adverse selection, even during a financial crisis, by mitigating moral hazard risks and information asymmetry. This body of literature has shown the importance of reducing information asymmetry and promoting information sharing in banking systems, which may be achieved using authorized credit bureaus. This reference may be used to develop a strategy to mitigate banks' hazard risks, enabling them to protect themselves during economic volatility, as relevant in the context of Burkina Faso (Ibrahim & Alagidede, 2017; Kusi et al., 2016).

Information asymmetry is central to banking because lenders are asked to commit funds before the future can be known. Banks invest heavily in screening, verification, covenant design, and monitoring precisely because borrowers typically know more about their own prospects than the bank does. Where this informational gap widens, credit becomes more expensive to originate and more difficult to supervise.

Modern banking attempts to narrow that gap through internal databases, credit registries, scoring tools, audited statements, collateral registries, and increasingly digital payment histories. These mechanisms do not eliminate uncertainty, but they change its cost. They determine whether the bank can transform uncertain commercial activity into a file that is actionable at the branch level and defensible at the committee level (Asongu & Moulin, 2016).

Banking is fundamentally an information business. Even when capital is plentiful, a lender still needs ways to screen borrower quality, verify claims, structure contracts, and monitor repayment. Internal databases, credit bureaus, collateral registries, financial statements, tax records, and digital transaction histories all exist because the bank can never know enough about the future; yet it must commit funds. In that sense, information asymmetry is not an occasional disturbance in credit markets. It is their normal operating condition, and the entire banking apparatus can be read as a response to it (Boateng et al., 2018; Berger & Udell, 2006).

For that reason, the cost of information matters as much as its existence. Some borrowers are expensive to understand. They require branch visits, repeated conversations, contextual interpretation, and judgment about the credibility of incomplete records. Others fit easily within standardized systems. The difference is not only economic; it is organizational. Banks will naturally gravitate toward

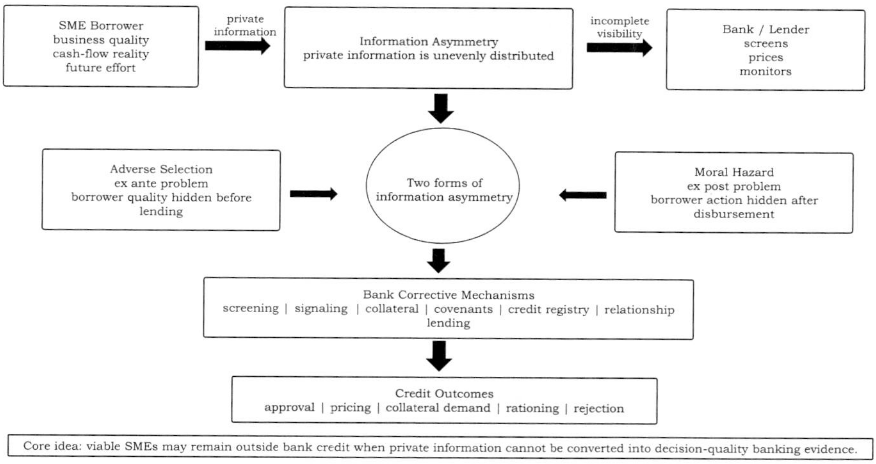

Fig. 3.4 Information asymmetry in banking. Legend: Information asymmetry shapes banking decisions through adverse selection, moral hazard, and the institutional mechanisms used to transform borrower information into usable credit evidence. Source: Author's conceptual synthesis based on Sect. 3.4 and the banking literature on information asymmetry, adverse selection, and moral hazard

clients whose information is cheaper to verify and easier to transmit upward. That tendency is rational from a prudential perspective, but it also helps explain why the financing gap persists even in well-capitalized, commercially active systems.

Information asymmetry is one of the most influential concepts in banking theory because it explains why credit markets do not function like ordinary spot markets. In lending relationships, the borrower usually knows more than the lender about the project's true quality, the reliability of cash flows, the use of funds, and the likely behavior after loan disbursement. Figure 3.4 summarizes this structure and highlights the two major forms of asymmetry: adverse selection before lending and moral hazard after lending.

The figure shows that information asymmetry is the central mechanism linking the borrower, the lender, and the final outcome in the credit market. Before the loan is granted, the bank faces adverse selection because it cannot perfectly identify which applicants are genuinely creditworthy and which present hidden weaknesses. After the loan is granted, the bank faces moral hazard because it cannot continuously monitor how the borrower uses the funds or how much effort is devoted to the project's success. These problems explain why banks rely on screening, signaling, collateral, documentation, monitoring, and relationship lending. They also help explain why credit may be rationed even when firms demand productive finance.

3.5 Information Asymmetry and Small and Medium-Sized Enterprises

Information asymmetry affects SMEs' access to credit. Researchers have identified information asymmetry as a common factor hindering lending to SMEs (Fontes et al., 2018; Howe & Morillon, 2020). The authors have delved into this topic and noted the value of information asymmetry in ensuring access to loans for SMEs in need of funding. Yoshino et al. explored this topic when investigating how a credit rating scheme for SMEs could be developed with bank lending data. The authors focused on SMEs and banks located in Thailand, employing statistical techniques to examine the data. The findings showed that reducing information asymmetry could increase funding and lending ceilings for SMEs. Song et al. (2018) also noted the value of information asymmetry, specifically based on banks' financing of SMEs.

The authors gathered and analyzed various case studies using interviews with lenders in China (Song et al., 2018). The authors examined commercial banks and financial service providers and found that reducing information asymmetry improved SME financing. Their findings showed that by acquiring transaction information and business credit from financial service providers, information asymmetry could be reduced. This body of knowledge showed the role of information asymmetry in helping guarantee funding for SMEs, which might be attained through the acquisition of transaction information and business credit in financial service providers (Song et al., 2018). Implementing financial service provider solutions within banking systems may help ensure SMEs receive the funding they need by addressing information asymmetry.

Decision-makers at banks should increase the share of performing loans in the SME sector. To do so, Fontes et al. (2018) and Yoshino et al. proposed and concluded that banks needed to decrease information asymmetry as they provided financing to healthy SMEs. A. Rahman et al. also underscored the need to increase funding for SMEs, given the importance of this sector in boosting the national economy in Bangladesh. The authors examined SMEs with long-term relationships with small banks, investigating factors related to bank size, relationship lending, and SME financing in Bangladesh. The findings showed that small banks often lacked the capacity or comparative advantage to process soft information. In another study, A. Rahman et al. found that small banks had no additional incentives to provide loans to SMEs, particularly regarding collateral security, than large banks. This body of findings showed the need for banks, both small- and large-scale, to develop lending techniques further to extend SME loans. Both small- and large-scale bank managers need additional techniques for extending loans to SMEs (Rahman et al., 2016a; Yoshino et al., 2016).

Various factors impact banks' willingness to lend to SMEs. According to researchers, some factors that impact SME access to bank financing include commitment of an SME to its credit obligations, financial information of the SME, the profitability of the SME, the borrower's debt ratio and current ratio, market share and competition of the SMEs, ability of the SME to generate cash flow, length of the

SME's relationship with the bank, the SME's line of industry, and the age of the SME (Erdogan, 2018; Fridhi et al., 2019).

Research from Turkey has shown that SMEs with long-term relationships with banks, as well as older SMEs, are more likely to have access to bank financing (Erdogan, 2018). Furthermore, interviews with bankers in Turkey revealed that SMEs in the manufacturing sector were more likely to obtain bank financing and loans than SMEs in other industries. Erdogan conducted a similar study, examining the determinants of perceived accessibility of bank financing for SMEs. The authors studied 492 Turkish SMEs using semi-structured interviews. Erdogan's study found that older and more innovative SMEs are more likely to obtain bank loans. Additionally, profitable SMEs with longer relationships with banks were found to have more positive perceptions of the accessibility of bank financing. Additionally, SMEs in the service industry had a better chance of obtaining bank financing and loans (Erdogan, 2019), which contrasted with Erdogan's finding that the manufacturing sector had a better chance of securing bank loans.

Similarly, Lussuamo and Serrasqueiro (2020) examined this topic to identify restrictions on SMEs' access to bank finance in Cabinda, Angola. The authors conducted semi-structured interviews with 15 SME owners and managers. The findings revealed that having close relationships with the bank manager and credit managers did not significantly drive SMEs' access to bank finance. Rather, factors such as high interest rates on bank loans and high collateral requirements have been identified as key constraints on SMEs' access to bank financing. In contrast to the findings of Erdogan (2019), Erdogan, Lussuamo, and Serrasqueiro found that the profitability of the SME, the borrower's debt ratio and current ratio, the ability of the SME to generate cash flow, and the SME's relationship with the bank did not significantly impact SMEs' access to bank financing.

This body of findings shows the various factors associated with SMEs' access to funding, highlighting the need for further examination of the setting, demographics, and other factors that might impact SME access to bank funding (Erdogan, 2018, 2019). More research is needed on the factors that influence banks' willingness to provide funding and loans to SMEs, considering the setting, demographic factors, and related factors, which justified the current study in Burkina Faso (Fridhi et al., 2019; Shaban et al., 2016).

The lack of collateral impacts SME owners' access to credit. Researchers have examined collateral requirements as a determinant for SMEs' access to credit (Fanta, 2016; Rahman et al., 2016b). Saito and Tsuruta in Japan, and Fanta in Ethiopia, noted that bank managers viewed SMEs as high-risk borrowers and demanded collateral for SMEs to access bank credit. However, Fanta noted that SME owners often lacked collateral, which deterred their access to bank credit. Administering a survey among 102 randomly selected manufacturing SMEs in Ethiopia, Fanta found that Ethiopian banks sparingly extended credit to SMEs, specifically due to the lack of collateral requirements. A. Rahman et al. noted other results, showing that having more collateral requirements did not guarantee or increase access to credit for SMEs, regardless of bank size. Liang et al. (2017) added that banks' cost efficiency declined as lending or funding to SMEs increased, thereby inhibiting South Korean banks' lending to SMEs. This body of findings identified a collateral factor that might be significant in determining banks' willingness to grant SMEs access to credit and funding. More research is needed to determine whether banks in Burkina Faso grant loans and funding to SMEs based on their collateral.

For SMEs, the problem of information asymmetry is typically more acute. Many smaller firms produce thinner financial records, operate with partially formalized systems, and rely on owner-managed practices that leave fewer documentary traces. As a result, the bank confronts not only the risk of default but also the cost of making the borrower intelligible in the first place.

This is where the distinction between hard and soft information becomes analytically decisive. Hard information travels easily within large institutions; soft information often depends on repeated contact, local sector knowledge, and branch-level judgment. SME credit is therefore shaped not just by borrower quality but also by whether the bank has workable ways to collect, transmit, and trust the kinds of information that smaller firms can realistically provide.

Informational opacity is often cumulative. Smaller firms tend to combine thinner accounts, shorter histories, fewer formal assets, irregular cash cycles, and a closer overlap between enterprise and household finance. None of these features automatically makes the business unviable, but together they increase the cost of interpretation. The missing middle persists in part because many viable firms generate rich soft information but insufficient standardized hard information for centralized credit processes (Berger & Udell, 2002; Angori et al., 2019).

A shared banking union, such as WAMU, does not eliminate this problem. Common prudential rules, regional monetary policy, and cross-border banking groups may standardize many aspects of supervision and balance sheet management, but they do not eliminate borrower opacity on the ground. Branches still operate in specific towns, sectors, and local commercial ecologies. Some markets generate cleaner documentary traces than others. This means that common institutions can coexist with varied lending outcomes. The union matters because mechanisms travel; the local market still matters because information remains unevenly produced and unevenly interpretable.

The literature reviewed so far points to a common analytical problem. Risk, distance, and information asymmetry are often discussed separately, yet in actual lending, they reinforce one another.

Figure 3.5 brings these dimensions together and shows how they converge on borrower legibility.

Seen in this way, the missing middle is not simply the residual category left after banks have funded the largest firms and ignored the smallest. It emerges where economically important borrowers remain difficult to classify, document, and process within formal lending routines. The figure, therefore, links the conceptual discussion of this chapter to the institutional reading developed throughout the book.

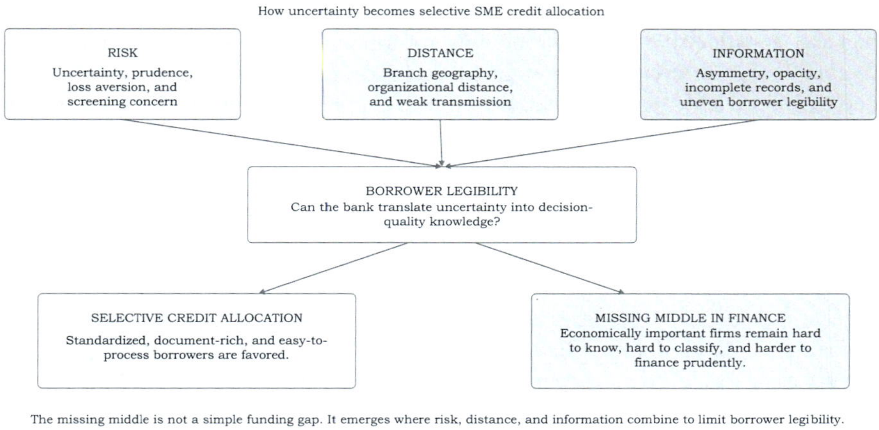

Fig. 3.5 The missing middle is not a simple funding gap. It emerges where risk, distance, and information combine to limit borrower legibility. Source: Author's conceptual synthesis based on Sect. 3.5, Information Asymmetry and Small and Medium-Sized Enterprises

3.6 Synthesis

The literature reviewed in this chapter draws on evidence from Africa, Asia, Europe, North America, and Oceania. However, the African evidence is particularly important for this book because it confirms that SME credit constraints are not only borrower-side problems, but also institutional, informational, and relational problems within bank-based financial systems.

The conceptual discussion also points toward a more disciplined way of talking about bank caution. Risk aversion, by itself, is too broad to explain how SME lending is organized. Agency theory identifies the contractual tensions at the heart of lending, while information asymmetry explains why those tensions intensify for smaller, less-documented firms. Behavioral and risk-oriented perspectives then help explain why uncertainty is interpreted unevenly by organizations and by the people who work within them.

That is why the evidence from Burkina Faso can speak beyond Burkina Faso without overclaiming. The book does not assume identical coefficients across WAMU member states; instead, it argues that where banks share supervisory architecture, business models, and borrower-opacity problems, the same mechanisms warrant sustained attention.

The value of combining these lenses is that it prevents the analysis from collapsing into either pure structure or pure psychology. SME credit decisions are neither fully mechanical nor fully personal. They emerge from institutional settings in which documentation, collateral, branch reach, internal controls, and decision-making authority interact with lenders' judgments. In this sense, theory is useful here not because it offers a single formula, but because it clarifies the layered nature of the financing problem.

The chapters that follow, therefore, use theory as an instrument of ordering rather than as a rigid doctrine. Agency problems, information frictions, soft and hard information, lender discretion, and organizational design are treated as interlocking mechanisms. The empirical material from Burkina Faso is then used to show which of these mechanisms appear most consequential in practice.

The conceptual conclusion is that SME lending should be understood as a problem of institutional legibility. Agency theory explains why incomplete contracts matter; behavioral finance reminds us that judgment is not frictionless; and information asymmetry shows why the cost of knowing a borrower is often as important as the price of funding.

In a shared banking space such as the West African Monetary Union, these mechanisms matter doubly. Banks operate under common prudential rules and, in many cases, inside cross-border groups. That does not make national outcomes identical. It does, however, make it plausible that similar organizational and informational bottlenecks recur across markets.

References

Amin, S., & Pirzada, S. S. (2014). Theory of behavioral finance and its application to property market: A change in paradigm. *Research Journal of Finance and Accounting, 5*(13), 132–134. https://core.ac.uk/download/pdf/234630024.pdf

Angori, G., Aristei, D., & Gallo, M. (2019). Lending technologies, banking relationships, and firms' access to credit in Italy: The role of firm size. *Applied Economics, 51*(58), 6139–6170. https://doi.org/10.1080/00036846.2019.1613503

Asongu, S. A., & Moulin, B. (2016). The role of ICT in reducing information asymmetry for financial access. *Research in International Business and Finance, 38*, 202–213. https://doi.org/10.1016/j.ribaf.2016.04.011

Bekerman, Z., & Zembylas, M. (2018). Emotion, emotional intelligence and motivation. In *Psychologized language in education* (pp. 67–78). Palgrave Macmillan. https://doi.org/10.1057/978-1-137-54937-2_8

Bendickson, J., Muldoon, J., Liguori, E. W., & Davis, P. E. (2016). Agency theory: Background and epistemology. *Journal of Management History, 22*(4), 437–449. https://doi.org/10.1108/JMH-06-2016-0028

Berger, A. N., & Udell, G. N. (2002). Small business credit availability and relationship lending: The importance of bank organization structure. *The Economic Journal, 112*(477), 32–53. https://doi.org/10.1111/1468-0297.00682

Berger, A. N., & Udell, G. N. (2006). A more complete conceptual framework for SME finance. *Journal of Banking & Finance, 30*(11), 2945–2966. https://doi.org/10.1016/j.jbankfin.2006.05.008

Bergh, D. D., Ketchen, D. J., Jr., Orlandi, I., Heugens, P. P., & Boyd, B. K. (2019). Information asymmetry in management research: Past accomplishments and future opportunities. *Journal of Management, 45*(1), 122–158. https://doi.org/10.1177/0149206318798026

Boateng, A., Asongu, S., Akamavi, R., & Tchamyou, V. (2018). Information asymmetry and market power in the African banking industry. *Journal of Multinational Financial Management, 44*, 69–83. https://doi.org/10.1016/j.mulfin.2017.11.002

Borch, K. (1967). The theory of risk. *Journal of the Royal Statistical Society: Series B (Methodological), 29*(3), 432–452. https://doi.org/10.1111/j.2517-6161.1967.tb00707.x

Campbell, D., Loumioti, M., & Wittenberg-Moerman, R. (2019). Making sense of soft information: Interpretation bias and loan quality. *Journal of Accounting and Economics, 68*(2-3), 101240. https://doi.org/10.1016/j.jacceco.2019.101240

Damasio, A. R. (1994). *Descartes' error: Emotion, reason, and the human brain*. Putnam.

Dias, R., & Mroczkowski, N. A. (2012). Do banks use credit default swaps to hedge or speculate? An agency theoretic perspective. *International Journal of Critical Accounting, 4*(3), 283–299. https://doi.org/10.1504/IJCA.2012.047365

Dickason, Z., Nel, I., & Ferreira, S. J. (2017). Gender: Behavioural finance and satisfaction of life. *Gender & Behaviour, 15*(3), 22–29. https://hdl.handle.net/10520/EJC-c3912944f

Erdogan, A. I. (2018). Factors affecting SME access to bank financing: An interview study with Turkish bankers. *Small Enterprise Research, 25*(1), 23–35. https://doi.org/10.1080/13215906.2018.1428911

Erdogan, A. I. (2019). Determinants of perceived bank financing accessibility for SMEs: Evidence from an emerging market. *Economic Research-Ekonomska Istraživanja, 32*(1), 690–716. https://doi.org/10.1080/1331677X.2019.1578678

Fanta, A. B. (2016). Complementarity between relationship lending and collateral in SME access to bank credit: Evidence from Ethiopia. *Journal of African Business, 17*(3), 308–318. https://doi.org/10.1080/15228916.2016.1177785

Fontes, J. C., Panaretou, A., & Peasnell, K. V. (2018). The impact of fair value measurement for bank assets on information asymmetry and the moderating effect of own credit risk gains and losses. *The Accounting Review, 93*(6), 127–147. https://doi.org/10.5539/ibr.v13n9p55

Fridhi, B., Trabelsi, W. B. A., & Zerai, M. T. (2019). Information asymmetry and credit rationing: An empirical study on Tunisian SMEs. *Transylvanian Review, 1*(1) http://www.transylvanian-reviewjournal.org/

Grandell, J. (2012). *Aspects of risk theory*. Springer. https://doi.org/10.1007/978-1-4613-9058-9

Hammond, R. C. (2015). *Behavioral finance: Its history and its future* [Theses, Southeastern University]. https://firescholars.seu.edu/cgi/viewcontent.cgi?article=1030&context=honors

Heckerman, D. G. (1975). Motivating managers to make investment decisions. *Journal of Financial Economics, 2*, 273–292. https://doi.org/10.1016/0304-405X(75)90016-1

Hill, C. W., & Jones, T. M. (1992). Stakeholder-agency theory. *Journal of Management Studies, 29*(2), 131–154. www.faratarjome.ir/u/media/shopping_files/store-EN-1485783393-748.pdf

Hillson, D., & Murray-Webster, R. (2007). *Understanding and managing risk attitude*. http://mcast.edu.mt

Howe, J. S., & Morillon, T. G. (2020). Do mergers and acquisitions affect information asymmetry in the banking sector? *Managerial Finance, 46*(12), 1521–1547. https://doi.org/10.1108/MF-03-2020-0127

Ibrahim, M., & Alagidede, P. (2017). Financial development, growth volatility and information asymmetry in sub-Saharan Africa: Does law matter? *South African Journal of Economics, 85*(4), 570–588. https://doi.org/10.1111/saje.12176

Ismail, A. G. (2011). The theory of Islamic banking: Look back to original idea. *Journal of Islamic Economics, Banking and Finance, 113*(453), 1–14. https://platform.almanhal.com/

Kahneman, D., & Tversky, A. (1979). Prospect theory: An analysis of decision under risk. *Econometrica, 47*(2), 263–291.

Karanja, N. N. (2018). *Effect of fraud risk management practices on level of activity by agent banks in Nairobi County* [Doctoral dissertation, Strathmore University]. Strathmore University Repository. https://su-plus.strathmore.edu/bitstream/handle/11071/6068

Kiburi, M. M. (2016). *Assessment of factors determining the performance of bank-led agent bank businesses in Kenya: Case of Kiambu County* [Doctoral dissertation, Strathmore University]. Strathmore University Repository.

Kusi, B. A., & Opoku-Mensah, M. (2018). Does credit information sharing affect funding cost of banks? Evidence from African banks. *International Journal of Finance & Economics, 23*(1), 19–28. https://doi.org/10.1002/ijfe.1599

Kusi, B. A., Agbloyor, E. K., Fiador, V. O., & Osei, K. A. (2016). Does information sharing promote or detract from bank returns: Evidence from Ghana. *African Development Review, 28*(3), 332–343. https://doi.org/10.1111/1467-8268.12209

Kusi, B. A., Agbloyor, E. K., Ansah-Adu, K., & Gyeke-Dako, A. (2017). Bank credit risk and credit information sharing in Africa: Does credit information sharing institutions and context matter? *Research in International Business and Finance, 42*, 1123–1136. https://doi.org/10.1016/j.ribaf.2017.07.047

Lee, J. J. (2013). Dancing with the enemy? Relational hazards and the contingent value of repeat exchanges in M&A markets. *Organization Science, 24*(4), 1237–1256. https://doi.org/10.1287/orsc.1120.0786

Liang, L. W., Huang, B. Y., Liao, C. F., & Gao, Y. T. (2017). The impact of SMEs' lending and credit guarantee on bank efficiency in South Korea. *Review of Development Finance, 7*(2), 134–141. https://doi.org/10.1016/j.rdf.2017.04.003

Loomes, G., & Sugden, R. (1982). Regret theory: An alternative theory of rational choice under uncertainty. *The Economic Journal, 92*(368), 805–824. https://doi.org/10.2307/2232669

Lussuamo, J. M., & Serrasqueiro, Z. (2020). Restrictions on access to bank finance for SMEs in Cabinda–Angola. *Small Enterprise Research, 1*, 1–14. https://doi.org/10.1080/13215906.2020.1835705

Mas-Colell, A., Whinston, M. D., & Green, J. R. (1995). *Microeconomic theory* (Vol. 1). Oxford University Press.

Mitnick, B. M. (1973). Fiduciary rationality and public policy: The theory of agency and some consequences. In *Paper presented at the 1973 Annual meeting of the American Political Science Association, New Orleans, LA*.

Mitnick, B. M. (2019). Origin of the theory of agency: An account by one of the theory's originators. *SSRN*. https://poseidon01.ssrn.com/

Nyoni, T. (2018). Information asymmetry in the banking sector: A Zimbabwean scenario. *International Journal of Marketing & Financial Management, 6*(1), 45–51. https://www.researchgate.net/profile/Thabani_Nyoni2/publication/325194833_INFORMATION_ASYMMETRY_IN_THE_BANKING_SECTOR_A_ZIMBABWEAN_SCENARIO/links/5afd4e150f7e9b98e03eb293/INFORMATION-ASYMMETRY-IN-THE-BANKING-SECTOR-A-ZIMBABWEAN-SCENARIO.pdf

Panda, B., & Leepsa, N. M. (2017). Agency theory: Review of theory and evidence on problems and perspectives. *Indian Journal of Corporate Governance, 10*(1), 74–95. https://doi.org/10.1177/0974686217701467

Patra, S. (2019). *Essays in bank dividend signaling, smoothing and risk shifting under information asymmetry and agency conflict* [Doctoral dissertation, University of Glasgow]. University of Glasgow Repository. http://www.theses.gla.ac.uk/41017/

Pawłowska-Szawara, E. (2016). Bank debt recovery in Poland as a determinant of information asymmetry. *World Scientific News, 57*, 465–473. https://www.infona.pl/resource/bwmeta1.element.psjd-eb8773f3-fc91-4815-8fa1-bb6204b1f6f6

Pirolo, L. (2020). Corporate boards. In *Corporate governance and diversity in boardrooms*. Springer. https://doi.org/10.1007/978-3-030-56120-8_2

Rahman, A., Rahman, T. M., & Ključnikov, A. (2016a). Bank size, relationship lending and SME financing: Evidence from Bangladesh. *Actual Problems of Economics, 183*(9), 294–307. https://publikace.k.utb.cz/

Rahman, A., Rahman, T. M., & Ključnikov, A. (2016b). Collateral and SME financing in Bangladesh: An analysis across bank size and bank ownership types. *Journal of International Studies, 9*(2), 112–126. https://doi.org/10.14254/2071-8330.2016/9-2/8

Rauchhaus, R. W. (2009). Principal-agent problems in humanitarian intervention: Moral hazards, adverse selection, and the commitment dilemma. *International Studies Quarterly, 53*(4), 871–884. https://doi.org/10.1111/j.1468-2478.2009.00560.x

Ross, S. A. (1973). The economic theory of agency: The principal's problem. *The American Economic Review, 63*(2), 134–139. https://www.jstor.org/stable/1817064

Shaban, M., Duygun, M., & Fry, J. (2016). SME's lending and Islamic finance. Is it a "win–win" situation? *Economic Modelling, 55*, 1–5. https://doi.org/10.1016/j.econmod.2016.01.029

Song, H., Yu, K., & Lu, Q. (2018). Financial service providers and banks' role in helping SMEs to access finance. *International Journal of Physical Distribution & Logistics Management, 48*(1), 69–92. https://doi.org/10.1108/IJPDLM-11-2016-0315

Sory, K. A. (2021). *Risk aversion behaviors in the bank-SMEs relationship: Predictors of credit in Burkina Faso* [Doctoral dissertation, Franklin Hudson International School of Management].

Stiglitz, J. E., & Weiss, A. (1981). Credit rationing in markets with imperfect information. *American Economic Review, 71*(3), 393–410. https://www.jstor.org/stable/1802787

Tran, D. V., Hassan, M. K., & Houston, R. (2019). Activity strategies, information asymmetry, and bank opacity. *Economic Modelling, 83*, 160–172. https://doi.org/10.1016/j.econmod.2019.02.008

Tupangiu, L. (2017). Information asymmetry and credit risk. *Finance: Challenges of the Future, 1*(19), 153–157. https://www.semanticscholar.org/paper/Information-Asymmetry-and-Credit-Risk-Tupangiu/214c4712409d553ed7da9a79186a7ac4f20a064f?p2df

Von Neumann, J., & Morgenstern, O. (1944). *Theory of games and economic behavior*. Princeton University Press.

Wilde, G. J. S. (1994). *Target risk*. PDE Publications.

Yosano, T., & Nakaoka, T. (2019). Soft information's role in lending decisions. In *Utilization of soft information on bank performance* (pp. 93–105). Springer.

Yoshino, N., Taghizadeh-Hesary, F., Charoensivakorn, P., & Niraula, B. (2016). Small and medium-sized enterprise (SME) credit risk analysis using bank lending data: An analysis of Thai SMEs. *Journal of Comparative Asian Development, 15*(3), 383–406. https://doi.org/10.1080/15339114.2016.1233821

Zeelenberg, M. (2018). Anticipated regret: A prospective emotion about the future past. In G. Oettingen, A. T. Sevincer, & P. M. Gollwitzer (Eds.), *The psychology of thinking about the future* (pp. 276–295). The Guilford Press.

Zhao, T., & Jones-Evans, D. (2017). SMEs, banks and the spatial differentiation of access to finance. *Journal of Economic Geography, 17*(4), 791–824. https://doi.org/10.1093/jeg/lbw029

Zhao, T., Luintel, K. B., & Matthews, K. (2020). Soft information and the geography of SME bank lending. *Regional Studies, 1*, 1–14. https://doi.org/10.1080/00343404.2020.1851024

Zhigang, L., Xianwang, S., & Lixian, G. (2016). CSR information disclosure and bank loan contract: From the perspective of information asymmetry. *Journal of Finance and Economics, 1*, 10. http://www.cnki.com.cn/

Chapter 4
Banks, Branches, and Borrowers in Burkina Faso and the WAMU Banking Space

This chapter repositions Burkina Faso as the book requires. The country is not introduced here as a shorthand for fragility or deficiency. It is introduced as a resilient, productive, and regionally connected economy whose banking system has become too important—and too dynamic—to be understood through older, overly pessimistic narratives. That is precisely why Burkina Faso is such a revealing empirical core for a book on risk, distance, and small and medium-sized enterprise (SME) credit in the West African Monetary Union (WAMU).

The argument of the chapter is straightforward. Burkina Faso matters to this book not only because it was the site of the original fieldwork (Sory, 2021), but because it combines three features that make the financing of the "missing middle" analytically significant. First, the country has a real productive base: Agriculture, trade, services, transport, construction, industry, and mining together create strong demand for working capital, investment finance, and payment services. Second, it sits within a shared monetary and supervisory architecture that gives national lending decisions broader regional relevance. Third, its banking sector has developed to a point where the central question is no longer whether banks exist but how they allocate information, proximity, and risk across firms of different sizes.

4.1 A Resilient Economy Inside a Shared Monetary Union

Burkina Faso belongs to the West African Monetary Union, an eight-country monetary area with a common central bank, currency, and framework for organizing and supervising banking activities. From this book's standpoint, that institutional fact is decisive. It means that the country's banking sector must be read at two levels: as a national market with its own structure and as part of a wider Union in which prudential rules, monetary conditions, and many banking groups are shared regionally (BCEAO, 2026a).

K. A. Sory, *Banking the Missing Middle*, Research Series on Responsible Enterprise Ecosystems, https://doi.org/10.1007/978-3-032-34582-0_4

Within that common framework, Burkina Faso has shown more resilience than many narratives acknowledge. The World Bank estimates that real gross domestic product (GDP) growth accelerated from 3.0% in 2023 to 4.9% in 2024, driven mainly by services and agriculture. Services alone contributed 3.1% points to overall growth, while agriculture contributed 1.9% points, supported by better weather conditions, improved access to land, and more effective public support. International Monetary Fund (IMF) staff subsequently estimated that growth strengthened further to 5.0% in 2025, supported by mining reforms, higher gold prices, and a response in artisanal and industrial production (IMF, 2026; World Bank, 2025a).

This resilience matters because it changes the meaning of SME finance. In a stagnant economy, weak credit demand can sometimes explain low lending. Burkina Faso is not that case. It is a country where growth has returned to around 5%, where the services economy is expanding, and where agricultural and extractive value chains continue to generate commercial opportunities. The financing question is therefore not whether there is anything to finance. It is whether the banking system can intermediate that activity beyond the largest and easiest-to-document clients (IMF, 2026; World Bank, 2025a).

The union-wide frame is analytically valuable because it prevents two symmetrical errors. One is to treat Burkina Faso as if it operated in isolation from regional banking institutions; the other is to assume that a common currency automatically produces identical credit markets. Neither is correct. WAMU creates a shared monetary and prudential architecture, but it does not dissolve national differences in economic structure, sectoral composition, or the quality of borrower information. Burkina Faso is therefore best read as a national market embedded in a common institutional order—precisely the kind of setting in which a case study can illuminate both local mechanisms and regional lessons (BCEAO, 2026a, 2024b).

Resilience, moreover, should not be romanticized. It does not mean the absence of shocks or constraints. It means that the economy has continued to generate growth, labor demand, and entrepreneurial activity even under demanding conditions. That distinction matters for this book because a resilient economy is one in which the question of SME finance becomes more—not less—important. Where firms continue to form, trade continues to expand, and services and agriculture continue to drive output, the financing gap cannot be dismissed as a side effect of economic inactivity. It becomes a central institutional bottleneck in an otherwise active, productive system (IMF, 2026; World Bank, 2025a).

4.2 Productive Strengths, Resources, and Demographic Potential

A more balanced reading of Burkina Faso must begin with its strengths. The country has a rapidly growing population of 23.5 million, and the World Bank projects the working-age population will reach 13.5 million in 2025, up 3.3% in a single year. This demographic profile creates pressure but also entrepreneurial energy, labor supply, and demand for new firms, markets, and financial services. In other words, the country's human resource base is not merely a social variable in the background of this book; it is part of the reason why SME finance has macroeconomic significance (World Bank, 2025b).

Burkina Faso also retains a diversified productive profile that is more substantial than caricatures of a narrow or exhausted economy suggest. Agriculture remains foundational and still employs about 60% of the workforce, while services are now the principal engine of measured growth. Gold mining remains strategic as well, accounting for 80% of exports, according to the World Bank's 2025 macro-poverty outlook. Cotton and broader agropastoral activities continue to matter to rural incomes and local commerce, while trade, logistics, repair services, and urban distribution link the country's primary and tertiary sectors in ways that directly concern SME financing (World Bank, 2025a, 2025b).

Even the security narrative should be handled with greater precision than is often the case. The point is not to deny constraints. It is worth observing that 2024 brought measurable improvements: The World Bank reports that incidents fell by 26.1% and fatalities by 11.5%. Those shifts do not eliminate risk, but they reinforce the central message of this book: Burkina Faso is not a space devoid of economic agency. It is a country in which households, firms, banks, and public institutions continue to adapt, invest, produce, and transact under demanding but evolving conditions. A book about the financing of the missing middle should therefore begin from resilience as much as from risk (World Bank, 2025a).

This more constructive framing also has a socioeconomic implication. The World Bank estimates that strong growth in agriculture and services reduced the extreme poverty rate by 3% points in 2024, to 23.2%. That matters for the present study because SME finance is not only a firm-level issue. Where smaller enterprises gain better access to working capital, equipment finance, or trade credit, the gains can flow into employment, household incomes, and local demand. In an economy where productive momentum is real, credit allocation becomes part of the mechanism through which growth is widened or narrowed (World Bank, 2025a).

The country's demographic profile reinforces that point. A growing, young population increases pressure on labor markets, but it also broadens the entrepreneurial base from which future borrowers emerge. New firms are created where markets deepen, towns expand, and households diversify income sources. In practice, that means the demand for financial services is likely to broaden long before all firms become fully legible in formal accounting terms. The book's concern with the missing middle is therefore not merely about current SMEs. It is also about how a growing population is converted—or not converted—into a future financeable enterprise (World Bank, 2025b).

Regional location adds a further dimension. Burkina Faso is landlocked, but it is not economically disconnected. Trade, migration, and financial relationships bind it to the wider Union. That regional embeddedness helps explain why lessons from the country matter beyond its borders. Many of the firms that seek credit in Burkina Faso operate in commercial circuits that extend into neighboring WAMU states, and many of the banks that evaluate them are themselves part of cross-border groups. The case, therefore, sits at a useful intersection between local borrower realities and a wider regional banking architecture.

4.3 A Banking Sector that Is Broader, Stronger, and More Innovative than Older Accounts Imply

The same rebalancing is required in any description of Burkina Faso's banking sector. Over 2020–2024, the system became demonstrably larger, denser, and more institutionally significant within the Union. The annual reports of the WAMU Banking Commission show that Burkina Faso moved from 19 credit institutions in 2020–2022 to 20 in 2023–2024, and by end-2024 accounted for 13.3% of total WAMU banking assets, ranking behind only Côte d'Ivoire and Senegal. At that date, the country's market comprised 16 banks, 4 nonbank financial institutions, and 2 financial holding companies. This is not a peripheral banking market. It is one of the Union's principal banking systems.

The expansion was also evident in the sector's operating footprint. Branches and offices increased from 324 in 2020 to 373 in 2024; ATMs rose from 503 to 610; and banking employment moved from 3823 to 4259. Customer penetration widened materially, with the number of bank accounts rising from about 2.20 million in 2020 to 3.27 million in 2024, while corporate accounts grew from 109,817 to 195,970. For the purposes of this book, those figures matter because distance is not only geographical. It is institutional. A denser banking network changes the conditions under which firms can be seen, screened, and monitored.

Balance-sheet growth reinforces the same point. Total banking assets rose from West African CFA francs (CFAF) 6633.6 billion in 2020 to CFAF 9574.1 billion in 2024, while share capital increased from CFAF 221.6 billion to CFAF 328.7 billion. Own funds and similar resources strengthened substantially over the period, and by 2024, deposits and borrowings stood at CFAF 6107.6 billion. Yet the post-2022 conversion of growing resources into credit was more restrained than the increase in institutional capacity might suggest. After rising strongly earlier in the period, net customer credit remained broadly flat between 2022 and 2024. That divergence is analytically important. It suggests that the missing middle cannot be explained by a simple shortage of banking resources. The more relevant issue is how available resources are filtered through lending routines, documentation requirements, and risk screens before they become available to smaller firms as credit.

Profitability remained positive throughout the period, but portfolio quality became more demanding. Net banking income increased from CFAF 300.1 billion in 2020 to CFAF 436.8 billion in 2024, while net profit, after climbing from CFAF 81.4 billion in 2020 to CFAF 158.6 billion in 2022, remained positive at CFAF 135.5 billion in 2024. Over the same horizon, however, the gross portfolio deterioration ratio moved from 9.6% in 2020 down to 5.7% in 2022, then back up to 9.0% in

2024, and the net deterioration ratio rose from 1.2% in 2022 to 3.3% in 2024. These are not signs of systemic failure. These are signs that credit risk has become more visible and more costly to manage. In such a setting, prudence toward smaller and less fully documented borrowers becomes easier to understand, even if it remains economically restrictive (BCEAO, 2024a, 2025b).

What is especially striking, however, is that this more difficult credit environment coexisted with durable prudential strength. The total solvency ratio stood at 13.8% in 2020, 13.4% in 2021, 14.2% in 2022, 14.2% in 2023, and 14.5% in 2024. The leverage ratio ranged from 6.6% to 7.6%, while the liquidity ratio remained above 111% throughout the period. On a 5-year average basis, Burkina Faso's banks posted a total solvency ratio of about 14.0%, a leverage ratio of 7.2%, and a liquidity ratio of 113.8%. In other words, the banking system was not structurally undercapitalized or illiquid. The challenge of SME finance arose within a system that was broadly resilient (BCEAO, 2024a, 2024b, 2025b).

The profitability profile over the same 5 years points in the same direction. Burkina Faso's banks recorded an average return on equity of about 15.4% and an average return on assets of 1.5%. The average net margin ratio was approximately 33.2%, while the net operating coefficient averaged 51.1%. Yet these results coexisted with an average gross portfolio deterioration ratio of about 7.9%, an average net deterioration ratio of 2.5%, and a nonperforming loan coverage ratio of roughly 71.4%. Read together, these ratios describe a system that was commercially viable and prudently sound, but one in which credit risk management remained active and costly (BCEAO, 2024a, 2024b, 2025b).

Market structure further sharpens the point. Burkina Faso's nationally systemically important banking institutions (établissements bancaires d'importance systémique, EBIS) gained weight over the period and, by 2024, collectively accounted for 66.9% of local market share in total assets, 63.5% in credit, 70.1% in deposits, and 91.8% of local net profit. At the regional level, Burkina Faso's banking groups also mattered, with some banks ranking among the Union's leading banks, placing Burkina Faso visibly within the upper tier of WAMU financial groups. This concentration does not negate market dynamism. It clarifies where decision-making power sits. In an expanding but concentrated market, SME credit outcomes depend disproportionately on the internal architecture of the institutions that dominate assets, deposits, and profit (BCEAO, 2024b, 2025a, 2025b).

The result is a banking sector that is broader, stronger, and more innovative in its possibilities than older accounts imply. It is broader because the network, customer base, and organizational reach have deepened. It is stronger because capital, liquidity, and profitability remained broadly robust. And it is more innovative in potential because this institutional deepening has occurred alongside the wider regional modernization of payments, financial infrastructure, and cross-border banking groups. For the purposes of this book, that is the key conclusion. Burkina Faso is not analytically useful because it lacks banking. It is useful because it has sufficient banking depth, regional integration, and institutional capacity to sharpen the central puzzle: Why, in a more capable system, does SME credit remain so selective?

A 5-year reading of the data makes the shift in scale unmistakable. Over 2020–2024, Burkina Faso's banking system recorded ratios typically associated with institutional solidity rather than marginality: an average total solvency ratio of around 14.0%, an average leverage ratio of about 7.2%, and an average liquidity ratio of about 113.8%. Profitability was also meaningful on average, with return on equity around 15.4% and return on assets around 1.5%. These are important facts for the book's argument. They show that the country's banking sector cannot be described convincingly as too weak, too illiquid, or too undercapitalized to lend. The deeper problem lies elsewhere—in how a prudentially solid system selects among borrowers whose information quality differs sharply (BCEAO, 2024a, 2024b, 2025b).

The same 5-year period also reveals a more subtle pattern: Balance-sheet growth and capital deepening did not translate evenly into customer credit growth after 2022. Assets, own resources, and institutional scale continued to strengthen, but lending expanded more cautiously, and portfolio quality became more demanding. That divergence is analytically important. It indicates that the constraint facing SMEs cannot be inferred from aggregate banking strength alone. A larger banking system does not automatically become a more inclusive one. It may simply become more selective, especially when rising portfolio stress encourages institutions to retreat toward borrowers they already know how to read and monitor.

Market concentration sharpens the same point. As national systemically important banks gained weight in total assets, deposits, credit, and profitability, a larger share of the country's financial intermediation became concentrated in institutions with strong internal hierarchies and powerful approval structures. That development is not inherently negative. Large banks bring scale, systems, and branch reach. But it does mean that the dynamics of SME credit increasingly depend on the routines of a relatively small number of dominant actors. In such a market, the missing middle is disproportionately shaped by the organizational choices of banks closest to the commanding heights of the system (BCEAO, 2024b, 2025b).

A final point concerns regional depth. Burkina Faso's place within financial holding structures reinforces the idea that the country is integrated into a wider banking order rather than operating on its margins. The presence of national and regional groups means that local credit decisions are influenced not only by domestic borrower conditions but also by cross-border governance, portfolio discipline, and strategic allocation inside multicountry institutions. This is precisely why the book moves from evidence from Burkina Faso to WAMU lessons. The country's banking sector is large enough, connected enough, and regionally entangled enough to be analytically significant beyond a single national balance sheet (BCEAO, 2024a, 2024b, 2025b).

Chapter 3 argues that Burkina Faso should not be approached as a marginal or purely distressed banking case. The more revealing point is that resilience, productive potential, banking depth, and regional embeddedness coexist with persistent selectivity in SME credit. Figure 4.1 condenses that apparent paradox.

The figure sharpens the chapter's central puzzle. If the banking system has broadened, deepened, and modernized, the persistence of selective SME credit

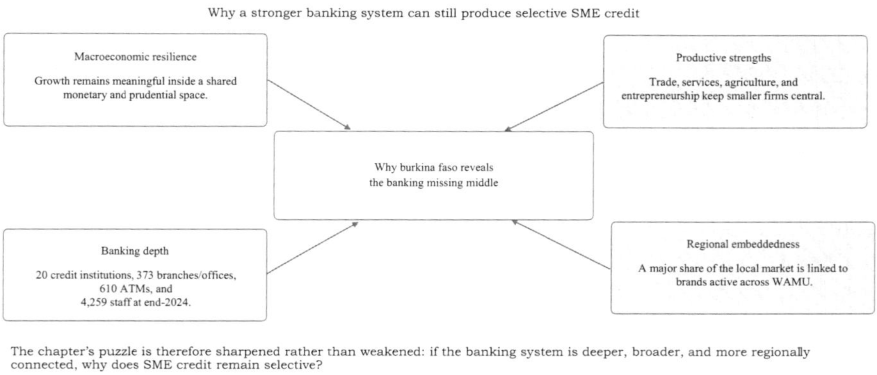

Fig. 4.1 Burkina Faso as a revealing banking case within WAMU. *Source: author's conceptual synthesis based on this section, a banking sector that is broader, stronger, and more innovative than older accounts imply*

cannot be explained by simple scarcity alone. It must also be explained by how prudence is organized inside a system that has become more capable without becoming equally inclusive.

4.4 Fidelis Finance as a Practitioner Vignette: Product Innovation and SME Finance in Burkina Faso

The argument of this chapter is not that Burkina Faso is merely a constrained or marginal banking case. It is also a setting in which specialized financial institutions have attempted to develop instruments adapted to the financing needs of smaller firms. For this reason, Fidelis Finance's experience is useful as a practitioner vignette. It should not be read as the book's central empirical proof. The empirical core remains the survey and banking evidence analyzed later in the manuscript. Rather, Fidelis Finance is used here as an illustrative case showing how one institution operating in Burkina Faso has sought to address the same problems that structure the book's central argument: risk, distance, borrower legibility, collateral constraints, and the difficulty of matching SME financing needs with conventional credit products.

The company's annual management report as of the end of 2025 presents the institution as a lending institution registered in Burkina Faso and Côte d'Ivoire. It describes an institution with approximately three decades of activity in West Africa, offering adaptive lending products to businesses and focusing on job creation and value addition. The document reports that Fidelis Finance has deployed more than 250 billion West African CFA francs (XOF) across its instruments and sectors, with the stated ambition to expand its loan book and strengthen its regional reach. This positioning makes the institution relevant to this book's argument, not because it represents the entire financial system, but because it illustrates how specialized institutions can broaden the range of technologies available for SME finance (Fidelis Finance, 2025).

The historical trajectory of Fidelis Finance also reflects the broader evolution of specialized SME finance in the region. The institution began operations in 1998 under the name Burkina Bail, at a time when leasing and asset-backed finance were still relatively specialized instruments in the Burkinabè market. The timeline presented in the report identifies several institutional milestones: ISO 9001 certification in 2006; the opening of a branch in Bobo-Dioulasso; a change of corporate name from Burkina Bail to Fidelis Finance; expansion into Côte d'Ivoire; authorizations to broaden activities; and, later, bond-market operations linked to SME finance based on a credit rating of A for long-term investments and A1 for short-term investments, both with stable outlooks.

This history matters because it shows that SME finance is not limited to the ordinary bank loan. Fidelis Finance's stated thesis is to provide innovative, flexible, and affordable financing to priority sectors, including agriculture, construction, renewable energy, technology, tourism, transportation, industry, education, and health. The product range presented in the report includes short-term financing, medium-term financing, medium-term investment, long-term investment, rental, factoring, purchase-order financing, equipment financing, furniture leasing, real-estate leasing, real-estate financing, and simple rental or rental with purchase option. These instruments are analytically important because each responds to a different configuration of risk, information, maturity, and collateral.

For the purposes of this book, the main lesson is not that any single institution can solve the SME financing gap. The lesson is that the missing middle cannot be addressed by a single product. Conventional bank lending is often ill-suited to firms whose financing needs are tied to equipment, receivables, contracts, inventory cycles, or small-ticket inclusion. Leasing can reduce collateral weakness by linking finance to a specific asset. Factoring and bill discounting can transform receivables into liquidity. Purchase-order financing can support firms that have commercial opportunities but insufficient working capital. Rental and leasing arrangements can give SMEs access to assets without immediate ownership. Guarantees can help firms participate in markets where contractual commitments exceed their immediate collateral capacity.

The Fidelis Finance vignette also illustrates the importance of process. The report describes an investment process that involves financial, operational, and legal analyses; evaluation of collateral, lease contracts, and repayment terms; risk assessment and credit scoring; and approval by a credit committee or relevant governance body. It also emphasizes deal structuring through leasing or loan agreements tailored to clients' cash flows and assets, contract finalization, disbursement of funds, delivery of leased equipment, and regulatory compliance. This process-based description aligns closely with the book's argument: SME credit is not simply a bilateral transaction between a bank and a borrower. It is an institutional chain through which information is collected, verified, interpreted, approved, monitored, and transformed into a financeable exposure.

The report further describes a regional footprint across Burkina Faso, Côte d'Ivoire, Benin, Mali, and Togo, as well as an institutional structure that includes Fidelis Finance's operations and AfriCred, a microfinance entity focused on responsible and inclusive finance for economic agents excluded from traditional financing institutions. AfriCred's products include women-focused accounts, group activity financing, microinsurance-linked products, and a mobile savings collection account that allows users to request a microloan. These elements are relevant because they show how the frontier between formal SME finance, microfinance, and inclusion-oriented products can be organized within a broader financial group.

The impact figures reported in the study are significant. The report presents more than 4545 impacted businesses, five countries reached, 82,075 direct jobs created or active in the portfolio, an average ticket size of XOF 55 million, XOF 125 billion specifically invested in SMEs, 5000 SME projects impacted, more than 12,000 direct and indirect jobs created in SMEs, and 18% of SME investment directed toward women-led SMEs. These figures are useful for understanding the scale of the institution's stated activities and ambitions, but they are not used here as the empirical basis for the book's statistical findings.

The vignette must therefore be interpreted with transparency. Because the author has held executive responsibilities in Fidelis Finance, the institution is presented here as a practitioner illustration rather than as neutral external evidence. Its role in the book is to show how the theoretical problems discussed earlier—information asymmetry, collateral weakness, monitoring cost, distance, and borrower legibility—can be addressed through a diversified set of financial instruments. The book's empirical claims remain grounded in survey evidence, archival bank data, and the regional banking analysis developed in the later chapters.

This distinction is important. The purpose of the vignette is not to promote Fidelis Finance, but to use its history as a concrete example of how SME finance can evolve when specialized institutions move beyond conventional lending. The broader implication is that banking the missing middle requires more than encouraging banks to lend more. It requires a richer financial infrastructure: asset leasing, receivables factoring, contract guarantees, working capital credit for operating cycles, rental products for flexible access to assets, and inclusive finance channels for smaller or women-led enterprises. In this sense, the Fidelis Finance experience reinforces the book's central argument: SME credit depends on financial institutions' capacity to transform SME activity into credible, monitorable, and financeable information.

The Fidelis Finance vignette, therefore, strengthens the case for treating Burkina Faso as an analytically revealing market. It shows that the country is not only a site of credit constraint, but also a space of institutional experimentation in SME finance. This dual character is precisely what makes the Burkinabè case valuable for a book on risk, distance, and SME credit in the West African Monetary Union.

4.5 Burkina-Based Banking Brands and Their Weight in the WAMU Financial Space

A further reason why Burkina Faso is analytically important to this book is that its banking market is not nationally isolated. At the end of 2024, Burkina Faso counted 20 credit institutions, comprising 16 banks and 4 nonbank financial institutions, within a Union-wide system of 160 credit institutions, including 135 banks and 25 nonbank financial institutions. Based on total assets, Burkina Faso represented 13.3% of WAMU banking assets, ranking behind only Côte d'Ivoire and Senegal. This makes Burkina Faso not merely a national case, but one of the Union's major banking systems (BCEAO, 2025b).

The regional importance of the Burkinabè market is reinforced by the number of institutions active in Burkina Faso that are also present elsewhere in the Union. On a conservative brand-matching basis, the 11 banking brands and two nonbank financial brands identified from Burkina Faso correspond to 70 local entities across WAMU at end-2024, comprising 64 banks and six nonbank financial institutions. Their geographic spread reaches all eight member states and is heaviest in Burkina Faso, Côte d'Ivoire, Senegal, Benin, and Mali. This is not a peripheral footprint. It is one of the institutional channels through which regional banking power is organized and exercised. Table 4.1 summarizes the country-by-country coverage of this Burkina-present cross-border core.

The quantitative weight of this cross-border core is substantial. The 11 banking groups alone account for CFAF 39,671.0 billion in total assets, CFAF 19,931.3 billion in credit to the economy, and CFAF 27,399.6 billion in deposits and borrowings. Relative to Union totals, this corresponds to roughly 55.0% of total banking assets, 54.0% of credit to the economy, and 56.8% of deposits and borrowings. Once the two nonbank financial brands are added, the perimeter reaches CFAF 39,882.1 billion in total assets, 1769 branches or outlets, 18,446 staff, and 13,506,951

Table 4.1 Country coverage of the 13 Burkina-present cross-border brands in WAMU, end-2024

Country	Local entities
Benin	9
Burkina Faso	13
Côte d'Ivoire	11
Guinea-Bissau	4
Mali	8
Niger	7
Senegal	10
Togo	8
Total	70

Source: Author's calculations from the 2024 WAMU Banking Commission country annexes and brand matching across member states

Table 4.2 Union-wide footprint of the 11 banking groups present in Burkina Faso, end-2024

Banking brand	Local entities	Total assets (CFAF bn)	Credit (CFAF bn)	Deposits/borrowings (CFAF bn)
Ecobank	8	6721.0	2831.5	4942.6
Coris Bank International	8	6213.1	2863.1	3868.7
Société Générale	5	6170.5	4116.9	4622.1
Bank of Africa	7	4977.5	2392.3	3712.2
Banque Atlantique	8	4414.5	2389.6	2895.3
Orabank	8	2972.8	1349.2	2173.8
United Bank for Africa	5	2383.2	684.8	1366.5
BSIC Group	7	2291.2	1169.5	1250.2
CBAO/Attijariwafa	4	1762.0	1170.0	1400.9
Banque de l'Union	2	980.9	540.8	634.6
IB Bank/International Business Bank	2	784.3	423.6	532.8
Total	64	39,671.0	19,931.3	27,399.6

Source: Author's calculations from Annex II.1.1.a part of the 2024 report

Table 4.3 Union-wide footprint of the two nonbank financial brands present in Burkina Faso, end-2024

Nonbank financial brand	Local entities	Total assets (CFAF bn)	Capital/dotation (CFAF bn)	Branches/ outlets	Staff
Fidelis Finance	2	116.2	27.5	6	71
Alios Finance	4	94.9	8.2	10	92
Total	6	211.1	35.7	16	163

Note: The 2024 report does not publish institution-level credit, deposits, or net banking income for these six local nonbank financial entities in a form that permits exact consolidation for this selected perimeter

disclosed accounts. The institutions that help define SME finance in Burkina Faso are not only local lenders. They are part of a banking core that already operates at Union scale. Tables 4.2, 4.3, 4.4 and 4.5 report this footprint in detail (author's calculations based on BCEAO, 2025b).

A methodological caution is required. The 2024 report allows exact institution-level aggregation for assets, credit, and deposits for banks, and exact reconstruction of capital—or dotation—branches, staff, and accounts from the country annexes. It does not, however, publish institution-level net banking income or institution-level credit and deposit aggregates for the six local nonbank financial entities in a form that permits exact consolidation for the full 13-brand perimeter. For that reason, the tables below report exact Union-wide totals for the 11-bank subset, exact absolute totals for the 13-brand perimeter where reconstructible, and transparent notes where the report does not provide a directly aggregable denominator.

Analytically, this matters to the book's argument because it sharpens the meaning of distance. Distance is not only the physical space between a borrower and a branch. It is also organizational distance: the distance between local commercial

Table 4.4 Consolidated weight of the 13 Burkina-present cross-border brands in WAMU, end-2024

Indicator	13-brand total	WAMU total	Share of WAMU
Local entities	70	160 credit institutions	43.8%
Total assets (CFAF bn)	39,882.1	72,068.3	55.3%
Capital/dotation (CFAF bn)	1210.6	n.a.	n.a.
Branches/outlets	1769	3220	54.9%
Staff	18,446	41,741	44.2%
Accounts*	13,506,951	22,202,263	60.8%

**Accounts correspond to the banking entities disclosed in the report. A comparable account count is not published for the six nonbank financial entities*
Source: Author's calculations from Annex II.1.1.a, the 2024 country annexes, and the Union totals reported for end-2024

Table 4.5 Banking-only weight of the 11 banking groups in WAMU, end-2024

Indicator	11-bank total	WAMU total	Share of WAMU
Total assets (CFAF bn)	39,671.0	72,068.3	55.0%
Credit to the economy (CFAF bn)	19,931.3	36,888.3	54.0%
Deposits/borrowings (CFAF bn)	27,399.6	48,243.5	56.8%

Source: Author's calculations from Annex II.1.1.a of the 2024 report and the Union totals reported for end-2024

knowledge and the regional or head-office structures that validate, reprice, or reject credit. In a system dominated by cross-border groups, branch-level decisions are shaped by multicountry governance, portfolio constraints, internal hierarchies, and supervisory expectations that extend beyond one national market. Burkina Faso's banking system is therefore not simply local in its consequences. It is regional in its organizational logic.

The implication for the "missing middle" is direct. If the institutions that dominate SME finance in Burkina Faso already account for more than half of WAMU banking assets, credit, deposits, and branch infrastructure, then SME underfinancing cannot be treated as a narrowly domestic puzzle. It must be read as a problem produced within a regional banking architecture whose routines, approval structures, and information standards span borders. That is precisely why evidence from Burkina Faso can support broader regional lessons without claiming pooled econometric proof for all member states.

The regional significance of Burkina Faso becomes clearer once the banking landscape is read across borders. Many institutions active in the Burkinabè market belong to brands and groups that operate elsewhere in the Union. Figure 4.2 visualizes that cross-border footprint.

This regional footprint matters because the mechanisms studied in this book are not confined to a single national banking market. They are embedded in a shared monetary and supervisory space in which organizational routines, approval structures, and portfolio logics travel across borders. The Burkinabè case is therefore nationally grounded but regionally illuminating.

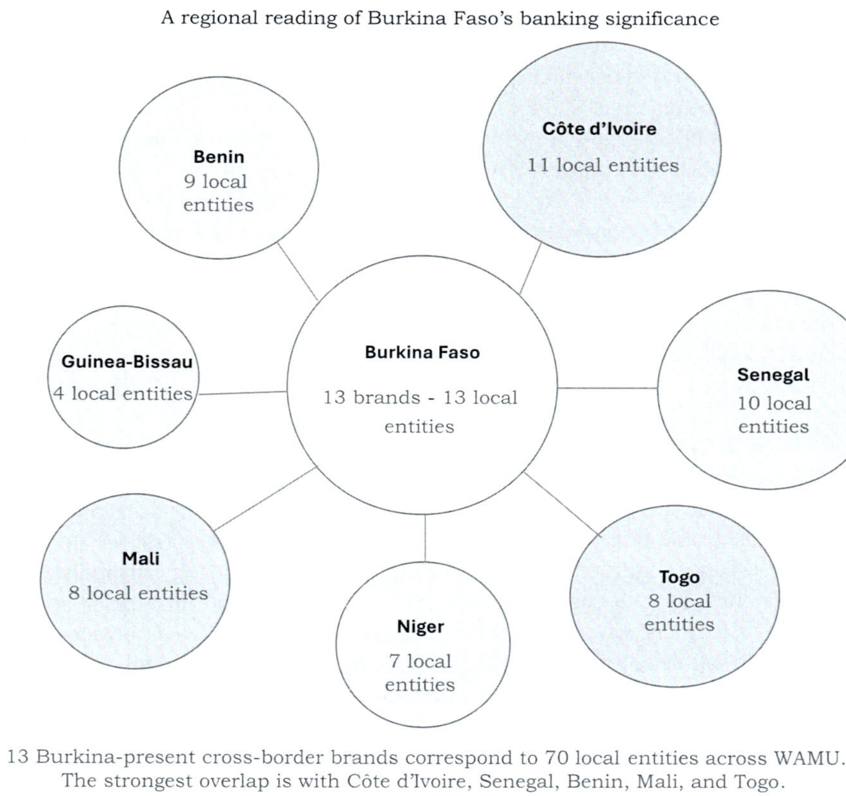

Fig. 4.2 Cross-border banking footprint of Burkina-linked brands in WAMU. *Source: Author's conceptual synthesis based on this section, Burkina-based banking brands and their weight in the WAMU financial space*

4.6 Digital Modernization and Regional Connectivity

Another positive development, highly relevant to the book's regional horizon, is the acceleration of financial digitalization. The 2024 digital financial services report of the Central Bank of West African States (Banque Centrale des États de l'Afrique de l'Ouest, BCEAO) estimates the Union's overall financial inclusion rate at 73.6%, with digital financial services contributing 57.2% of that total. The same report records 69 electronic-money initiatives in the Union in 2024, including 52 bank-led initiatives and two national treasuries—those of Côte d'Ivoire and Burkina Faso. In value terms, electronic-money transactions reached CFAF 160,415 billion in 2024, equivalent to 118.94% of Union GDP (BCEAO, 2026b).

Burkina Faso's place in this regional financial circulation is notable. The BCEAO reports that in 2024, Burkina Faso accounted for 22 million intra-Union cross-border payment operations with a total value of CFAF 1459 billion, ranking just behind Côte d'Ivoire on this measure. For the purposes of this book, that statistic is more than descriptive. It signals that Burkina Faso is deeply embedded in regional payment, trade, and transfer circuits. A banking system operating in such an environment cannot be understood only as a set of domestic balance sheets. It is part of a regional financial geography in which information, payments, savings, and credit increasingly travel across borders (BCEAO, 2026b).

Digital modernization has expanded the informational possibilities of banking, but not all digital depth translates immediately into credit depth. Payment accounts, electronic-money platforms, transaction trails, and intra-Union transfers all increase the volume of potentially usable data. They can, in principle, help banks estimate turnover stability, supplier relationships, and customer flows. Yet those possibilities become real only when such information is incorporated into risk assessment systems and accepted by committees as credible evidence. The crucial distinction is therefore between digital activity and digital bankability. Burkina Faso and the wider Union have progressed significantly on the first dimension; the second remains more uneven.

This distinction is especially important for SMEs. Many smaller firms now generate more electronic traces than older accounts of African enterprise would suggest. They receive digital payments, move funds across mobile channels, and increasingly interact with customers through hybrid formal and informal systems. But as long as loan underwriting continues to privilege conventional balance-sheet evidence above all else, these new traces remain underused. The promise of digital modernization for SME finance lies not simply in more transactions, but in developing lending models that translate transactional visibility into prudently usable credit information.

4.7 Why Burkina Faso Is a Revealing Case for This Book

All of this—including the cross-border banking footprint just examined—brings the argument back to the book's title and objectives. A study of risk, distance, and SME credit requires a setting in which there is both genuine demand for finance and a banking system capable of responding to it, yet the translation of economic activity into formal credit remains incomplete. Burkina Faso fits that requirement particularly well. The economy is resilient, the productive base is real, the entrepreneurial and demographic potential is substantial, and the banking sector is both nationally meaningful and regionally embedded. Precisely because these strengths exist, persistent SME underfinancing becomes analytically revealing rather than unsurprising.

The chapter, therefore, treats Burkina Faso not as an outlier of weakness but as a strategic observatory of the missing middle problem in the West African Monetary Union. The country's commercial geography, its mix of domestic and cross-border banks, its rising deposit base, and its growing integration into digital and intra-Union financial flows make it an especially useful setting for studying how branch presence, institutional distance, information quality, and lending technologies affect

SMEs. In that sense, the evidence from Burkina Faso developed later in this book does not narrow the regional conversation. It sharpens it.

The value of Burkina Faso as a case is therefore not accidental. It combines a banking system of real scale, a productive economy with visible entrepreneurial demand, and a regional institutional setting that makes the mechanisms under study relevant beyond one jurisdiction. In other words, the country offers the right mix of national specificity and regional portability. That is precisely what a book on risk, distance, and SME credit requires: a case grounded enough to support careful empirical argument yet institutionally connected enough to generate lessons for the wider West African Monetary Union.

It is also a revealing case because it does not allow easy explanations. The economy is not inert. The banking system is not absent. Prudential ratios are not collapsing. Digital modernization is advancing. And yet the financing gap persists. When those simpler explanations are removed, the analytical spotlight falls more sharply on organizational design, information frictions, and branch-level knowledge. That is why Burkina Faso works so well for the present inquiry. It forces the problem of SME credit to be analyzed at the level where the book wants to analyze it: the organization of prudence itself.

4.8 Synthesis

The broader lesson of this chapter is that context should not be written only in the language of deficiency. Burkina Faso enters this book as a country with economic resilience, demographic momentum, resource endowments, entrepreneurial demand, and banking dynamism within a highly integrated monetary union. Those strengths are not incidental to the financing problem; they are what make it important. The cross-border banking core documented in the preceding section reinforces that point. A large share of the institutions that structure SME credit in Burkina Faso are also actors in a wider WAMU banking space, meaning that local lending decisions are filtered through regional group strategies, supervisory routines, and organizational distances that extend beyond a single market. Where growth potential, domestic resource mobilization, and banking depth are all present, the persistence of a missing middle in formal credit becomes a question of organizational design, informational reach, and risk management under distance. That is the precise question the next chapters take up.

References

BCEAO. (2024a). *Rapport annuel de la Commission Bancaire de l'UMOA—2022*. https://www.bceao.int/sites/default/files/2024-03/Rapport_Annuel_SGCB_2022.pdf

BCEAO. (2024b). *Rapport annuel de la Commission Bancaire de l'UMOA—2023*.

BCEAO. (2025a). *Paysage bancaire de l'UMOA à fin décembre 2024*. https://www.bceao.int/fr/content/paysage-bancaire

BCEAO. (2025b). *Rapport annuel de la Commission Bancaire de l'UMOA—2024*. https://www.bceao.int/fr/publications/rapport-annuel-de-la-commission-bancaire-de-lumoa-2024

BCEAO. (2026a). *Presentation of the BCEAO / WAMU*. https://www.bceao.int/en/content/presentation-bceao

BCEAO. (2026b). *Rapport annuel sur l'évolution des services financiers numériques dans l'UEMOA—Année 2024*. https://www.bceao.int/sites/default/files/2026-03/Rapport%20annuel%20sur%20les%20services%20financiers%20num%C3%A9riques%20dans%20l%27UEMOA%20-%202024.pdf

Fidelis Finance. (2025). *Management 2025 annual report fidelis finance Burkina Faso*.

International Monetary Fund (IMF). (2026). *Burkina Faso: Fourth review under the extended credit facility arrangement, financing assurances review, and request for an arrangement under the resilience and sustainability facility—Press release; staff report; and statement by the executive director for Burkina Faso*. IMF Country Report No. 26/64. https://www.imf.org/-/media/files/publications/cr/2026/english/1bfaea2026001-source-pdf.pdf

Sory, K. A. (2021). *Risk aversion behaviors in the bank-SMEs relationship: Predictors of credit in Burkina Faso* [Doctoral dissertation, Franklin Hudson International School of Management].

World Bank. (2025a). *Burkina Faso economic update: Energy for economic growth*. https://documents1.worldbank.org/curated/en/099070725193540162/pdf/P507242-d1d2d1e3-c63b-49ba-a5da-c9994d3e747a.pdf

World Bank. (2025b). *Macro poverty outlook: Burkina Faso, October 2025*. https://documents1.worldbank.org/curated/en/099746010032519147/pdf/IDU-a40d865c-cdbc-4bef-b176-b97561a7ac76.pdf

Chapter 5
How Banks Decide in the WAMU Banking Space

If small and medium-sized enterprise (SME) finance matters because it shapes survival, investment, and growth, the next question is how banks decide. That question is national in its immediate evidence but regional in its relevance. Across the WAMU banking space, banks and banking groups repeatedly confront the same underlying problem: how to transform incomplete, uneven, and sometimes fragile information on smaller firms into a decision that is commercially defensible and prudentially acceptable.

A useful starting point is the idea of lending technology. Banks do not lend in a purely intuitive way. They lend through identifiable systems that combine sources of information, screening procedures, contract structures, monitoring methods, and approval routines. In this sense, a lending technology is not a machine. It is an institutional method for transforming uncertainty into judgment. Different lending technologies rely on different forms of evidence, and they therefore favor different kinds of borrowers (Angori et al., 2019; Berger & Udell, 2006).

The most important distinction is between transaction-based lending and relationship lending. Transaction-based lending relies primarily on hard information: formal financial statements, collateral records, credit histories, ratings, standardized scoring, and other data that can be verified, compared, and transmitted easily within the bank. It works best when firms are already legible in documentary terms. Large firms, or smaller firms with stronger accounting practices and clearer asset positions, fit this model more easily. For banks, transaction lending has obvious attractions. It is more standardized, more scalable, and more compatible with centralized decision-making.

Relationship lending addresses a different reality. Many SMEs do not produce the volume or quality of formal information that transaction-based systems require. Their accounts may be incomplete, their governance informal, their revenues variable, and their collateral imperfectly documented. Yet these firms are not unknowable. They become knowable through repeated contact, local presence, site visits, repayment history, supplier and customer reputation, and the cumulative

K. A. Sory, *Banking the Missing Middle*, Research Series on Responsible Enterprise Ecosystems, https://doi.org/10.1007/978-3-032-34582-0_5

observations of bank staff. This is the domain of soft information. Relationship lending is therefore not a lesser form of rationality. It is a different way of producing knowledge under conditions where formal records alone are insufficient (Berger & Udell, 2002; Boulanouar et al., 2020).

This distinction helps explain why proximity matters. The closer a bank is to the commercial life of SMEs, the easier it becomes to collect soft information and update it over time. Distance is not only geographic. It is informational. A branch that knows the local market, visits clients regularly, and understands local business rhythms can often interpret a borrower more accurately than a distant decision center relying solely on files. This is one reason why the architecture of branch networks matters so much in SME finance.

Technology modifies this landscape, but it does not eliminate the underlying problem. Information technology can improve data collection, reduce screening time, broaden lenders' reach, and support decision-making for geographically distant borrowers. Digital tools, scoring systems, platform lending, and data-processing models can all increase the speed and apparent objectivity of credit allocation. For banks, this is attractive: Technology lowers costs, standardizes procedures, and can make it easier to process large numbers of smaller applications.

Yet the effects of technology are not uniformly inclusive. The same systems that make lending more efficient can also make it more selective. A bank that relies heavily on standardized information may become less capable of lending to firms whose main problem is not poor quality, but poor documentation. Technology can reduce some forms of opacity, but it can also penalize enterprises that fail to leave the right digital or accounting traces. In this sense, fintech does not automatically solve the SME credit problem. It changes the terms on which legibility is produced.

For the borrower, this means that access to credit depends partly on becoming readable to the bank. SME-side factors matter for this reason. Entrepreneurs who understand the logic of lending procedures, can present more coherent information, maintain better records, and engage more effectively with bank requirements are more likely to navigate the application process successfully. Educational attainment, familiarity with banking practices, the ability to explain the business model, and the capacity to provide usable documentation all affect how the firm appears inside the lending process.

Bank-side factors are equally important. Even where formal procedures exist, loan decisions involve interpretation. Loan officers assess files, read inconsistencies, weigh character against documentation, and translate local knowledge into institutional recommendations. Their judgment can add value, especially when soft information matters. But discretion also introduces variability. Different officers may read the same borrower differently. Perceptions of trust, competence, seriousness, or risk may shape outcomes even when formal requirements appear to be met (Benvenuti et al., 2017; Bouwens & Kroos, 2019).

This is where the literature on individual cognition becomes relevant, but only up to a point. Emotional intelligence (EI), cognitive constraints, and behavioral tendencies may influence how officers process information and respond to uncertainty. However, this book does not treat those factors as the central explanation of SME credit allocation. Their importance is mediated by organizational structure. A loan officer does not make decisions in an empty space. Judgment is shaped by delegation rules, approval hierarchies, branch responsibilities, reporting systems, portfolio pressures, and the availability of hard information.

The stronger analytical claim is therefore institutional. SME credit depends on the interaction between lending technologies and organizational judgment. When banks rely solely on hard information, opaque yet viable firms may be excluded. Where banks rely only on informal impressions, credit allocation may become inconsistent, biased, or overly dependent on personal ties. The practical challenge is to combine discipline with flexibility: objective information where possible, relationship-based assessment where necessary, and approval structures that translate local knowledge into defensible lending decisions.

Seen in this way, the bank-SME relationship is neither purely transactional nor purely relational. It is a structured process in which documentary evidence, local knowledge, branch geography, screening tools, and officer judgment interact. This interaction determines not only whether a firm receives credit but also the terms, cost, and degree of monitoring. The scarcity of SME finance is therefore best understood not as a simple shortage of willingness, but as a problem of institutional information processing.

5.1 Technology in Lending Decisions

Technology is a vital factor to consider in understanding lending decisions. Various researchers have noted the significant role of technology in underpinning SME lending (Berger & Udell, 2002; Brighi et al., 2019). According to the literature, a lending technology can be defined as a unique combination of primary data sources, assessment and guaranteeing policies, loan contract structures, and monitoring tools. Further to this, Burger and Udell reported that seven technologies significantly underpin SME lending: financial statement lending, credit-score microbusiness, asset-based lending (leasing), factoring, trade credit, credit insurance, and, most importantly, relationship lending. In more recent studies, researchers have outlined two common lending techniques: transaction-based lending and relationship lending (Ferri et al., 2019; Yosano & Nakaoka, 2019a).

Transaction lending technologies include financial statement lending, small-business credit scoring, asset-based lending, factoring, fixed-asset lending, and leasing (A. N. Berger & Udell, 2002). Transaction lending technologies also focus more on hard quantitative information. On the other hand, relationship lending focuses more on soft qualitative information, which is often affected by data collection processes and by bank and loan officer characteristics (Ferri et al., 2019).

The outlined lending techniques are vital because they influence banks' lending decisions (Ferri et al., 2019; Yosano & Nakaoka, 2019a). Yosano and Nakaoka, for one, noted that banks commonly use soft information in their lending decisions. The authors found this among Japanese banking institutions, where survey data showed that technology is a vital factor in understanding banks' lending decisions. Yosano and Nakaoka added to this finding, noting that although soft information was often uncertain at the start of the loan application process, its use in lending decisions generally increased bank profitability. This profitability effect of soft information is observed in both competitive and noncompetitive markets (Yosano & Nakaoka, 2019b).

In addition to these assertions by Yosano and Nakaoka (2019a), Yosano and Nakaoka, along with Brighi et al. (2019), highlighted the predictive power of lending technologies for SMEs. Brighi et al. further examined this topic and noted the key role of lending technologies in addressing adverse selection in banking institutions. Viewing this topic through an intertemporal framework, Brighi et al. found that loan decision-making processes are based on financial information about SMEs and that lending technologies can provide empirical analyses of correct and incorrect lending choices. A review of empirical literature on technologies and lending decisions, and their role in banking for SMEs, indicates that lending technologies focused on soft information require further analysis to better understand and expand SME access to credit.

Similarly, Yosano and Nakaoka (2019a) and Filomeni et al. underscored similar findings regarding the vital role of lending technologies (specifically, soft information) in a more recent study. Filomeni et al. examined credit score lending in banking organizations using technology and soft information. Using lending technologies that focus on soft information, Filomeni et al. examined factors related to bank organizational frictions and borrowers' credit availability in relation to loan approval decisions. The findings showed that geographically distant borrowers were less likely to be granted a loan by banks. This finding was significant when loan officers provided their subjective opinions about the borrower. Similarly, Degryse et al. reported similar findings in the United Kingdom, examining SMEs and access to bank credit. Their findings showed that SME borrowers who are closer to the bank's branches and headquarters are more likely to be granted access to credit. Many SMEs are not geographically close to their banks; however, they need bank credit, especially during financial crises. These findings provided initial evidence on the relevance of technology in lending decisions, which could help in understanding how SMEs are granted loans by banking organizations (Brighi et al., 2019; Degryse et al., 2018).

In line with lending technologies, relationship lending is a crucial part of access to credit. Various researchers have noted that relationship lending is ideal for SMEs (S. Berger & Udell, 2012; Jakšič & Marinč, 2019). Jakšič and Marinč further delved into this topic, examining factors in relationship banking and information technology, particularly the role of artificial intelligence (AI) and financial technology. The authors noted that information technology and artificial intelligence offer banks competitive advantages in making lending decisions, especially when customers or borrowers are geographically distant. However, despite the relevance of technology in lending decisions, relationship banking remains equally important, as it ensures close relationships between banks and their clients. Sutherland concurred, as the author examined credit reports and relationship lending in the context of information-sharing technology. The author noted that information sharing through technology has mixed results for SMEs' access to credit. Despite the transparency and efficiency that technology offers banks, there is a strong likelihood that client relationships with banks will grow more distant and often shorter. This finding showed the need for bank managers to remain focused on relationship lending rather than solely on technology lending or on relying on technology for lending decisions (Jakšič & Marinč, 2019; Sutherland, 2018).

Similarly, Ekpu (2016) and Ferri et al. noted the impact of soft information on improved access to credit for SME firms. Leeuw and Ekpu noted that SME owners commonly relied on relationship lending techniques. Leeuw explained this finding while examining survey data collected from 14,000 SMEs across seven European countries. The author determined the lending technology and financial constraints of SMEs. The findings showed that SMEs often used relationship lending techniques, especially when they had longer relationships with their banks. Leeuw explained that this issue occurred because intensive relationships were more relevant for larger SMEs. As a result, larger SMEs with longer relationships with their banks were less likely to be financially constrained. Also, S. Nguyen and Wolfe (2016) noted this finding in their examination of the determinants of successful access to bank loans for SMEs in Vietnam. The authors examined survey results from 20 banks and 180 SMEs and found that both collateral and relationship lending positively affected SMEs' access to credit (S. Nguyen & Wolfe, 2016). The results also showed that relationship lending helped loosen stringent contract terms and credit approval requirements for SMEs (S. Nguyen & Wolfe, 2016). However, Ferri et al. added that there was a significant benefit to using both soft information and hard information jointly, leading to increased access to credit for SMEs. As such, combining relationship- and transaction-based lending is worth examining further to determine how SME lenders can increase their chances of accessing bank credit (Ekpu, 2016; Ferri et al., 2019).

In summary, a lending technology is best understood as an organized method for turning uncertainty into a credit decision. It combines sources of information, screening rules, collateral practices, approval sequences, and monitoring arrangements. Seen in this way, banks do not simply "lend"; they lend through specific architectures of judgment.

The most important divide is between transaction-based lending and relationship lending. Transaction lending relies on hard information that can be standardized and transmitted easily across the institution. Relationship lending relies more heavily on context, repeated interaction, and locally gathered knowledge. SMEs often do not fit standardized models and cannot always be managed by informal judgment.

This is why lending technology is central to the book's argument. The missing middle persists not only because smaller firms are risky, but because many institutions are configured for borrowers who are easier to document and cheaper to process.

A useful way to make this concrete is to think of the lending process as a chain rather than a single decision point. Applications are sourced, pre-screened, documented, scored or discussed, checked against collateral requirements, escalated to

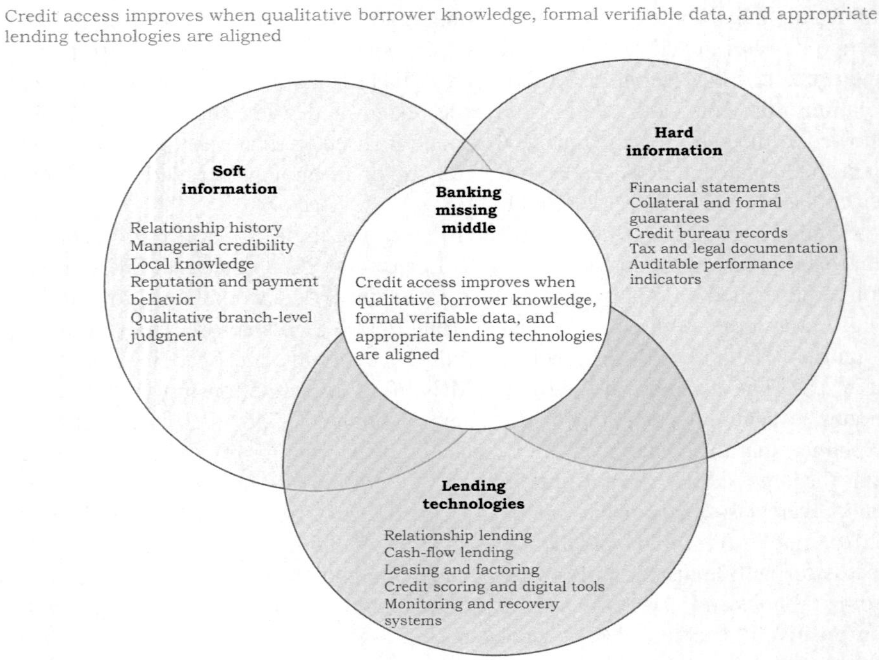

Fig. 5.1 Banking missing middle: soft information, hard information, and lending technologies. *Source: Author's conceptual synthesis based on Sect. 5.1*

committees, priced, monitored after disbursement, and reviewed when signals deteriorate. SMEs can fall out of this chain at many stages. Some are screened out because their documentation is too weak, others because branch knowledge cannot be translated into committee language, and still others because monitoring seems too costly relative to the expected return. A lending technology is therefore a sequence of organized filters, not merely a scoring model or a yes-or-no decision at the end (Berger & Udell, 2006). The distinction between lending technologies becomes clearer when viewed as an infrastructure problem rather than a simple menu of bank products. In practice, SME lending depends on the extent to which banks can combine three elements: soft information drawn from proximity, repeated interaction, and qualitative judgment; hard information derived from financial statements, collateral records, and formal documentation; and lending technologies capable of translating both forms of information into workable credit decisions. Figure 5.1 illustrates this complementarity and shows why upgrading lending infrastructure is central to widening prudent access to SME credit.

The figure clarifies that the missing middle is not only a question of risk appetite. It is also a question of whether banks can combine qualitative knowledge of borrowers with formal, verifiable information and appropriate lending tools into a usable credit infrastructure. Where these elements remain disconnected, smaller firms are more likely to remain economically visible but financially unreadable.

Product choice as a lending technology: matching SME needs with risk, information, and collateral conditions

Product family	SME need	Best used when	Risk/information logic
Working-capital credit	Operating cycle	Recurring sales and cash-flow visibility	Supports inventory, payroll, supplier payments
Factoring/bill discount	Receivables liquidity	Verifiable invoices and reliable buyers	Turns receivables into monitorable cash flows
Purchase-order financing	Contract execution	Valid purchase order or supply contract	Credit decision anchored in a transaction
Equipment leasing/ finance	Productive assets	Identifiable equipment, vehicle, machinery	Asset-backed control reduces collateral gap
Real-estate leasing/ finance	Premises/facilities	Clear title, valuation, long-term use	Long maturity linked to tangible property
Rental/rent-to-own	Flexible asset use	Need to use asset without immediate ownership	Access over ownership; lower entry burden
Guarantees/market bonds	Market access	Tender, contract, or performance obligation	Substitutes or complements collateral

Source: Author's synthesis based on Fidelis Finance's Product Program, including key instruments, investment process, priority sectors, risk-management framework, and inclusive finance products.

Fig. 5.2 SME financing products and conditions of use. *Source*: *Author's synthesis based on his experience*

This distinction is central to the book's argument. The missing middle is not only underserved because banks are cautious. It is also underserved when the available financial products are poorly matched to the SME's risk and information profile. A firm with weak collateral but identifiable equipment needs may be better served by leasing than by an ordinary term loan. A firm with reliable customers but delayed payments may be better served by factoring than by an overdraft. A firm with a public or private contract may need a guarantee or a purchase-order facility rather than a generic loan.

Figure 5.2 summarizes these instruments and indicates the conditions under which each product is most appropriate for SMEs. The figure draws on the Fidelis Finance practitioner vignette, but its purpose is conceptual: to show how diversified SME finance products respond to different configurations of risk, information, cash-flow visibility, and asset structure (Fidelis Finance, 2025).

The figure clarifies why SME credit should be understood as a portfolio of financing technologies rather than as a single conventional loan product. A working capital loan is appropriate when the firm faces operating-cycle pressures and can demonstrate recurring cash flows. Factoring and bill discounting are more appropriate when the SME has receivables or invoices that can be verified. Purchase-order financing addresses a different need: The firm has a contract or commercial opportunity but lacks the liquidity to execute it. Leasing and equipment finance are more closely tied to productive assets and are therefore useful when the credit decision can be anchored in identifiable equipment, vehicles, machinery, or productive infrastructure.

The practical implication is that widening SME finance requires more than increasing credit volume. It requires a richer credit infrastructure capable of matching financing instruments to the actual structure of SME activity. In this sense, leasing, factoring, guarantees, purchase-order financing, rental products, and equipment finance are not peripheral to SME credit. They are part of the institutional architecture through which risk, distance, and information can be managed.

5.2 Beyond Conventional Loans: Leasing, Factoring, Guarantees, and Risk-Capital Channels

The financing of SMEs should not be reduced to conventional bank loans. Although the title of this book refers to SME credit, credit should be understood as a broader framework of financing technologies through which banks and specialized financial institutions evaluate, structure, secure, monitor, and recover exposure to smaller firms. Different instruments transform risk, distance, and information in different ways.

A conventional term loan requires the bank to assess the borrower's overall repayment capacity, collateral position, cash-flow stability, and managerial credibility. This remains important, but it is not always the most appropriate instrument for smaller firms. SMEs often need financing that is more closely tied to the asset, contract, receivable, or transaction being financed. In such cases, specialized instruments can reduce information problems by anchoring the credit decision in a more observable economic object.

Leasing is one such instrument. It allows finance to be linked to an identifiable productive asset. This can mitigate the weakness of conventional collateral by keeping the financed asset central to the transaction structure. For SMEs seeking equipment, vehicles, machinery, or productive assets, leasing may therefore be better suited than an unsecured or weakly secured term loan. Within this book's analytical framework, leasing reduces distance by connecting the lender to the financed asset and reduces risk by improving control over that asset.

Factoring addresses a different problem. Many SMEs are not short of commercial activity; they lack liquidity as they wait for customers to pay. Factoring can transform receivables into working capital by shifting attention from the SME's balance sheet alone to the quality of invoices, buyers, payment histories, and commercial flows. It therefore converts business activity into verifiable information. In this sense, factoring is not merely a product; it is an information technology for credit.

Guarantees also play an important role. A guarantee can help a viable SME overcome the gap between economic potential and insufficient collateral. It does not eliminate risk, but it reallocates or shares part of the risk in a way that may make the loan acceptable to the bank. For this reason, guarantee mechanisms can be particularly useful where prudential discipline is necessary but collateral markets are incomplete.

Risk-capital channels, including venture capital and, where available, structures known as sociétés d'investissement en capital à risque (SICARs; risk-capital investment companies), should be treated differently from credit but not separately from the financing problem. Equity and quasi-equity instruments improve firms' financial structure and may make future borrowing more viable. They are especially relevant for firms with high growth potential but whose cash flows, collateral, or repayment history do not yet support conventional debt. In the West African Economic and Monetary Union (WAEMU) and Organization for the Harmonization of Business Law in Africa (OHADA) contexts, capital investment and venture capital discussions are increasingly relevant to enterprise financing, particularly where debt alone is ill-suited to innovation or early-stage expansion.

The policy implication is straightforward. Better SME finance in WAMU requires a portfolio of instruments rather than a single lending model. Conventional bank credit, leasing, factoring, guarantees, equipment finance, and risk-capital channels each address a different configuration of risk, distance, and information. The challenge is not to replace banking but to enrich the credit infrastructure that makes smaller firms financeable.

This broader understanding of lending technologies prepares the next part of the chapter. If instruments differ in how they process risk and information, then SME credit decisions must be analyzed as institutional processes rather than isolated approval decisions.

5.3 Information Technology and the Infrastructure of Credit Assessment

If lending technologies define the architecture of credit decisions, the actual allocation of credit depends on how applications move through the decision chain. From sourcing to recovery, each stage introduces filters, losses, delays, and reinterpretations of borrower information. Figure 5.3 maps the chain and highlights the points at which SME applications are most often narrowed, reformatted, or discounted.

The figure shows why exclusion often occurs inside the lending process rather than only at the final approval stage. Information can be weakened, discounted, or reformatted as it travels from branch to committee, especially where SME files rely on mixed evidence rather than standardized documentation. The missing middle thus appears as much a process outcome as a portfolio outcome.

Researchers have noted the significance of information technology in determining loan decisions (Flögel & Beckamp, 2020; Metawa et al., 2017). According to

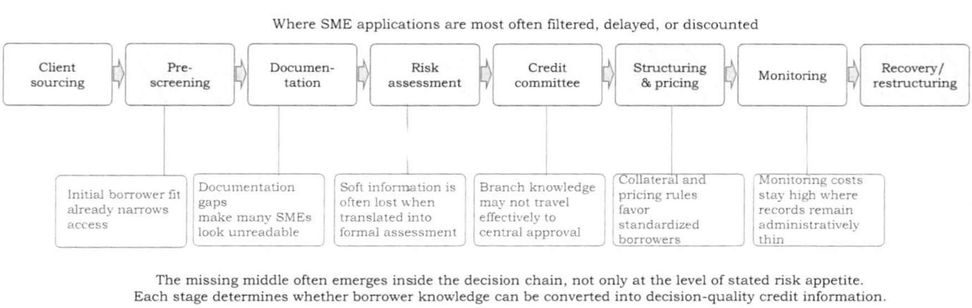

Fig. 5.3 The SME credit decision chain. *Source: author's conceptual synthesis based on this section, Information technology and the infrastructure of credit assessment*

the literature, banks' access to technology significantly determines their use of hard information and soft information.

Additionally, Z. L. Song and Zhang (2018) noted the role of information technology in SMEs' decision-making across different types of loans. The authors examined data from China on different types of loans, using SME loan data from 2010 to 2013. The authors found that banks used financial technology to determine credit loans and other types of lending to SMEs (Z. L. Song & Zhang, 2018). However, Z. L. Song and Zhang cautioned against the risks associated with the risk-sharing mechanism of financial technologies.

More research is needed on the use of technology in decision-making to grant SMEs access to credit, particularly regarding its benefits and risks (Z. L. Song & Zhang, 2018). Further to the findings of Z. L. Song and Zhang, Santoso et al. underscored the relevance of information technology in lending to firms. Santoso et al. investigated this topic to identify factors that determine platform interest rates and borrowers' default status. The findings showed that financial technology was used to determine access to loans and loan rates given to small firms, specifically through online peer-to-peer lending platforms. Technology is employed to calculate borrowers' loan amounts and loan rates (Santoso et al., 2020).

This body of findings demonstrated the use of financial technology to provide SMEs with access to loans (Santoso et al., 2020; Z. L. Song & Zhang, 2018). According to the literature, technology affects banks' lending decisions for SME firms. In fact, technological development in bank organizations is primarily driven by lending decisions. As a result, banks use less soft-information lending and employ more transaction-based lending techniques. Zhao et al. delved into this topic by examining soft information and SME bank lending. The authors examined data from Great Britain on bank lending to SMEs and showed that bank technology improved the assessment of lending to SMEs, especially for geographically distant firms. Metawa et al. concurred in their examination of the impact of a genetic algorithm-based model for optimizing bank lending decisions. The authors proposed a model to determine bank lending decisions under limited access to credit. Using genetic algorithms and mathematical programming techniques, their study found that the proposed technology-based framework could optimize banking profits when granting loans to SME firms, increasing them by 3.9–8.1%. The results showed that the intelligent tool yielded less loan-screening time by 12–50%. Hence, information technology can be used as a strategy to improve lending decisions for SMEs in various settings, even when geographically distant from the bank branch and headquarters, which can be beneficial during economic crises (Metawa et al., 2017; Sedunov, 2017).

The role of technology on the borrower's side is also relevant to the determination of lending decisions. Kariuki-Njogu et al. (2018) examined this topic by focusing on smallholder farmers and their adoption of technology. The authors determined how the adoption of technology impacted access to credit among 243 small-scale dairy farmers. A double-hurdle analysis showed that the borrower's level of technology adoption influenced banks' probability of granting loans and credit. Borrowers who frequently utilized mobile banking platforms and adopted technology within their business were more likely to attain loan approvals from their banks. Overall, technology adoption affected both access to credit and the amount of credit extended to borrowers. Twine et al. reported similar findings in their examination of the impact of technology adoption and collective action on access to credit. The authors focused on milk producers in Tanzania and showed that the adoption of technology and collective action increased the chances of obtaining bank loans for this cohort. However, the authors found that adopting new technologies would require increased cash flow, which could hinder most small-scale borrowers and business owners from doing so. The findings of Twine et al. and Kariuki-Njogu et al. could be further expanded by future researchers focusing on SMEs in African countries, particularly small-scale borrowers from the agricultural sector. Nonetheless, small-scale borrowers and business owners need additional support, especially when seeking loans and credit from banks, as technology adoption is costly for this cohort (Kariuki-Njogu et al., 2018; Twine et al., 2019).

For SME firms, the findings of Kariuki-Njogu et al. (2018) on technology adoption and its link to credit access remain applicable. Flaminiano and Francisco noted this finding when examining credit constraints of SMEs in the Philippines. Flaminiano and Francisco examined firm characteristics such as firm size, fixed assets, and technology adoption and showed that these factors significantly affected the probability of obtaining credit. The results showed that the use of technology reduced the significance of firm size and fixed assets and their impact on access to credit. This finding further showed the significant value of technology adoption by SME firms, which could increase their probability of accessing credit from banking institutions (Flaminiano & Francisco, 2019).

According to various scholars, SME firms with technological advancements are more likely to be granted loans and credit by their banks (Jayasooriya, 2020; R. Wang et al., 2019). For instance, R. Wang et al. noted the relationship between the adoption of blockchain technology, bank credit, and SME financing. The authors examined this topic further by evaluating bank loans and credit patterns for SME firms. The authors found that SMEs using blockchain technology are more likely to have access to loans and credit, even when they cannot meet standard collateral requirements. Jayasooriya added to this by examining the role of technology among SMEs in Sri Lanka, analyzing 1200 SMEs that adopted technology and innovation. The author found that technology is an enabling mechanism that helps increase capital and the likelihood of external loans for SME firms. The findings also showed that adopting technology facilitates information flow within SMEs and thus increases financial capacity. Jayasooriya further noted the relevance of technology adoption within SME firms, which could help expand their networks, enhance their creditworthiness, and thus attain sustainable growth. This body of knowledge highlighted the role of technology in SMEs and its impact on access to credit. SME owners seeking credit and loans from their banks could adopt technology and innovation to increase the likelihood of loan approval, thereby facilitating their growth and development in the market (Jayasooriya, 2020; R. Wang et al., 2019).

Digital infrastructures have changed the mechanics of credit assessment. Internal databases, credit bureaus, payment histories, and increasingly automated scoring systems allow banks to compare borrowers more quickly, centralize records, and reduce some screening costs. These tools can widen reach, especially where branch networks are stretched.

Yet digitization does not neutralize the underlying problem. It can also intensify selectivity by rewarding borrowers who already leave clean administrative traces and by discounting firms whose relevant strengths remain embedded in relationships, local reputation, or semiformal business practice. Technology, in other words, can reduce opacity for some firms while deepening it for others.

The practical issue is not whether banks should digitize. It is whether digital systems are designed to complement rather than displace context-sensitive assessment.

Information technology can reduce some of the frictions in that chain by making it easier to aggregate customer histories, compare sector exposures, and track repayment performance across portfolios. It can also shorten processing times and support more consistent treatment of borrowers across branches. In a regional banking space such as WAMU, these advantages are significant because large groups often need common systems that can handle clients across multiple jurisdictions. Better data infrastructure can therefore expand banks' ability to act at scale without relying exclusively on idiosyncratic, branch-level judgment.

Yet the same infrastructure can intensify exclusion if it is designed only around what is already easy to measure. Soft information often fails to travel upward, not because branches have learned nothing, but because centralized systems are poorly designed to absorb that learning. A borrower known locally as disciplined, commercially embedded, and temporarily cash-constrained may still look weak when translated into a file dominated by thin statements and limited collateral. This is one of the central organizational challenges in SME lending: how to formalize local knowledge without either losing it or converting it into arbitrary discretion.

5.4 Small and Medium Enterprise-Side Factors in Lending Decisions

According to the literature, various factors affect lending decisions. In addition to technology and lending technologies, H. T. Nguyen et al. (2020) and Kozubikova et al. argued for the importance of SME-side factors and other bank-side factors that impact lending decisions. For instance, Kozubikova et al. examined this topic among SMEs, focusing on the impact of the business environment and entrepreneurs' gender on the perception of financial risk in the SME sector. Kozubikova et al. analyzed data from questionnaire surveys in the Czech Republic in 2015, and their findings showed that entrepreneurs' ability to secure credit for their SMEs was strongly affected by their understanding of and engagement with the credit process and criteria used by banks. Dvorský et al. added to these findings by reporting similar results. The authors conducted a study evaluating market and financial risks in

SMEs by interviewing SME managers in the Zilina region of Slovakia. The findings showed that managers' ability to understand both market and financial risks was vital to SMEs' access to credit (Dvorský et al., 2018).

Furthermore, SME managers are often uninformed about the process and requirements for obtaining credit, specifically because these factors are opaque and poorly telegraphed by banks (Dvorský et al., 2018). This body of findings provided empirical evidence on the role of SME-side factors in lending decisions and access to credit within the SME sector. Further examination of this topic could increase access to credit for SMEs, as SMEs also work on developing their ability to understand and engage with the credit processes of banking organizations (Dvorský et al., 2018; Kozubikova et al., 2017).

In line with the conclusions of Dvorský et al. (2018) and Kozubikova et al., others underscored the importance of SMEs' understanding of lending practices. H. T. Nguyen et al. (2020) explained that a lack of understanding of, or information about, banks' lending practices is one of the most significant factors in whether a given SME can secure the necessary levels of funding. The authors also found that borrowers with lower educational attainment tended to utilize less formal credit, as they reported challenges during the credit application processes (H. T. Nguyen et al., 2020). L. T. Nguyen et al. (2019) concurred with this finding in their examination of SME credit constraints in Vietnam. H. T. Nguyen et al. examined survey data on manufacturing SMEs from 2005 to 2013, focusing on credit-constrained SMEs. The findings of their study showed that various SME characteristics significantly influenced banks' lending decisions. Some SME factors that impact banks' lending decisions include firm size, age, education, and knowledge of credit constraints and processes (L. T. Nguyen et al., 2019).

Hence, SMEs' understanding of banks' lending practices and processes was linked to their access to bank credit (H. T. Nguyen et al., 2020; L. T. Nguyen et al., 2019). Aside from SME owners' ability to understand bank managers' lending practices and processes, researchers have identified SME managers' age and experience as significant factors in access to bank credit. Djousta Wamba et al. examined this topic by focusing on the dimensions of the bank-SME relationship and their influence on banks' decisions to grant credit. In the context of asymmetric information, the authors examined data from 262 SME loan applications at a bank in Cameroon and found that SME managers' ages and experience influenced the bank's credit-granting decisions. Specifically, SMEs with young and inexperienced managers were less likely to be granted credit. Beyina concurred that bank managers consider the identity profiles of SME owners and managers when making funding decisions for SMEs. The author examined SMEs in Cameroon using qualitative methods and showed that bank financing for SMEs depended on a borrower's ethnic origin, experience, and age (Beyina, 2019).

The findings showed a clear association between SME managers' characteristics and loan size (Beyina, 2019). This body of knowledge highlighted the specific SME-side factors associated with lending decisions, particularly SME managers' characteristics, such as age, gender, work experience, and level of education (Beyina, 2019; Chin et al., 2020).

In line with Beyina's (2019) and Djousta Wamba et al.'s findings, Chin et al. indicated similar results when examining the role of managerial characteristics among Malaysian manufacturing SMEs and their funding. The authors examined SME managers' characteristics, such as age, gender, work experience, and level of education, using qualitative methods with 219 respondents. The findings showed that managers with higher levels of experience and educational attainment, and who were male, were more likely to be granted loans by banking institutions. De Andrés et al. concurred and even underscored the gender gap in access to bank credit. The authors examined more than 80,000 Spanish SMEs and found that women entrepreneurs were significantly less likely to obtain loans than their male counterparts in the same sector (De Andrés et al., 2020). This finding was apparent when the authors analyzed the company's profit-and-loss history. De Andrés et al. found that this gender gap in access to bank credit disappeared over time; however, the researchers did not examine how women entrepreneurs obtained capital or credit.

Nonetheless, De Andrés et al. (2020) further found that women entrepreneurs who were granted access to credit were less likely to default than their male counterparts. This body of findings highlighted the need for bank decision-makers to ensure access to loans and credit to avert potential gender biases and discrimination, especially because women SME owners and managers might yield better results than their male peers (Chin et al., 2020; De Andrés et al., 2020).

More research is needed on access to credit among men and women SME owners and managers in African countries, as gender may influence lending decisions in such contexts. In addition to SME managers' specific characteristics, innovative SMEs may be more likely to secure loan approvals. According to the literature, SMEs in countries such as the Czech Republic, the Slovak Republic, Hungary, and Poland are more likely to secure bank and other external financing when they present innovative ideas. Also, van der Zwan (2016) noted this finding, as the author examined the success of bank loan applications by innovative and non-innovative SME firms across 29 European countries. The author examined and tested the relationship between innovative behavior and successful loan applications. The results showed that SMEs engaged in innovative activities were more likely to seek loans from financial institutions than non-innovative SMEs. The findings also indicated that SMEs that adopted innovations were more likely to have access to credit than SMEs without them, consistent with Belas et al. (2017).

Contrary to the findings of Belas et al. (2017) and van der Zwan, Wellalage et al. noted that innovative SME firms face greater challenges in accessing external funding and credit, especially when smaller. Wellalage et al. further underscored the role of firm size as a key determinant in decision-making for SME lending. Given these conflicting findings on the role of innovation in SMEs' access to bank credit, more research is needed to examine whether innovative SMEs are more likely to receive bank loans and grants, particularly in African countries such as Burkina Faso (Belas et al., 2017; van der Zwan, 2016).

Researchers have also noted the size of SMEs as a key factor in lending decisions. According to the literature, as previously outlined, larger SMEs are more likely to receive loan grants than their smaller counterparts. In a more recent study, Borish

(2020) reached a similar conclusion regarding the effects of firm size on SME financing. The author examined at least 31,000 SME firms, both small and large. The findings showed that bank credit allocation frequently favored larger SMEs over smaller ones. It was also found that midsized SMEs had more limited access to credit than larger SMEs, while small or emerging SMEs faced the greatest financing constraints. Hence, based on the findings of Borish and Wellalage et al. (2019), firm-size bias in bank lending allocation is present, affecting banks' lending decisions for SMEs.

Angori et al. (2019) explained this phenomenon by examining SME firms' access to credit at Italian banks. The authors explained that SMEs had higher levels of debt, which decreased their chances of loan approval. The findings of their study also showed that medium-sized firms have the greatest exposure to credit limitations, particularly as the duration of the bank-SME relationship increases, due to lock-in. Chodorow-Reich et al. further added that smaller SME firms obtain shorter credit lines than their larger counterparts. In addition, smaller SME firms commonly face significantly higher collateral requirements and spreads than larger SME firms. Given these effects of firm size, Chodorow-Reich et al. highlighted the need to support smaller SMEs, especially during economic downturns. As such, these findings provide a more in-depth explanation of the role of firm size in bank credit allocation, with larger SMEs favored. More support is needed for SMEs, particularly because these firms have higher debt levels and are more vulnerable to financing constraints (Angori et al., 2019; Borish, 2020).

In addition to firm size, another factor to consider in lending decisions is geographic proximity. That is, SME firms located farther from their bank branches and headquarters are less likely to obtain credit (Degryse et al., 2018; Filomeni et al., 2020). Several researchers have further observed this in their studies, noting that SMEs' access to bank finance is significantly impacted by the functional distance between bank headquarters and branches. Zhao and Jones-Evans attempted to explain these findings, showing that SMEs were more likely to form productive credit-based relationships when they were geographically closer to their banks. Lee and Brown also noted this finding when examining SMEs and the liability of distance to investigate the demand and supply of bank funding in peripheral regions of the United Kingdom. The authors analyzed surveys collected from 40,000 SMEs between 2011 and 2013. Their findings revealed that credit applications filed in regions closer to the bank were more likely to be accepted and granted loans than those filed farther away. N. Lee and Brown (2017) found this even when controlling for the SME firm's credit score. N. Lee and Brown identified this phenomenon as the liability of distance that far-flung SME firms might face, especially under credit constraints.

This body of research highlights the role of an SME's geographic proximity to the bank branch to which its loan application is submitted (N. Lee & Brown, 2017; Zhao & Jones-Evans, 2017). There are bank-side factors that also impact bank lending decisions to SME firms. One of these factors is emotional intelligence among loan officers. According to the literature, loan officers' emotional intelligence affects their information processing. The researchers conducted experiments with selected loan officers, examining their overall risk rating, overall trend rating, loan-granting decisions, and decision-making processes for determining interest rates.

The findings showed that emotional intelligence served as a personal variable influencing their credit-granting decisions. Bucciol et al. similarly noted that trait emotional intelligence affects financial risk-taking. The authors further noted that trait emotional intelligence had been linked to cognitive processes. Given the significance of emotional intelligence in cognitive processes and decision-making, further research is needed in this area to determine whether the emotional intelligence of loan officers can be significant in impacting the likelihood of SME firms' access to credit and loan approvals (Bucciol et al., 2020; Lagrange et al., 2017).

So, on the borrower side, bankability often depends on legibility. Recordkeeping, separation of business and household accounts, tax and registration status, collateral quality, managerial coherence, and the ability to explain the business model all affect how an application is evaluated within the bank. These are not superficial details; they shape whether the borrower can be incorporated into the bank's routines at a reasonable cost.

Size matters for the same reason. Very small firms often combine thinner documentation, shorter operating histories, and more volatile cash cycles. Distance matters as well: The farther the firm is from the branch or decision center, the more expensive it becomes to verify soft information through visits and repeated contact. These conditions do not automatically disqualify SMEs, but they do raise the institutional burden of lending to them.

On the SME side, legibility is achieved through a set of practices that are more administrative than glamorous: separating business and household accounts, keeping usable records, formalizing supplier relationships, documenting inventories, clarifying ownership, and presenting a coherent financing request aligned with the business logic. None of these practices guarantees credit, but their absence often increases the cost of interpretation. Banks not only judge projects; they also judge how much work will be required to understand the project well enough to defend approval. In that sense, borrower preparedness is itself part of the lending technology (Amoako-Adu & Eshun, 2018).

It is also important not to homogenize SMEs. Sector, firm age, and cash-flow rhythm matter. A trading firm with rapid turnover, visible transactions, and modest inventory behaves differently from a small processor whose revenues are seasonal or a service business with thin fixed assets. The problem of SME credit is therefore not a single borrower problem repeated many times. It is a family of borrower situations that place different demands on documentation, collateral, monitoring, and local knowledge. Recognition of that heterogeneity is essential if the missing middle is to be treated as a problem of lending design rather than borrower stigma.

5.5 Managerial Capability and Borrower Legibility

The success of an SME depends on many factors, but the capacity of its manager is especially important. In the context of bank lending, however, managerial capability matters not only because it improves business performance. It matters because it affects borrower legibility. A capable manager is better able to translate business activity into documentation, projections, explanations, and commitments that a bank can evaluate.

This point is central to the missing middle problem. Many smaller firms are not invisible in the economy. They trade, employ, produce, import, distribute, and invest. Yet they may remain financially unreadable because their activity is poorly documented, their accounts are incomplete, their contracts are informal, or their financing needs are not clearly matched to their business cycle. The manager is the person who can reduce this gap between economic activity and bankable information.

Managerial capability influences SME credit in at least five ways. First, the manager determines whether the firm keeps usable financial records. Second, the manager decides whether contracts, invoices, taxes, payroll, and inventory records are formalized. Third, the manager identifies the financing instrument most appropriate to the problem: working capital credit, leasing, factoring, guarantee-backed lending, equipment finance, or equity support. Fourth, the manager maintains the relationship with the bank and provides explanations when performance changes. Fifth, the manager anticipates risk and communicates corrective action before problems become defaults.

For banks, this means managerial capability is a form of soft information. It can be observed through repeated interaction, repayment discipline, transparency, business planning, and responsiveness to information requests. Yet the value of this soft information depends on whether the bank has internal processes capable of transmitting it from the branch to the credit committee. If managerial quality is known only at the relationship manager level, it may not influence the final credit decision. If it is translated into decision-quality information, it can improve the borrower's creditworthiness.

This is where the book's themes converge. Managerial capability reduces information asymmetry by improving documentation. It reduces distance by making the firm easier to understand. It reduces perceived risk by increasing confidence in the borrower's discipline and adaptability. It also improves the fit between financing instruments and business needs. In this sense, the SME manager is not simply a beneficiary of finance. The manager is a producer of bankability.

The implication is not that banks should lend on personality alone. Rather, they should develop credit processes that recognize managerial capability when supported by evidence, documentation, and consistent behavior.

5.6 Bank-Side Factors, Lender Discretion, and Trust

Loan officers have a substantial impact on borrowers' access to credit. Researchers have noted the significance of loan officers in loan decision-making (Campbell et al., 2019; Gao et al., 2017). Gao et al. explored this topic when investigating the lending terms and loan performance of corporate loans issued by at least 7000 loan officers in the United States. The authors analyzed data gathered from 1994 to 2012 and found that loan officers had a substantial impact on the lending process, including contract terms such as loan spreads, maturities, loan performance, and loan rates. From 1994 to 2012, Gao et al. did not show any decline in loan officers' influence over lending decisions. Similarly, Campbell et al. noted that loan officers had a significant impact on private lending, primarily due to personal biases and cognitive constraints. Through the subjective processes and views of loan officers, soft information in private lending is processed and interpreted differently. Campbell et al. further identified three main constraints and biases that influenced lending decisions: limited attention, task-specific human capital, and common identity. The authors also found that loan officers' experiences, schedules, and gender affected lending decisions. Specifically, loan quality is worse when loan officers review soft information before weekends and during holidays. Additionally, other work found that loan quality was worse when both loan officers and borrowers were men and when loan officers had sales experience. This body of knowledge revealed further insights into the impact of loan officers on lending decisions, beyond the cognitive processes and biases that might be present during decision-making (Campbell et al., 2019). These findings could serve as empirical evidence for researchers examining this topic in the context of SME firms' loan applications.

Similarly, earlier work noted the influence of bank officers on lending decisions. The authors investigated the screening and monitoring processes of corporate loan officers and found that distracted loan officers were more likely to issue loans with lower spreads to borrowers, who were then more likely to default (Gao et al., 2018). This aspect led to increased future default rates. Their findings also revealed that distracted loan officers rarely incorporated soft information into loan terms, leading to poor decisions and misallocated credit. Alibhai et al. added to this finding, noting that loan officers had their own biases in SME lending decisions. The authors examined factors affecting SME lending in Turkey, using data from 77 loan officers at Turkish banks. The findings of their experimental research showed that loan officers often had gender biases. For example, 35% of the loan officer participants were less likely to grant loans to female applicants. Further, women borrowers received significantly lower loan amounts than their male counterparts by at least $14,000 (Alibhai et al., 2019).

This body of knowledge further provided significant insights into how loan officers could have a vital influence on SME lending decision-making, including gender biases and loan officer characteristics (Alibhai et al., 2019; Gao et al., 2018). Loan officers are more likely to rely on hard information than on soft information when granting SME loans. Researchers have noted that, despite banking frameworks for loan assessments that also emphasize hard information, loan officers are more focused on hard-information analyses and assessments. Palazuelos et al. delved further into this topic and conducted a case study on how bank loan officers processed and evaluated information for SME firms. The authors examined 75 experienced bank loan officers in Sweden and made 7425 observations of assessments of SME loan applications. The findings showed that loan officers paid significantly more attention to hard information than to soft information. Rad et al. added to these findings, noting that loan officers placed great importance on the quality of the borrower's accounting information. The quality of the borrower's accounting information significantly affects the loan officer's willingness to grant loans (Rad et al., 2018).

Rad et al. (2018) further examined this topic based on Spanish banks and surveyed 471 bank loan officers to gather information on audited and non-audited firms. The findings showed that being audited as a borrower firm is significant for improving the firm's willingness to facilitate SMEs' access to credit. Factors such as SME firms' trust and benevolence did not significantly influence loan officers' willingness to grant loans to SMEs in need of credit. This body of knowledge showed how loan officers found significance in using hard information when granting loans to SMEs. These findings are significant for SMEs seeking access to credit from loan officers, who focus more on preparing pertinent hard information, such as accounting information quality, rather than soft information (Palazuelos et al., 2018; Rad et al., 2018).

Several researchers have also underscored the power of loan officers in SME lending decisions. For one, Benvenuti et al. (2017) examined the real authority of loan officers in lending decisions for small businesses. The authors examined the factors that constrain loan approvals for small businesses. The authors examined a dataset from Italian banks and showed that loan officers' authority played a significant role in explaining loan approvals and lending to small businesses. Their analysis also showed that loan officers commonly determine loan interest rates and the types of information used for loan assessments and monitoring (Benvenuti et al., 2017).

Bouwens and Kroos (2019) concurred in their examination of loan officers' decision rights and control over lending decisions for small firms. Bouwens and Kroos studied how loan officers granted loans to small businesses using proprietary data from their bank. The authors of the study, including Benvenuti et al., explored the factors that constrain loan approvals for small businesses. The findings showed that loan officers exhibited biases in their loan decisions, particularly when soft information was used for monitoring and screening. These findings provided further empirical evidence on the extent of loan officers' influence over loan approvals and terms for SMEs. Various factors limit loan approvals for small businesses; however, loan officer biases consistently pose the major hindrance to SME access to credit (Benvenuti et al., 2017; Bouwens & Kroos, 2019).

Trust is a vital factor to consider in understanding loan decisions. According to the literature, banks and loan officers who have low trust in SMEs are less likely to approve loans. Chuong et al. (2020) examined this topic to determine SMEs' access to bank loans in Vietnam. The authors identified barriers to SMEs' access to bank loans among 695 SMEs in Vietnam's manufacturing industry. The findings identified firm size, collateral requirements, the need for bribery, and high interest rates as factors that negatively affected SMEs' access to bank loans. Their findings also showed that SMEs' access to bank loans was more challenging when loan officers had low trust in the SMEs. Additionally, Moro et al. examined loan managers' decisions and their trust toward small firms. Moro et al. conducted surveys and semi-structured interviews with 450 bank–entrepreneur relationships; their findings revealed that trust was a positive factor in lending relationships, even in varying institutional contexts. Hence, the authors also noted that trust could be used as leverage for small business owners to increase the likelihood that loan managers approve their loan applications. These findings showed the significant positive role of trust in lending relationships, especially for SME firms (Chuong et al., 2020; Moro et al., 2018).

Other researchers have examined trust and noted its positive impact on loan approvals for SME firms (Kervinen, 2019; Moro & Fink, 2013). For one, Moro and Fink examined the role of loan managers' trust and its influence on SMEs' access to credit. The authors gathered data from six banks and examined loan managers' trust in SME managers applying for loans. Their findings showed that SMEs with higher levels of trust from loan officers were more likely to obtain credit and loans from their banks than SMEs with lower levels of trust. Moro and Fink also found that SME owners who enjoyed greater trust from loan managers had lower agency and transaction costs, as loan officers seemed to rely on trust when assessing SMEs' creditworthiness. This finding highlighted the need for SME owners and managers to forge and maintain trusting relationships with their banks, as this could reduce their credit constraints. Kervinen similarly examined the role of trust in bank-SME relationships in Finland. Kervinen found that trust played a key role in bank-SME relationships, which facilitated SME financing. The findings further revealed that SME managers may be hesitant to share growth projections with banks; however, SMEs should not be concerned about doing so, as transparency is key to strengthening SME-bank relationships. Additionally, Jude and Adamou contributed to these findings and attempted to explain the factors behind SME firms' decisions on bank loan financing. The authors employed a mixed-method approach to examine this topic among 450 Cameroonian SMEs. The findings showed that bankers' trust in SME managers influenced loan and financing decisions, consistent with other findings by Moro, Fink, and Kervinen. The findings indicated that managerial behaviors shaped trust within the bank-SME relationship, including attitudes and behaviors characterized by control aversion and overconfidence (Jude & Adamou, 2018).

Consistent with earlier work, Zhou et al. (2018) noted the importance of trust in SME-bank relationships. In their study, the authors examined 389 SME firms in China. Their findings showed that trust in SME-bank relationships could significantly improve SMEs' access to bank loans, as well as the rates, costs, and terms. The authors also highlighted how the trust mechanism could act as a stabilizer for SME loans, maintaining the credit standing of SME firms and reducing overall loan default rates. Palazuelos et al. reported similar findings in a model of loan and credit approvals for SME firms, focusing on loan officers' risk and trust factors. Palazuelos et al. administered survey questionnaires to 471 bank loan officers in Spain and found that perceived risk and trust significantly influenced SMEs' chances of obtaining approved loans. In addition, their findings revealed that high-quality information significantly and positively increased bank loan officers' perceived trust in SMEs, consistent with Kervinen's findings. High levels of perceived trust lead to better credit granting for SMEs, whether audited or not. These findings highlighted the importance of perceptual variables of trust in the context of SME lending relationships, which help ensure better credit terms and secure loan approvals for SME firms. More research is needed to examine the role of trust in SME lending relationships, particularly in African countries, a gap that motivates the current study. Nonetheless, this body of knowledge highlighted the role of trust in SME lending within banking institutions, which was crucial to bank-SME relationships and SME financing (Jude & Adamou, 2018; Kervinen, 2019).

To summarize, on the bank side, discretion is unavoidable. Loan officers interpret files, read inconsistencies, evaluate collateral narratives, and decide when missing documentation is tolerable or disqualifying. Their judgment is shaped by experience, as well as by delegation limits, portfolio targets, branch responsibilities, and the degree of centralization in the approval process.

Trust enters here in a precise sense. It is not blind confidence in the borrower; it is the institutional willingness to act on incomplete but credible information. Banks lend more effectively to SMEs when they can transform local knowledge into disciplined trust—trust that is documented, reviewable, and compatible with risk management rather than opposed to it.

On the bank side, one of the most consequential tensions is between branch-level knowledge and head-office validation. Branches often see borrowers first, collect initial information, and observe local commercial behavior over time. Headquarters, by contrast, must protect portfolio quality, maintain consistency, and defend decisions across a wider institutional horizon. The challenge is not to choose one over the other, but to connect them. Where that connection fails, local opportunity can be lost through excessive caution at the center, while central standards can be undermined by poorly documented local advocacy. The quality of that organizational bridge is a decisive determinant of SME credit outcomes.

In this context, trust should be defined precisely. It is not sentimental confidence in the borrower, nor the abandonment of verification. It is the institutional willingness to act on incomplete but credible evidence once that evidence has been appropriately interpreted. A bank capable of disciplined trust can lend to firms that are not perfect on paper but are understandable in practice. A bank incapable of it will remain dependent on the narrow set of borrowers who already resemble large, standardized clients. The missing middle persists largely because many institutions have not yet solved how to make trust both scalable and prudent.

5.7 Emotional Intelligence, Soft Information, and Officer Behavior

Emotional intelligence (EI) can be defined as the ability to recognize, interpret, and manage one's emotions and navigate interpersonal relationships successfully (Goleman, 1998). The history of EI is complicated, with iterations dating back to Charles Darwin, who argued that EI was essential for existence and reproduction

(Karthikeyan & Lalwani, 2017). However, within the past few decades, EI has been considered in more specialized ways, often with increased practical implications.

Goleman (1998) built on the foundations of EI to develop a paradigm linking EI to organizational leadership and business performance.

Within Goleman's (1998) current conceptualization of EI, five competencies comprise it: self-awareness, motivation, empathy, self-regulation, and prosocial skills. According to the literature, self-awareness can facilitate the examination of one's emotions for situational appropriateness and authenticity. Furthermore, self-aware individuals can recognize and use others' emotional cues to make sounder business- or leadership-related decisions. According to the literature, individuals with strong self-awareness can also more easily persuade or influence others in their environment.

The second competency of EI is motivation (Goleman, 1998, 2019). Within this context, motivation refers to the ability to drive employees and leadership to work harder to achieve organizational goals. Motivating factors are often unique to individuals and can be compensatory or driven by personal goals. Management's ability to recognize motivating factors and effectively promote productivity is essential for organizational success (Goleman, 1998, 2019).

The third component of EI is empathy (Goleman, 1998, 2019). Empathetic leaders can recognize, both cognitively and emotionally, how others feel in a given situation. According to the literature, EI-inclined leadership can set more reasonable organizational policies and ensure that employees are more likely to succeed by providing them with adequate tools and resources to achieve their goals (Goleman, 2019).

The fourth dimension of EI is self-regulation (Goleman, 2019; Nyerere & Wawire, 2015). According to the literature, self-regulation can inform individuals about which emotions are appropriate in a given situation, to what degree they should be expressed, and for how long. Self-regulation has also been shown to be critical to decision-making, as individuals with high self-regulation are better decision-makers because they are less easily influenced by emotion (Goleman, 2019).

The last EI competency is the possession of prosocial skills (Bekerman & Zembylas, 2018). These skills include the personality and temperament to facilitate teamwork and foster a positive environment for stakeholders. Within this context, prosocial skills can foster interpersonal relationships and promote positive interactions among those involved (Bekerman & Zembylas, 2018; Fernández-Abascal & Martín-Díaz, 2019). Thus, this final EI competency is especially important in service-based businesses such as banking. Furthermore, prosocial skills can be crucial for consumer-facing bank employees, such as loan managers, who need them to assess risks and benefits when successfully providing loans.

All EI competencies are necessary within service-driven sectors, such as banking. EI competencies are often associated with effective leadership and business acumen (Karthikeyan & Lalwani, 2017; Prentice, 2016). There is also a strong positive correlation between EI proficiency and increased satisfaction with service delivery (Nyerere & Wawire, 2015; Prentice, 2016). Thus, when management and

Table 5.1 A practical reading of emotional intelligence in SME lending

EI competency	Influence on loan officer behavior
Self-awareness	Increased comfort with loan-related decisions (Lagrange et al., 2017)
Empathy	Important for navigating interactions between loan officers and borrowers (IFC, 2011)
Motivation	Needed to review and complete risk assessments and distinguish willingness to repay from capacity to repay (IFC, 2011)
Self-regulation	Reduced risk-taking and lending mistakes (Ibtissem, 2015)
Prosocial skills	Needed to navigate interpersonal relationships and collect soft data (Abraham & Schmukler, 2017)

employees have higher EI scores, consumers are more satisfied with the services and experiences they receive.

The impact of EI on loan officers' decisions to lend to SMEs has been examined. According to the International Finance Corporation (IFC, 2011), loan officers' ability to navigate the complex interactions between borrowers and lenders is essential for mitigating risk and ensuring lenders' success. Proficient EI skills are also necessary for collecting the soft information needed to lend money to SMEs. Within this context, soft information refers to forecasts, projections, reputational assessments, and viability judgments collected through private, qualitative interactions between the loan officer and the borrower. Conversely, lending to large firms usually relies on hard information—that is, quantitative data that can be readily compiled and shared—which typically makes credit decisions easier. As SMEs are often less able than larger firms to obtain funding from banking institutions, the ability to successfully collect and interpret soft data becomes paramount for both lenders and borrowers (Abraham & Schmukler, 2017).

Although EI is essential for all organizational leaders to motivate employees and achieve organizational goals, it is also necessary for loan officers who make lending decisions. However, the extent to which EI influences loan officer behavior has been mixed (Ibtissem, 2015). According to the literature, improved EI competencies, especially self-regulation, have been shown to reduce lending mistakes and risk-taking behaviors. In a similar study, Lagrange et al. (2017) examined EI and loan officers' decisions regarding loan provision, interest rates, trend rating, and risk assessment. Lagrange et al. found that EI was not significantly related to any dimension of the decision-making process but was helpful for feeling comfortable with their decisions. However, a review of the literature clarifies the importance of EI for loan officers' behavior. Table 5.1 below summarizes the key EI competencies and the associated lending behaviors, particularly in the context of SMEs.

The conclusion is that the literature on emotional intelligence is relevant to SME lending only to a limited extent. Officers who can listen carefully, manage difficult borrower interactions, and distinguish between confidence and noise may be better placed to gather and interpret soft information during interviews and site visits.

Even so, these capabilities should be treated as supportive rather than decisive. Emotional intelligence cannot substitute for documentation, branch knowledge, or coherent approval systems. It matters most where institutions already rely on interpersonal judgment and need staff who can collect qualitative signals without confusing empathy with leniency.

The table should therefore be read as an interpretive aid. It highlights relational capabilities that may improve the handling of soft information, while leaving the book's main explanatory burden on organizational structure and information processing.

The bounded relevance of emotional intelligence follows from this broader institutional reading. Officers who listen well, manage tension, and distinguish between overconfidence and genuine commercial clarity may indeed extract better soft information from SME borrowers. Those abilities can improve file quality, reduce misunderstanding, and help preserve useful relationships. But they are valuable chiefly when institutions know how to use the information thus gathered. Emotional intelligence improves the handling of uncertainty; it does not substitute for systems capable of converting that uncertainty into justified credit decisions (Bekerman & Zembylas, 2018).

5.8 Behavioral Finance and Other Factors Related to Lending Decisions

Behavioral finance is relevant to SME lending because credit decisions are made by human beings operating inside organizations, not by neutral calculators alone. Under uncertainty, loan officers and committees may overweight recent defaults, react strongly to salient sector failures, or prefer files that are easier to defend after the fact. These tendencies can make ambiguous SME applications appear riskier than they would under a purely mechanical assessment.

For this book, however, behavioral finance is treated as a complementary lens rather than as the master explanation. The financing gap cannot be solved by changing mindsets alone. Risk perception is embedded in procedures, incentives, delegation rules, collateral practices, and supervisory expectations. A cautious officer within a well-designed information system may support prudent SME lending, whereas an optimistic officer within a weak system may lead to poor risk selection.

Other factors also shape lending decisions: sector concentration, audit quality, collateral enforceability, the length and quality of bank-SME relationships, and the way branch recommendations are interpreted by central committees. Behavioral considerations therefore complete the institutional analysis. They explain why prudence can harden into excessive selectivity, but they do not replace the need to study the lending architecture itself.

5.9 AI, Alternative Data, and the Future of SME Credit Decisions

The future of SME credit decisions will increasingly be shaped by artificial intelligence, alternative data, and digital credit infrastructure. This development is directly relevant to the argument of this book. AI will not eliminate risk, distance, or information asymmetry. It will change how these dimensions are measured, combined, governed, and contested inside financial institutions.

In principle, AI-assisted credit assessment can help banks process larger quantities of information at lower cost. Transaction histories, mobile payments, invoice data, account flows, tax records, procurement contracts, repayment behavior, and digital footprints can all contribute to a richer credit file. For SMEs that lack conventional collateral or audited financial statements, this may create new pathways toward bankability. The promise of AI is therefore not that it removes uncertainty, but that it may reduce the cost of interpreting dispersed information.

This promise is particularly important in African banking systems, where many SMEs operate with limited formal documentation but increasingly leave digital traces. If these traces can be collected, verified, and interpreted responsibly, they may help narrow the gap between borrowers' realities and bank decision-making. Digital finance can therefore contribute to transforming soft, fragmented, and transaction-based information into evidence that supports credit decisions.

Yet AI also creates risks. A model can reproduce bias if the data used to train it are incomplete, unrepresentative, or historically discriminatory. A model can be difficult to explain if its internal logic is opaque. A bank can become dependent on third-party technology providers. Cybersecurity, data privacy, model validation, and accountability all become central to prudential governance. These risks are not theoretical. The Basel Committee's work on the digitalization of finance identifies artificial intelligence, machine learning, cloud computing, distributed ledger technology, and open banking as key technologies with implications for banks and supervisors. It also stresses that such developments affect supervision and require attention to emerging risks and coordination.

Explainability is especially important in SME credit. If a bank rejects an SME because an AI model produces an adverse score, the borrower, the credit officer, the risk committee, and the supervisor must be able to understand the basis of the decision. Recent supervisory work on AI explainability emphasizes that opaque models can raise systemic, governance, data quality, and consumer protection concerns.

The WAMU context is already moving into this debate. In 2025, the BCEAO organized an international conference, Artificial Intelligence: Opportunities and Challenges for Central Banks, bringing together central bank representatives, financial institutions, academics, and experts to discuss AI in economic policy, central bank missions, monetary policy, and financial stability. This confirms that AI is no longer a distant topic for the region. It is becoming part of the institutional agenda.

For the missing middle, the right conclusion is cautious optimism. AI can support SME finance only if it is embedded in sound governance, explainable models, reliable data, and human accountability. The future of SME lending should therefore not be imagined as a replacement of bank judgment by machines. It should be understood as a hybrid architecture: AI-assisted credit analysis, human-accountable credit judgment, and supervisory oversight strong enough to preserve trust.

The policy question is therefore not whether AI will make banks lend more. The question is whether AI will help banks know smaller firms better, at lower cost, and with sufficient fairness, transparency, and prudential discipline.

5.10 Synthesis

The literature reviewed in this chapter shows that lending is best understood as a technology of judgment. What banks know about a borrower depends on the tools they use, the information they collect, the routines through which that information is transmitted, and the discretionary room left to staff. Technology, relationships, internal authority, and borrower characteristics are therefore not isolated explanations. They are part of a wider architecture that determines what a bank can know and act upon.

For SMEs, this architecture matters profoundly because their financing problem is rarely one of demand alone. It is also a problem of representation. A firm may possess customers, ambition, and local credibility, yet still lack the standardized signals that many lending systems require. In such settings, relationship lending, officer discretion, and soft information can partially compensate for weak formal records—but only if institutions are designed to use them productively rather than arbitrarily.

This is the interpretive frame that informs the empirical chapters and the regional lessons drawn from them. The book is less interested in the generic claim that many factors affect lending than in the more disciplined question of how shared banking routines, branch structures, and information-processing constraints shape SME credit across a common monetary space.

The literature reviewed in this chapter points to a simple but powerful conclusion: SME lending is best understood as a system of organized interpretation. Information technology, borrower preparedness, officer discretion, institutional trust, and behavioral filters all matter because they determine how uncertainty is processed.

That interpretive architecture is what links the conceptual discussion to the empirical evidence from Burkina Faso. The next chapter turns from theory to method and explains how the book observes these mechanisms in practice.

References

Abraham, F., & Schmukler, S. L. (2017). *Addressing the SME finance problem*. World Bank Research and Policy Briefs. http://documents1.worldbank.org/curated/en/809191507620842321/pdf/Addressing-the-SME-finance-problem.pdf

Alibhai, S., Donald, A., Goldstein, M., Oguz, A. A., Pankov, A., & Strobbe, F. (2019). *Gender bias in SME lending: Experimental evidence from Turkey*. The World Bank.

Amoako-Adu, B., & Eshun, J. P. (2018). SME financing in Africa: Collateral lending vs cash flow lending. *International Journal of Economics and Finance, 10*(6), 111–123. https://doi.org/10.5539/ijef.v10n6p151

Angori, G., Aristei, D., & Gallo, M. (2019). Lending technologies, banking relationships, and firms' access to credit in Italy: The role of firm size. *Applied Economics, 51*(58), 6139–6170. https://doi.org/10.1080/00036846.2019.1613503

Bekerman, Z., & Zembylas, M. (2018). Emotion, emotional intelligence and motivation. In *Psychologized language in education* (pp. 67–78). Palgrave Macmillan. https://doi.org/10.1057/978-1-137-54937-2_8

Belas, J., Rahman, A., Rahman, M. T., & Schonfeld, J. (2017). Financial constraints on innovative SMEs: Empirical evidence from the Visegrad countries. *Engineering Economics, 28*(5), 552–563. https://doi.org/10.5755/j01.ee.28.5.18204

Benvenuti, M., Casolaro, L., Del Prete, S., & Mistrulli, P. E. (2017). The right to decide and the effective control over small business lending decisions: A look into loan officers' real authority. *Economic Notes: Review of Banking, Finance and Monetary Economics, 46*(2), 237–268. https://doi.org/10.1111/ecno.12079

Berger, A. N., & Udell, G. N. (2002). Small business credit availability and relationship lending: The importance of bank organization structure. *The Economic Journal, 112*(477), 32–53. https://doi.org/10.1111/1468-0297.00682

Berger, A. N., & Udell, G. N. (2006). A more complete conceptual framework for SME finance. *Journal of Banking & Finance, 30*(11), 2945–2966. https://doi.org/10.1016/j.jbankfin.2006.05.008

Berger, S., & Udell, A. (2012). Credit reporting and repayment behaviour in loan market. *Journal of Social Sciences and Research, 16*(2), 23–27. https://doi.org/10.2139/ssrn.968387

Beyina, E. (2019). Identity profile of ownership managers and SMEs funding modes: The case of Cameroon small and medium size enterprises. *Global Journal for Research Analysis, 8*(4), 24–30. http://www.worldwidejournals.net/index.php/GJRA/article/viewFile/380/376

Borish, M. S. (2020). *SME creditworthiness and financing: Firm size effects* [Doctoral dissertation, Carleton University]. https://curve.carleton.ca/38811583-1231-4234-9fae-2e1f5052dac4

Boulanouar, Z., Locke, S., & Holmes, M. (2020). An analysis of the SME–bank match made in heaven: The case of New Zealand main banks and their relationship-managed SMEs. *Qualitative Research in Financial Markets, 12*(4), 391–411. https://doi.org/10.1108/QRFM-12-2018-0139

Bouwens, J., & Kroos, P. (2019). The effect of delegation of decision rights and control: The case of lending decisions for small firms. *Management Accounting Research, 43*, 29–44. https://doi.org/10.1016/j.mar.2018.07.004

Brighi, P., Lucarelli, C., & Venturelli, V. (2019). Predictive strength of lending technologies in funding SMEs. *Journal of Small Business Management, 57*(4), 1350–1377. https://doi.org/10.1111/jsbm.12444

Bucciol, A., Guerrero, F., & Papadovasilaki, D. (2020). Financial risk-taking and trait emotional intelligence. *Review of Behavioral Finance, 13*, 259. https://doi.org/10.1108/RBF-01-2020-0013

Campbell, D., Loumioti, M., & Wittenberg-Moerman, R. (2019). Making sense of soft information: Interpretation bias and loan quality. *Journal of Accounting and Economics, 68*(2–3), 101240. https://doi.org/10.1016/j.jacceco.2019.101240

Chin, K. Y., Zakaria, Z., & Keong, C. C. (2020). The impact of managerial characteristics on capital structure in Malaysian manufacturing SMEs. International. *Journal of Banking and Finance, 15*(1), 21–37. www.e-journal.uum.edu.my

Chuong, P. H., Hung, N. V., Thanh, T. T., Hoa, H. Q., Dat, T. T., & Nam, P. X. (2020). Constraints of small and medium enterprises access to bank loans: Evidence from Vietnam manufacturing firms. *Academy of Accounting and Financial Studies Journal, 24*(1), 1–12. https://search.proquest.com/openview/c75d199c20b274dbc8d76babc84e78c6/1?pq-origsite=gscholar&cbl=29414

De Andrés, P., Gimeno, R., & de Cabo, R. M. (2020). The gender gap in bank credit access. *Journal of Corporate Finance, 71*, 101782. https://doi.org/10.1016/j.jcorpfin.2020.101782

Degryse, H., Matthews, K., & Zhao, T. (2018). SMEs and access to bank credit: Evidence on the regional propagation of the financial crisis in the UK. *Journal of Financial Stability, 38*, 53–70. https://doi.org/10.1016/j.jfs.2018.08.006

Dvorský, J., Schönfeld, J., Kotásková, A., & Petráková, Z. (2018). Evaluation of important credit risk factors in the SME segment. *Journal of International Studies, 3*, 204–216. https://doi.org/10.14254/2071-8330.2018/11-3/17

Ekpu, V. U. (2016). Supply-side factors affecting bank lending to SMEs. In *Determinants of bank involvement with SMEs* (pp. 45–72). https://doi.org/10.1007/978-3-319-25837-9_5

Fernández-Abascal, E. G., & Martín-Díaz, M. D. (2019). Relations between dimensions of emotional intelligence, specific aspects of empathy, and nonverbal sensitivity. *Frontiers in Psychology, 10*, 1066–1072. https://doi.org/10.3389/fpsyg.2019.01066

Ferri, G., Murro, P., Peruzzi, V., & Rotondi, Z. (2019). Bank lending technologies and credit availability in Europe: What can we learn from the crisis? *Journal of International Money and Finance, 95*, 128–148. www.docs.dises.univpm.it/web/quaderni/pdfmofir/Mofir135.pdf

Fidelis Finance. (2025). *Management 2025 annual report fidelis finance Burkina Faso*.

Filomeni, S., Udell, G. F., & Zazzaro, A. (2020). Communication frictions in banking organizations: Evidence from credit score lending. *Economics Letters, 195*, 109412. https://doi.org/10.1016/j.econlet.2020.109412

Flaminiano, J. P., & Francisco, J. P. (2019). *Firm characteristics and credit constraints across SMEs in the Philippines (Working Paper 2019-006)*. Asian Institute of Management, Rizalino S. Navarro Policy Center for Competitiveness. http://www.ssrn.com/abstact=3498019

Flögel, F., & Beckamp, M. (2020). *Digitalisation and (de) centralisation in Germany-a comparative study of retail banking and the energy sector*. IAT Discussion Paper. https://www.iat.eu/discussionpapers/download/IAT_Discussion_Paper_20_04.pdf

Gao, J., Karolyi, S. A., & Pacelli, J. (2018). *Screening and monitoring by inattentive corporate loan officers (Working paper)*. Indiana University. https://business.depaul.edu/about/centers-institutes/financial-services/Documents/9_3_Karolyi.pdf

Gao, J., Martin, X., & Pacelli, J. (2017). *Do loan officers impact lending decisions? Evidence from the corporate loan market*. https://www.lebow.drexel.edu/sites/default/files/1489607744-loanofficer20170314.pdf

Goleman, D. (1998). *Working with emotional intelligence*. Bantam.

Goleman, D. (2019). *The emotionally intelligent leader*. Harvard Business Press.

Ibtissem, B. (2015). "On the role of loan officers' psychological traits in predicting microcredit default accuracy," qualitative research in financial markets. *Emerald Group Publishing, 7*(3), 264–289. https://ideas.repec.org/a/eme/qrfmpp/v7y2015i3p264-289.html

International Finance Corporation (IFC). (2011). *Corporate and SME workouts: A manual of best practices*. World Bank Group.

Jakšič, M., & Marinč, M. (2019). Relationship banking and information technology: The role of artificial intelligence and FinTech. *Risk Management, 21*(1), 1–18. https://doi.org/10.1057/s41283-018-0039-y

Jayasooriya, S. (2020). *Roles of technology, innovation, and finance in small and medium-sized enterprises (SMEs) in Sri Lanka*. Munich Personal RePEc Archive. https://mpra.ub.uni-muenchen.de/104412/

Jude, F. A., & Adamou, N. (2018). Bank loan financing decisions of small and medium-sized enterprises: The significance of owner/managers' behaviours. *International Journal of Economics and Finance, 10*(5), 231–241. https://doi.org/10.5539/ijef.v10n5p231

Kariuki-Njogu, G., Njeru, A., & Olweny, T. (2018). Influence of technology adoption on credit access among small holder farmers: A double-hurdle analysis. *Africa International Journal of Management Education and Governance, E1813*, 1–15. https://www.oalib.com/

Karthikeyan, V., & Lalwani, S. (2017). Emotional intelligence in banking sector–an integrative literature review. *Journal of Business and Management, 19*(10), 9–14. www.iosrjournals.org

Kervinen, L. (2019). *Role of trust in bank-SME relationships* [Doctoral dissertation, Aalto University]. Aalto University Repository.

Kozubikova, L., Homolka, L., & Kristalas, D. (2017). The effect of business environment and entrepreneurs' gender on perception of financial risk in the SMEs sector. *Journal of Competitiveness, 9*(1), 36–50. https://doi.org/10.7441/joc.2017.01.03

Lagrange, B., Morin, E. M., & Viger, C. (2017). The moderating effect of emotional intelligence on loan officers' judgments and decisions. *Journal of Business and Management, 23*(1/2), 47–81. www.jbm.johogo.com/

Lee, N., & Brown, R. (2017). Innovation, SMEs and the liability of distance: The demand and supply of bank funding in UK peripheral regions. *Journal of Economic Geography, 17*(1), 233–260. https://doi.org/10.1093/jeg/lbw011

Metawa, N., Hassan, M. K., & Elhoseny, M. (2017). Genetic algorithm based model for optimizing bank lending decisions. *Expert Systems with Applications, 80*, 75–82. https://doi.org/10.1016/j.eswa.2017.03.021

Moro, A., & Fink, M. (2013). Loan managers' trust and credit access for SMEs. *Journal of Banking & Finance, 37*(3), 927–936. https://doi.org/10.1016/j.jbankfin.2012.10.023

Moro, A., Fink, M., Maresch, D., & Fredriksson, A. (2018). Loan managers' decisions and trust in entrepreneurs in different institutional contexts. *Entrepreneurship & Regional Development, 30*(1–2), 146–172. https://doi.org/10.1080/08985626.2017.1400115

Nguyen, H. T., Nguyen, H. M., Troege, M., & Nguyen, A. T. (2020). Debt aversion, education, and credit self-rationing in SMEs. *Small Business Economics, 1*, 1–19. https://doi.org/10.1007/s11187-020-00329-9

Nguyen, L. T., Su, J. J., & Sharma, P. (2019). SME credit constraints in Asia's rising economic star: Fresh empirical evidence from Vietnam. *Applied Economics, 51*(29), 3170–3183. https://doi.org/10.1080/00036846.2019.1569196

Nguyen, S., & Wolfe, S. (2016). Determinants of successful access to bank loans by Vietnamese SMEs: New evidence from the red river delta. *The Journal of Internet Banking and Commerce, 21*(1), 162. https://doi.org/10.4172/1204-5357.1000162

Nyerere, K. J., & Wawire, B. P. (2015). The influence of emotional intelligence on service delivery. *International Journal of Economics, Finance and Management, 4*(1), 8–13. http://erepository.kibu.ac.ke/handle/123456789/1107

Palazuelos, E., Crespo, Á. H., & del Corte, J. M. (2018). Accounting information quality and trust as determinants of credit granting to SMEs: The role of external audit. *Small Business Economics, 51*(4), 861–877. https://doi.org/10.1007/s11187-017-9966-3

Prentice, C. (2016). Leveraging employee emotional intelligence in casino profitability. *Journal of Retailing and Consumer Services, 33*, 127–134. https://doi.org/10.1016/j.jretconser.2016.08.011

Rad, A., Öhman, P., & Yazdanfar, D. (2018). *Loan officers' information focus in SME loan assessment: A case study* [Doctoral dissertation, Mid Sweden University]. Mid Sweden University Repository.

Santoso, W., Trinugroho, I., & Risfandy, T. (2020). What determine loan rate and default status in financial technology online direct lending? Evidence from Indonesia. *Emerging Markets Finance and Trade, 56*(2), 351–369. https://doi.org/10.1080/1540496X.2019.1605595

Sedunov, J. (2017). Does bank technology affect small business lending decisions? *Journal of Financial Research, 40*(1), 5–32. https://doi.org/10.1111/jfir.12116

Song, Z. L., & Zhang, X. M. (2018). Lending technology and credit risk under different types of loans to SMEs: Evidence from China. *International Review of Economics and Finance, 57*, 43–69. https://doi.org/10.1016/j.iref.2018.02.012

Sutherland, A. (2018). Does credit reporting lead to a decline in relationship lending? Evidence from information sharing technology. *Journal of Accounting and Economics, 66*(1), 123–141. https://doi.org/10.1016/j.jacceco.2018.03.002

Twine, E. E., Rao, E. J., Baltenweck, I., & Omore, A. O. (2019). Are technology adoption and collective action important in accessing credit? Evidence from milk producers in Tanzania. *The European Journal of Development Research, 31*(3), 388–412. https://doi.org/10.1057/s41287-018-0158-z

van der Zwan, P. (2016). Bank loan application success of innovative and non-innovative SMEs. *International Review of Entrepreneurship, 14*(4), 483–502. https://www.abacademies.org/journals/international-journal-of-entrepreneurship-home.html

Wang, R., Lin, Z., & Luo, H. (2019). Blockchain, bank credit and SME financing. *Quality & Quantity, 53*(3), 1127–1140. https://doi.org/10.1007/s11135-018-0806-6

Wellalage, N. H., Locke, S., & Samujh, H. (2019). Firm bribery and credit access: Evidence from Indian SMEs. *Small Business Economics, 55*, 283–304. https://doi.org/10.1007/s11187-019-00161-w

Yosano, T., & Nakaoka, T. (2019a). Survey data from Japanese regional banks and using soft information in lending decisions. In *Utilization of soft information on bank performance* (pp. 31–56). https://doi.org/10.1007/978-981-13-8472-1_3

Yosano, T., & Nakaoka, T. (2019b). Soft information's role in lending decisions. In *Utilization of soft information on bank performance* (pp. 93–105). Springer.

Zhao, T., & Jones-Evans, D. (2017). SMEs, banks and the spatial differentiation of access to finance. *Journal of Economic Geography, 17*(4), 791–824. https://doi.org/10.1093/jeg/lbw029

Zhou, Y., Zhao, H., & Xie, X. (2018, August). Study of the differences between government and bank in bank loans: Evidence from Chinese listed SMEs. In *3rd International Conference on Judicial, Administrative and Humanitarian Problems of State Structures and Economic Subjects (JAHP 2018)*. Atlantis Press.

Chapter 6
Data, Measurement, and Empirical Strategy: Burkina Faso Evidence, WAMU Relevance

This book examines how banks translate uncertainty about small firms into lending decisions. The methodological challenge is therefore practical before it is philosophical: What kind of evidence allows us to observe that process with enough precision to say something meaningful about small and medium-sized enterprise (SME) credit in Burkina Faso while still drawing disciplined lessons for the West African Monetary Union (WAMU)?

The empirical setting is Burkina Faso's two principal urban centers, Ouagadougou and Bobo-Dioulasso, where formal banking activity and SME concentration are most heavily clustered. All banks or bank branches in the target area were approached, resulting in a sampling frame of 53 institutions or branches. Within this frame, the study matched institutional information from participating banks with survey responses from lending officers and managers. The resulting analytical threshold was set at 127 respondents, a sample size justified through power analysis for multiple regression. This design places the analysis at the operational point where SME applications are screened, documented, interpreted, and either advanced or constrained (Sory, 2021).

The evidence comes from two sources. The first is archival information supplied by participating banks. The second is a researcher-designed survey administered to officers and managers involved in SME lending. This combination matters because each source compensates for the other's limitations. Administrative records provide observable lending outcomes and institutional characteristics. Survey responses provide access to the informational and perceptual dimensions of lending that do not appear directly in bank files. Together, they make it possible to examine not only what banks do, but under what informational and organizational conditions they do it.

A central improvement in the framing of this study concerns the dependent variable. In the dissertation language from which the book emerged, the outcome is described as "willingness to provide credit." Yet willingness is not directly observable. The data capture includes two proximate indicators: the number of SME loans

K. A. Sory, *Banking the Missing Middle*, Research Series on Responsible Enterprise Ecosystems, https://doi.org/10.1007/978-3-032-34582-0_6

approved and the share of lending directed to SMEs. In this book, these measures are therefore treated as indicators of SME lending intensity or of institutional engagement with SMEs, rather than as pure psychological intention. This distinction is important. Observed lending reflects not only attitudes, but also bank scale, branch reach, client mix, and organizational exposure to the SME segment.

The explanatory variables are organized into four blocks. The first captures the geospatial and organizational relationship between the bank and SME activity, including bank type, branch location, and the reach of the branch network. The second captures information asymmetry through survey items on the availability, reliability, and transparency of borrower information. The third block comprises demographic characteristics of bank officers, including age, gender, education, job level, and tenure. The fourth block captures bank perceptions of SMEs through Likert-scale items measured at both the institutional and individual levels. This structure allows the analysis to compare the explanatory power of organizational, informational, personal, and perceptual factors within a common empirical framework.

The empirical strategy proceeds in stages. It begins with descriptive statistics that map the sample's institutional composition and the distributions of the main variables. It then examines associations among variables through correlation analysis. The core inferential step is multiple linear regression (MLR). This method is used because the research problem is relational: The question is whether several sets of predictors are associated with variations in SME lending intensity, and, if so, which sets matter most. The reported coefficients are interpreted as associational rather than causal. This is a retrospective, nonexperimental design built on matched cross-sectional evidence, not a causal identification strategy.

One methodological clarification is especially important. The dissertation text gestures toward a multilevel logic in discussing the role of officers within the sample, yet the subsequent inferential strategy is a conventional regression framework. In the present book, the analysis is therefore presented transparently as a matched bank-officer design rather than as a fully hierarchical model. This is not a weakness if stated clearly. It simply defines the scope of inference: The findings illuminate patterned associations within the observed bank–officer environment, but they do not claim to estimate a fully nested organizational process.

Because part of the evidence relies on a researcher-developed survey instrument, questions of reliability and validity require direct treatment. A pilot test was used to refine the instrument before wider deployment, and internal consistency diagnostics, such as Cronbach's alpha, informed the final questionnaire. That is a reasonable strategy in a context where no ready-made instrument exactly fits the variables of interest. At the same time, the survey's contribution is not that it produces a universal psychometric scale of banker behavior. Its contribution is that it generates context-specific, original evidence on a banking environment and lending problem that remains understudied in the literature.

The limits of the design follow from the nature of the evidence. The study can observe recorded lending outcomes and the representations of participating bank staff, but it cannot fully observe discouraged borrowers who never apply, nor can it reconstruct every unrecorded interaction between banks and firms. The geographic

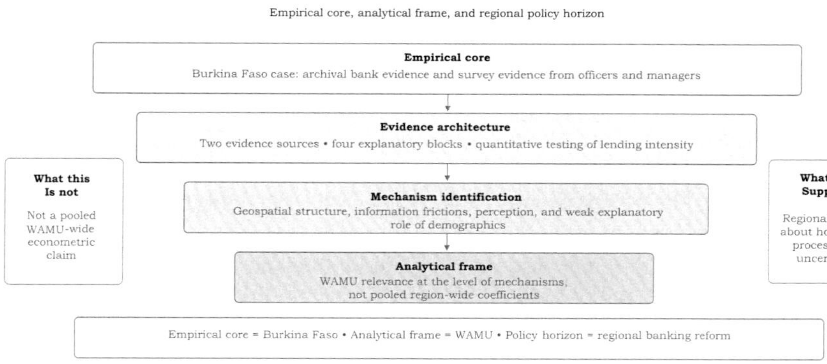

Fig. 6.1 From Burkina Faso evidence to WAMU relevance: the architecture of inference. *Source: author's conceptual synthesis*

focus on Burkina Faso's principal banking centers captures the core of formal intermediation, but it should not be mistaken for a complete map of the country's peripheral lending environments. These limits do not diminish the study's value. They specify the level at which its claims are strongest: the organizational and informational conditions under which SME lending is expanded, restricted, or selectively structured within the formal banking system.

Methodological chapters in dissertations often begin by defending a philosophical position. This book takes a different route. Its priority is to explain the evidence's architecture as clearly as possible. The reader does not need an extended defense of positivism to evaluate the argument. The reader needs to know what was measured, how the measures were constructed, why the case selection is credible, and how far the results can be trusted. That is the work of this chapter.

Because the empirical evidence comes from Burkina Faso while the book speaks to WAMU, the scope of inference must be made explicit. Figure 6.1 sets out the architecture of inference by distinguishing the empirical core, the analytical frame, and the regional policy horizon.

The figure makes clear that the book does not claim pooled econometric proof for all WAMU member states. Its regional contribution operates at the level of mechanisms: how banks process uncertainty, how knowledge from branches travels, and how institutions decide which smaller firms are financeable. This distinction preserves both analytical ambition and methodological discipline.

6.1 Research Philosophy and Methodological Choice

The study was carried out under a positivist research philosophy. Positivism is a research philosophy that focuses on hard, observable data rather than on abstract theory (Y. S. Park et al., 2020). Under a positivist approach, only propositions that can be empirically tested hold merit. Hence, though positivism does not exclude theory, it is less concerned with the generation of new theory than with the empirical validation of existing theory. Moreover, under positivism, theory must be falsifiable. A positivist approach is typically adopted when addressing concepts that are examined in detail, are well-defined, and for which a significant amount of concrete information can be collected (Y. S. Park et al., 2020). The present study aligned with all these criteria of the positivist approach to research. Behavioral finance is a field concerned with linking concrete human behavioral patterns to specific choices or financial outcomes. Though it does concern individual perceptions and choices, these factors are considered only as predictors of concrete financial outcomes rather than as an exploration of the human experience. Hence, a positivist approach was ideal for this study.

The alternative research philosophy to positivism is constructivism. Rather than empirically evaluating the world using data, a constructivist research philosophy examines and understands the socially constructed nature of human experience (Grant, 2016). Positivism, by nature, is less concerned with how well theory holds up in the abstract and more concerned with developing theory that accounts for social factors and perspectives. Such a philosophy does have a place in behavioral finance but would be more appropriate for a study examining the individual experiences of bank loan officers than for one like this, which is intended to empirically validate theoretical propositions.

The research methodology was quantitative. Quantitative research is aligned with a positivist research philosophy. Quantitative inquiry is used to assess relationships empirically between variables or to understand quantifiable problems. Quantitative inquiry draws on and tests existing theory and requires that the variables under study be defined concretely and quantitatively. A quantitative researcher cannot explore new ideas because of the closed-ended nature of the research approach. However, closed-ended quantitative data can be easily collected and analyzed for vast sample sizes, allowing a quantitative study to achieve strong statistical significance (Balnaves & Caputi, 2001).

The key focus of quantitative inquiry is on variables and how these relate to one another, meaning that statistical power translates into empirically verified relationships with real-world predictive implications (Balnaves & Caputi, 2001). All these criteria made quantitative research a strong fit for this study. First, it aligned with the chosen positivist research philosophy. Second, the study was relational, intended to measure the nature and strength of relationships among key study variables.

Third, the researcher addressed the variables under study through closed-ended inquiry, enabling the collection of large quantities of quantitative data to achieve statistical significance. Finally, the study was guided by theory-grounded hypotheses tested through a quantitative study. By contrast, a qualitative approach to research is descriptive and exploratory (Merriam & Tisdell, 2015). Qualitative research aligns with the constructivist philosophy of research, as qualitative researchers typically collect subjective data regarding participants' experiences and perceptions. Using these data, the qualitative researcher explores the phenomenon as experienced by those with firsthand knowledge. Qualitative research is accordingly open-ended, seeking to examine all perspectives present within the population under study. The trade-off for the richness of qualitative data is that it can only be collected from smaller samples. Qualitative research is widely used to develop new theory or, relatedly, to explore new territory where existing theory applies poorly (Merriam & Tisdell, 2015).

A qualitative approach to research would be a poor fit for the study for many of the same reasons that a quantitative approach was a strong fit. First, the present study focused on relationships among specific variables rather than on a broad phenomenon. Second, the present study used inherently quantified empirical data, such as banks' lending rates to SMEs. These issues would be difficult to explore in a descriptive fashion. Moreover, the present study addressed a topic, information asymmetry and risk aversion, universally understood through existing theory, making a qualitative exploration unnecessary.

6.2 Research Design

The research design for the study was nonexperimental, correlational, and retrospective. Quantitative research can be experimental or nonexperimental (S. M. Ross & Morrison, 2004). Experimental researchers provide the strongest evidence, as they can demonstrate causal relationships. However, experimental research requires that the researcher have control over the variables and be able to manipulate those variables. Hence, experimental research is rarely viable in disciplines such as economics or finance, which involve variables embedded in the study's economic context and are too large-scale or otherwise impactful to be feasible or ethically manipulated. Hence, a nonexperimental design must be employed. Nonexperimental researchers can only draw weaker correlational or associational conclusions, but this approach allows them to use real-world data in their analysis. Furthermore, a nonexperimental study can still yield important results that have real-world predictive value (Johnson, 2001).

Consequently, a nonexperimental design was the most appropriate choice for this study. Nonexperimental research can be descriptive, correlational, or causal-comparative (Johnson, 2001). In this study, a correlational design was the most appropriate. Correlational research is used to assess the relationships between variables at a functional or predictive level. Such a research design aligns with the purpose of examining the relationships between predictors of banks' willingness to extend credit to SMEs and their choice to offer credit. On the other hand, descriptive research would be a poor fit. Descriptive research is used to describe the population under study in quantitative terms. Descriptive quantitative researchers can provide valuable insight, but because such an approach only describes, it would not enable the present study's research questions to be answered. A causal-comparative design would also be a poor fit for the proposed study. Causal-comparative research is used to compare outcomes for one or more dependent variables across a binary or categorical independent variable (Johnson, 2001). For example, a causal-comparative researcher might determine whether large or small banks were more likely to lend to SMEs. Instead, this researcher addressed a continuous predictor.

Within correlational research, cross-sectional, retrospective, and longitudinal designs are possible (Johnson, 2001). For this study, a retrospective approach was best aligned. A retrospective researcher uses existing, historical data, possibly in concert with new data where necessary. The retrospective approach was appropriate to this study because the key decision variable, SME financing, was recorded in historical records of banks' crediting decisions regarding SMEs. Some additional data, such as bank types and bank officer demographics, could also be retrieved from historical records. Hence, a retrospective approach was most strongly aligned with the study purpose and variables. By contrast, a cross-sectional approach involves collecting a cross-sectional snapshot of the population at a given moment in time. Although this design could be a good alternative if no relevant historical data existed, such data were available and used in this study. A longitudinal design is instead used to compare changes over time (Johnson, 2001). However, the present study was not designed to examine how the bank-SME relationship evolved over time. Hence, a longitudinal design would be poorly aligned with the study's purpose.

6.3 Population, Sampling, and Fieldwork

Within this sample, data were collected from bank officers and managers. Because the officers were the lowest level in the multilevel analysis, they represented the sample size in the power analysis. Using G*Power for the multiple linear regression described below, the minimum necessary sample size was 127 bank officers or managers (Sory, 2021). This sample size corresponded to a medium effect size ($f^2 = 0.15$), a statistical power of 80%, and a significance level of 0.05. The recruitment effort began with banks. All banks and bank branches in Bobo-Dioulasso and Ouagadougou were contacted and asked to participate in the study, using either a blanket sampling approach or an exhaustive sampling approach, in which all members of the target population were approached (see Elfil & Negida, 2017).

For those banks that expressed a willingness to participate, the necessary secondary data points were requested. In addition, the banks were requested to distribute a recruitment letter or e-mail (whichever was more convenient) to all their officers or managers who handled SME loans, inviting them to participate in the study. Those who agreed to participate were asked to complete a survey. For the purposes of matching each respondent to their secondary data, the survey was not fully anonymous; only the researcher knew which participants and banks were connected. These data were used only to link the different data within the analysis, not to identify any participants. The banks were offered a copy of the study results to incentivize participation, while individual bank officers were offered a small incentive, such as a gift card.

6.4 Instrumentation and Variable Construction

Data for the study were collected from two key sources: survey questionnaires and secondary data. The secondary data were drawn from the banks that agreed to participate in the study. Surveys were distributed to individual participants via the Internet using an online survey host, such as SurveyMonkey. Data collected included the variables discussed in the following subsections. The SME loan history variable was collected at both the bank and individual bank officer levels. At each level, the number was collected in two forms: as the total number of SME loans approved and the percentage of all SME loans approved. The geospatial relationship variable was assessed using survey items that captured the bank's physical proximity to SMEs. It was constructed from bank type (large/small/international) and primary location (main branch/side branch/only location) and served as the predictor (independent variable) in the first research question. Information asymmetry was assessed using a series of Likert-scale items. Hence, it represented a continuous variable with two dimensions: banks' awareness of SME information and transparency of loan information. Each was treated as a continuous variable per analytical tradition. Information asymmetry was the predictor (independent variable) for the second research question. The demographics of bank officers represented the predictor variable in the third research question. Demographics collected included age, race, gender, job level, professional tenure, and education level. Each was collected as a categorical or continuous variable as appropriate. Bank perception of SMEs was the independent variable in the fourth research question. It was measured at two levels: the bank level and the individual bank officer level. The researcher used a series of 5-point Likert-scale items. In line with analytical tradition, these items were treated as continuous variables.

6.5 Data Collection, Analysis, and Model Specification

The data collection process for the study was carried out as follows. The first step in the study was to obtain approval from the university's Institutional Review Board (IRB). This process entailed submitting the study to the university's research board for review and making any requested changes to obtain approval. Following the review process, a list of all banks in Bobo-Dioulasso and Ouagadougou was compiled. As previously noted, there were 53 bank offices or branches in the sampling frame within this region.

Contact information for all these banks was compiled. Then, a recruitment e-mail was composed. This e-mail requested site authorization from each bank—permission to recruit participants from the bank and to collect data on the loan officers' and banks' ratings of SME loan approval. The banks were offered a copy of the study results to incentivize participation, while individual bank officers were offered a small incentive, such as a gift card.

Those banks that granted site authorization for the research received a secondary recruitment e-mail. This e-mail was distributed to the banks' loan officers and managers to request their participation. If more convenient for the banks, the participating banks could instead distribute the request for participation in letter form. For e-mail participation requests, the participants were directed to an online survey. If the participation requests were instead distributed in paper form, the surveys were provided to the banks in paper form. For the purposes of matching participant and bank data, each participant received a unique identifier.

Although the researcher was aware of which participant corresponded to each identifier, this information was not included in the study data. Each bank was assigned a coded identifier. In the actual analysis and reporting of data, the data were treated as anonymous and contained no identifying information about either the participants or the banks. All data were compiled in a spreadsheet and then imported into Statistical Package for the Social Sciences (SPSS) for statistical analysis.

Given the concentration of both banks and SMEs in the two cities under study, there was no backup population from which to draw data if the minimum sample could not be achieved within those cities. Accordingly, every reasonable, noncoercive effort was made to encourage the participation of both banks and individual employees within banks. If the minimum necessary sample size was not met, this issue must be regarded simply as a limitation of the study, as expanding the population would undermine the study's focus on Burkina Faso's specific context.

Because the study used a researcher-developed instrument, the first participating bank was used as a pilot site. The results were used to test reliability and validity and to refine the questionnaire before wider field deployment. Data analysis then proceeded with descriptive statistics and multiple linear regression to identify which bank-side factors were most strongly associated with SME lending intensity in Burkina Faso.

Four empirical questions guided the analysis: whether the geospatial relationship, information asymmetry, demographic characteristics of lending staff, and overall bank perception of SMEs were associated with SME lending intensity. Framed in book form, these are no longer treated as isolated doctoral hypotheses, but as competing explanations whose relative explanatory power can be compared within a common empirical design.

Following the descriptive analyses, multiple linear regression analysis was used to answer the research questions. Multiple linear regression (MLR) was the ideal method for testing multiple hypotheses simultaneously (Aiken et al., 2012). Though multiple simple linear regressions could be used to test the hypotheses individually, multiple linear regression offered two advantages. First, it helped reduce the likelihood of redundant results due to multiple highly correlated predictors (Aiken et al., 2012).

Second, it helped reduce Type I errors without the need to apply a Bonferroni or other correction because the same analysis included all predictors (Aiken et al., 2012). Before estimating the models, diagnostics for normality of residuals, homoscedasticity, and multicollinearity among predictors were examined. If these assumptions were not met, the data might be transformed as appropriate, or a non-parametric regression approach might be substituted.

Once the assumptions were verified, the analysis was conducted. The four sets of predictor variables corresponding to the four research questions were regressed against the different dimensions of the two outcome variables. First, the overall multiple R-squared of the multiple regression was tested to determine if the model had any predictive power. Then, if the multiple R-squared was significantly different from 0, the hypotheses were tested. If the coefficient of regression for any dimension of a research question was significantly different from 0 for any dimension of the outcomes, then the null hypothesis for that research question was rejected, and the alternative hypothesis was supported.

6.6 Reliability, Validity, and Research Ethics

Reliability refers to the extent to which a study measures outcomes accurately (Merriam & Tisdell, 2015). In quantitative research, this refers to the extent to which the scales used to measure the variables yield consistent scores, both across multiple tests and within the measure's factors. For the data in this study, drawn directly from banks, the reliability of the information rested solely on the assumption that banks maintained records with consummate accuracy, since these variables were intrinsic measures of the underlying construct. For the other variables, the reliability issue was more complex. Typically, a quantitative researcher uses existing, validated measures of a variable from the literature (Balnaves & Caputi, 2001). However, the specificity of the variables in this study necessitated a researcher-developed instrument. A pilot study was conducted at the first bank to agree to participate in testing the reliability of this new instrument. From this pilot study, key reliability statistics, such as Cronbach's alpha, were calculated. If necessary, the study instrument was revised to improve reliability.

Validity is another key aspect of research (Merriam & Tisdell, 2015). Validity is divided into internal and external validity. Internal validity addresses the alignment of key study components and the study's ability to answer the research questions (Merriam & Tisdell, 2015). Internal validity was achieved in several ways. First, the study components had been carefully aligned. The research purpose is derived from the research problem, whereas the research questions are derived from the research purpose. The variables for the study were selected in alignment with the research questions. Second, as noted above, internal validity was supported by a pilot study that tested the researcher-developed instrument used to collect some of the data. This process ensured that the instrument was an accurate measure of the key variables needed to answer the research question. Together, the measures ensured that the researcher addressed the foundational, motivating problem: risk aversion among banks in lending to SMEs in Burkina Faso.

External validity reflects the generalizability of the study (Balnaves & Caputi, 2001). There are two aspects of external validity: statistical power and representativeness. First, statistical power was assessed using G*Power. At least 127 participants were recruited to achieve the desired level of statistical power. If not, the failure to achieve the desired power was considered a limitation of the study, and a post hoc analysis was conducted to determine the study's actual statistical power. Second, representation in this study was achieved through exhaustion. Because there were only 53 bank branches in the two cities, which accounted for the vast majority of Burkina Faso's financial sector, it was possible to contact and recruit participants from almost all banks nationwide. In addition, the demographic profile showed whether the results were representative as desired.

The study was conducted with careful attention to ethical research practices at all stages. Because the data could not be collected with full anonymity, the study instead employed careful measures to protect participants' confidentiality. Even in internal study documents, participants and banks were referred to only by coded designators, which were used solely to match bank and survey data. During the analysis, all the data were anonymized and stripped of any identifying information. In this way, no personally identifying information regarding either banks or individuals was reported in the final study. Moreover, the individual loan officers' or managers' choices to participate were kept confidential from the banks, ensuring that neither participation nor nonparticipation posed a risk. Participants were compensated with a small item, such as a gift card, which was sufficient as an incentive but not coercive. All participating banks received a copy of the analysis results as soon as the analyses were completed, in case they were useful for improving operational practices. Participants also received informed consent documentation as the survey's cover page.

All data collected for the study were stored securely in password-protected files. The identifiers used to link participants to banks were kept separate from the analytical dataset and used only for matching. No personally identifying information about individual officers, managers, or institutions is reported in the book. These safeguards support the ethical use of the evidence while preserving the empirical value of linking organizational information to survey responses.

The population under study was all banks in Burkina Faso. The target population was further narrowed to Ouagadougou and Bobo-Dioulasso, the two centers that account for the overwhelming majority of bank offices and SMEs in the country. Hence, all 53 bank offices or branches in the sampling frame, were contacted. From these banks, the minimum necessary sample size was 127 bank officers or managers.

This is why the book maintains a strict distinction between the empirical core and the analytical horizon. The data do not license pooled claims about all WAMU member states. They do, however, identify mechanisms inside a shared banking space that can be compared, challenged, and refined in future regional research. That is a stronger and more defensible form of regionalization.

6.7 Synthesis

Methodologically, the study sits at the intersection of organizational evidence and lender perception. That positioning is deliberate. A purely archival design would have captured observed lending outcomes but not the informational routines and judgments that animate them. A purely survey-based design would have captured perceptions but risked detaching them from actual lending patterns. By combining both sources, the research design provides a more plausible basis for interpreting how institutions translate uncertainty into credit exposure.

At the same time, the design remains appropriately modest in its claims. This is not a causal identification strategy in the narrow econometric sense, nor does it seek to reconstruct every discouraged application or informal refusal. Its contribution lies elsewhere: in mapping a structured bank-side environment, pairing institutional characteristics with officer-level responses, and testing which clusters of variables are most strongly associated with observed SME lending intensity.

References

Aiken, L. S., West, S. G., Pitts, S. C., Baraldi, A. N., & Wurpts, I. C. (2012). Multiple linear regression. In *Handbook of psychology* (Vol. 2, 2nd ed.). https://doi.org/10.1002/9781118133880.hop202018

Balnaves, M., & Caputi, P. (2001). *Introduction to quantitative research methods: An investigative approach*. Sage.

Elfil, M., & Negida, A. (2017). Sampling methods in clinical research; an educational review. *Emergency, 5*(1), e52. https://www.ncbi.nlm.nih.gov/pmc/articles/PMC5325924/

Grant, C. B. (2016). Constructivism. In *The international encyclopedia of communication theory and philosophy* (Vol. 1–9). https://doi.org/10.1002/9781118766804.wbiect160

Johnson, B. (2001). Toward a new classification of nonexperimental quantitative research. *Educational Researcher, 30*(2), 3–13. https://doi.org/10.3102/0013189X030002003

Merriam, S. B., & Tisdell, E. J. (2015). *Qualitative research: A guide to design and implementation*. Wiley & Sons.

Park, Y. S., Konge, L., & Artino, A. R., Jr. (2020). The positivism paradigm of research. *Academic Medicine, 95*(5), 690–694. https://doi.org/10.1097/ACM.0000000000003093

Ross, S. M., & Morrison, G. R. (2004). Experimental research methods. In *Handbook of research on educational communications and technology* (Vol. 2, pp. 1021–1043). https://doi.org/10.30935/cedtech/5959

Sory, K. A. (2021). *Risk aversion behaviors in the bank-SMEs relationship: Predictors of credit in Burkina Faso* [Doctoral dissertation, Franklin Hudson International School of Management].

Chapter 7
What Drives SME Lending? Evidence from Burkina Faso and Lessons for WAMU

This chapter presents the empirical core of the book. Its purpose is not to ask whether banks dislike risk in the abstract, but to identify which observable features of the banking environment are most closely associated with the scale and structure of small and medium-sized enterprise (SME) lending in Burkina Faso. The chapter then interprets those findings as regional lessons for West African Monetary Union (WAMU), while keeping the distinction between measured evidence and plausible portability clear.

The descriptive evidence already points toward an institutional explanation. Most respondents come from privately owned banks, a majority from foreign-owned institutions, and a substantial share from medium-sized and large banks. Respondents also identify bank structure, officer competencies, the legal and contractual environment, macroeconomic conditions, and lending technology as major indicators of bank involvement in the SME segment (Sory, 2021). This is a revealing starting point. It suggests that SME finance is not treated simply as a matter of borrower quality. It is embedded in the broader organizational and contractual conditions within the banking system.

A second descriptive pattern concerns the organization of lending work itself. Many participating institutions report a separate unit for managing SME relations. Pre-screening is often conducted at branches, while approval, risk management, and nonperforming loan recovery are more frequently handled by both branches and headquarters. Banks also report that their involvement with SMEs is driven primarily by the segment's perceived profitability and by competitive pressure in markets for larger corporate clients. These patterns matter because they show that SME lending is neither accidental nor purely charitable. It is strategically relevant to banks but filtered through internal screening, routing, and approval processes.

The strongest empirical result concerns organizational geography. Among the geospatial variables, bank classification and the number of offices in Bobo-Dioulasso are both positively and significantly associated with SME lending intensity. The corresponding model explains 68.9% of the observed variation. This is the

K. A. Sory, *Banking the Missing Middle*, Research Series on Responsible Enterprise Ecosystems, https://doi.org/10.1007/978-3-032-34582-0_7

dominant result of the chapter. It indicates that the allocation of credit to SMEs is shaped above all by the scale and reach of the institution and by the local architecture through which banks encounter firms. Branch presence is therefore not a peripheral operational fact. It is part of the mechanism by which banks reduce uncertainty, gather soft information, and sustain lending relationships with smaller clients.

This finding is important because it shifts the interpretation of the SME credit problem. The main obstacle is not best described as generalized banker caution. It is better understood as a problem of institutional capacity. Larger or more extensively positioned banks appear better equipped to engage with the SME segment, not merely because they hold more resources, but because they can process local information more effectively. In that sense, geography becomes a proxy for informational reach. The missing middle in finance is produced in part by the uneven organization of proximity.

The second family of results concerns information asymmetry. Here, the evidence is more selective. Only one variable emerges as clearly significant: the impact of cost factors on SME loan contract terms. Its coefficient is negative, indicating that as informational and contractual frictions intensify, SME lending intensity declines. Yet the model explains only a small share of the variance. The proper conclusion is therefore not that information asymmetry is unimportant. On the contrary, it remains central to the logic of SME lending. But its effects appear thinner, more dispersed, and less institutionally decisive than the organizational-geographic factors identified in the first model.

The descriptive information on sources of reliable data reinforces this interpretation. Banks report heavy reliance on internal databases, credit bureaus, and rating agencies, while softer or more decentralized sources of information are used much less consistently. Participants also assign high importance to firm characteristics, market infrastructure, and relationship characteristics in credit assessment. Together, these patterns suggest that banks are actively trying to manage opacity, but that the available informational architecture remains uneven. SMEs become easier to finance where their documentary and relational traces can be converted into credible credit evidence.

By contrast, demographic characteristics of bank officers explain very little. Position, years of experience, education, competencies, and emotional intelligence do not significantly predict SME lending intensity in the reported model, which explains only 3.2% of the variance. This negative result matters. It weakens any interpretation that places the main causal burden on the observable personal profile of loan officers. The relevant problem is not primarily who the officer is in demographic terms. It is the institutional environment in which the officer operates, the information available, and the screening routines through which judgment is produced.

The final model turns to the bank's perception of SMEs. Here again, the evidence is limited but not irrelevant. The only significant coefficient concerns perceived obstacles to SME lending. This suggests that the way banks interpret barriers to SME finance affects observable lending outcomes. Yet the model's explanatory power remains weak. These results are best read cautiously. They indicate that perception matters, but not as a comprehensive theory of SME credit scarcity. Rather, perceptions operate as a selective channel through which restrictive screening practices may become more likely.

Taken together, the results establish a clear ranking. The strongest explanation lies in bank organization and branch geography. Information frictions matter, but more selectively. Perceptions of obstacles matter too, but only weakly and unevenly. Demographic characteristics of officers contribute the least. The most defensible interpretation is therefore institutional rather than psychological. SME credit scarcity in Burkina Faso is shaped first by how banks are organized spatially and how they process information, and only secondarily by the personal profiles of the individuals who work within those systems.

If the central obstacles to SME credit are organizational and informational, then the appropriate response is not simply to urge banks to be less risk-averse. The more serious question is how to redesign the infrastructure that makes smaller firms legible, credible, and financeable. That question is taken up in the conclusion.

7.1 The Architecture of the Evidence

One of the strengths of the empirical evidence is that it does not force a false symmetry among explanations. The results point to a ranking, and that ranking matters. Organizational geography stands out most clearly. Information asymmetry remains relevant, but its statistical footprint is weaker and more selective. Demographic characteristics contribute little. Perception matters, but not in a way that overrides institutional structure. This hierarchy helps move the discussion from anecdotal claims about conservative banking to a more precise account of how SME credit scarcity is produced.

The tables and figures reproduced in this chapter are not included merely for completeness. They show the architecture of the evidence on which the book's argument rests. Descriptive tables clarify the sample composition and the operational organization of SME lending. Regression tables locate the strongest signals. Diagnostic figures, reproduced in the appendix, document the adequacy of the models used. Taken together, they allow the reader to see not only what the conclusion is, but also why it is warranted.

The results do not place all explanations on the same level. Some mechanisms appear more powerful, more stable, and more institutionally consequential than others. Figure 7.1 summarizes the empirical hierarchy before the chapter turns to each explanatory block in detail.

The ranking reinforces one of the book's main conclusions. Organizational and geospatial structures matter more than the demographic profile of lending staff, while informational frictions and perception work more selectively, often through contract terms rather than binary approval alone. The financing gap is therefore

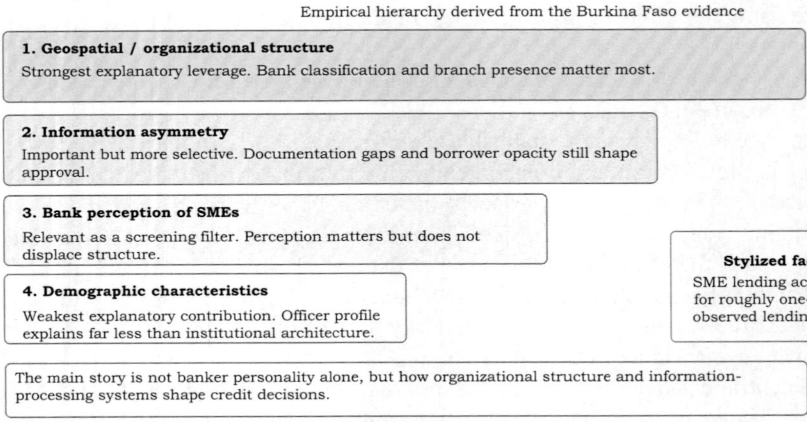

Fig. 7.1 What drives SME lending? A ranked architecture of explanations. *Source: author's conceptual synthesis based on this section, the architecture of the evidence*

better explained by institutional architecture than by banker temperament in the abstract.

7.2 Sample Composition and the Structure of Bank Involvement

The analytical sample comprises 127 bank officers and managers directly involved in SME-related lending activity (Sory, 2021). Most respondents came from privately owned institutions, a majority from foreign-owned banks, and a large share from medium-sized or large institutions. The sample, therefore, captures the decision environment of the dominant formal lenders rather than a peripheral niche.

Portfolio exposure to SMEs also varied meaningfully across institutions. The most common category was 1001 to 5000 SME clients, followed by banks financing 5001 to 10,000 and those financing 10,001 to 50,000. Respondents further emphasized organizational structure, officer competence, legal and contractual conditions, macroeconomic context, and lending technology as the main indicators shaping bank involvement in the SME segment.

Archival bank data supplied the broader portfolio context. Across the available reporting windows, SME loans accounted for roughly one-third of total loans—about 33 to 36%. The issue, therefore, is not the complete absence of SME lending but the uneven depth, structure, and selectivity of that lending.

A further implication of the sample profile is that the book is not describing a peripheral or exceptional corner of the market. The respondents sit inside banks that already carry much of the country's formal lending activity. That matters because it means the findings illuminate how the mainstream banking system approaches

SMEs, not simply how a niche institution or specialist development program does so. The structure of the sample, therefore, strengthens the case for reading the results as institutionally significant.

The composition of the sample is analytically revealing. A strong presence of privately owned, foreign-owned, and medium-to-large institutions means the evidence is drawn from the part of the market where formal procedures, portfolio discipline, and cross-border banking practices are most visible. That is important to the book's regional ambition. The findings do not emerge from a marginal niche of the system; they emerge from the institutional core of modern banking in Burkina Faso, which is precisely where WAMU-wide banking logics are most likely to be felt.

A second implication concerns how banks internally understand the SME segment. The prominence of dedicated structures, staff competencies, legal environments, and lending technologies in respondents' answers suggests that SME finance is not treated as a residual activity. Banks recognize it as a strategic segment, but one whose profitability and risk profile require specialized handling. That helps explain why the book repeatedly returns to organizational architecture. The issue is not whether banks notice SMEs. It is how they decide that the segment can be approached without compromising discipline (Table 7.1).

Table 7.1 Institutional composition of the sample

Category	Item	Frequency	Percent
Bank ownership equity shares	Privately owned bank	119	93.7
Bank ownership equity shares	Publicly owned bank	8	6.3
Bank ownership nationality	Locally owned bank	55	43.3
Bank ownership nationality	Foreign-owned bank	72	56.7
Bank classification according to the central Bank of West African States	A small bank (less than XOF 100 billion total assets)	17	13.4
Bank classification according to the central Bank of West African States	Medium-sized bank (from XOF 101 to XOF 200 billion total assets)	52	40.9
Bank classification according to the central Bank of West African States	Large bank (more than XOF 200 billion total assets)	58	45.7
Portfolio size (number of SMEs) financed by bank	Less than 1000	10	7.9
Portfolio size (number of SMEs) financed by bank	From 1001 to 5000	46	36.2
Portfolio size (number of SMEs) financed by bank	From 5001 to 10,000	31	24.4
Portfolio size (number of SMEs) financed by bank	From 10,001 to 50,000	23	18.1
Portfolio size (number of SMEs) financed by bank	Above 50,000	17	13.4
Key indicators for bank involvement with SMEs	Macroeconomic factors	102	80.3

(continued)

Table 7.1 (continued)

Category	Item	Frequency	Percent
Key indicators for bank involvement with SMEs	Regulations (prudential)	51	40.2
Key indicators for bank involvement with SMEs	Legal and contractual environment	103	81.1
Key indicators for bank involvement with SMEs	Bank-specific factors like organizational structure	111	87.4
Key indicators for bank involvement with SMEs	Bank-specific factors like loan officers' competencies	109	85.8
Key indicators for bank involvement with SMEs	Nature of the lending technology to SMEs	80	63.0
Key indicators for bank involvement with SMEs	Competition in the SME segment	40	31.5
Key indicators for bank involvement with SMEs	Lack of adequate demand	39	30.7

7.3 Geospatial Relationship

The first empirical block examines whether organizational geography helps explain SME lending intensity. The model combines variables related to bank size, classification, branch presence, and the location of operating units. The underlying question is whether proximity and organizational reach change the bank's ability to engage the SME segment.

Respondents reported the number of offices by location, allowing the analysis to distinguish between denser and thinner branch footprints (Table 7.2). The resulting distribution shows that the presence of branches in both Ouagadougou and Bobo-Dioulasso is not a neutral background variable. It shapes the frequency of borrower contact, the cost of monitoring, and the collection of locally grounded information.

The survey further documented how banks define SME clients, how they target them, and where key steps in the loan process occur (7.3 and 7.4). Many institutions reported dedicated SME units and hybrid approval chains in which branches participate in pre-screening while headquarters retain substantial control over final approval, risk management, or problem-loan oversight.

These descriptive patterns already point toward an organizational reading of the credit problem. Where branches identify and filter SME opportunities, but central units retain the power to validate or restrict them, distance inside the bank becomes part of the lending mechanism. Profitability considerations remain important, but they are mediated by internal routing and control structures (Tables 7.5 and 7.6).

This model delivers the clearest statistical result in the study. Bank classification and the number of offices in Bobo-Dioulasso emerge as significant predictors, and the model explains 68.9% of observed variation in SME lending intensity (Table 7.7). That makes organizational geography the dominant empirical result of the book.

Table 7.2 Branch network distribution by location

Location	Category	Frequency	Percent
In Ouagadougou	1 to 5	36	28.3
In Ouagadougou	6 to 10	35	27.6
In Ouagadougou	11 to 20	36	28.3
In Ouagadougou	21 to 40	20	15.7
In Bobo-Dioulasso	1 to 5	84	66.1
In Bobo-Dioulasso	6 to 10	32	25.2
In Bobo-Dioulasso	11 to 20	11	8.7
In total in Burkina Faso	1 to 5	10	7.9
In total in Burkina Faso	6 to 10	33	26.0
In total in Burkina Faso	11 to 20	29	22.8
In total in Burkina Faso	21 to 40	40	31.5
In total in Burkina Faso	More than 40	15	11.8

Table 7.3 Criteria used to define and target SME clients

Category	Item	Frequency	Percent
Important criteria to define SMEs	Other (please specify)	3	2.4
Important criteria to define SMEs	Client size in terms of average sales	69	54.3
Important criteria to define SMEs	Client size in terms of total assets	28	22.0
Important criteria to define SMEs	Client size in terms of total employees	21	16.5
Important criteria to define SMEs	Capital	6	4.7
Criteria to determine SMEs to target	Company size	37	29.1
Criteria to determine SMEs to target	Geographic area where the firm operates	43	33.9
Criteria to determine SMEs to target	Industry sector to which the firm belongs	14	11.0
Criteria to determine SMEs to target	Product needs of the firm	8	6.3
Criteria to determine SMEs to target	Expected profitability of the firm	16	12.6
Criteria to determine SMEs to target	Exposure size	2	1.6
Criteria to determine SMEs to target	Credit quality	7	5.5
Does your bank have a separate unit for managing SME relations?	Yes	87	68.5
Does your bank have a separate unit for managing SME relations?	No	40	31.5

The prominence of Bobo-Dioulasso in the model also deserves careful interpretation. The result does not simply imply that one city matters more than another. It suggests that secondary urban centers can play a strategic role in reducing the informational distance between banks and productive enterprises. Where commercial life is active enough to sustain repeated contact, but not so diffuse that local

Table 7.4 Location of key loan-processing functions

Process	Location pattern	Frequency	Percent
Loan pre-screening	Only done at headquarters	4	3.1
Loan pre-screening	Only done at branches	51	40.2
Loan pre-screening	Done primarily at headquarters	1	0.8
Loan pre-screening	Done primarily at branches	36	28.3
Loan pre-screening	Done at both headquarters and branches	35	27.6
Loan approval	Only done at headquarters	14	11.0
Loan approval	Only done at branches	20	15.7
Loan approval	Done primarily at headquarters	3	2.4
Loan approval	Done primarily at branches	39	30.7
Loan approval	Done at both headquarters and branches	51	40.2
Risk management	Only done at headquarters	18	14.2
Risk management	Only done at branches	3	2.4
Risk management	Done primarily at headquarters	1	0.8
Risk management	Done primarily at branches	41	32.3
Risk management	Done at both headquarters and branches	64	50.4
Nonperforming loan recovery	Only done at headquarters	3	2.4
Nonperforming loan recovery	Only done at branches	4	3.1
Nonperforming loan recovery	Done primarily at headquarters	3	2.4
Nonperforming loan recovery	Done primarily at branches	25	19.7
Nonperforming loan recovery	Done at both headquarters and branches	92	72.4
Sale of nonlending products	Only done at headquarters	2	1.6
Sale of nonlending products	Only done at branches	14	11.0
Sale of nonlending products	Done primarily at branches	15	11.8
Sale of nonlending products	Done at both headquarters and branches	96	75.6

knowledge disappears into anonymity, branch presence may become especially valuable. That insight is relevant beyond Burkina Faso because many WAMU economies depend on exactly such city networks to connect national markets to wider regional circuits.

The strength of the geospatial model should not be read narrowly as a matter of simple physical distance. Geography matters here because it stands in for organizational reach, informational proximity, and monitoring capacity. Branches are the institutional sites where soft information is first gathered, commercial rhythms are observed, and borrower histories become concrete. A denser local presence can therefore reduce uncertainty even before any formal credit decision is taken. What the model captures is less "map distance" in the abstract than the architecture through which a bank becomes capable of knowing smaller firms well enough to lend.

This interpretation also helps explain why bank classification matters alongside branch presence. Size, scale, and organizational category shape what a bank can do with proximity once it has it. A local footprint without systems may fail to generate usable credit; a large institution without proximity may fail to interpret the

Table 7.5 Reported drivers of bank involvement in SME finance

Category	Item	Frequency	Percent
Three important drivers of SME involvement	Perceived profitability in the SME segment	116	91.3
Three important drivers of SME involvement	Intense competition for large corporates	99	78.0
Three important drivers of SME involvement	Intense competition for retail customers	44	34.6
Three important drivers of SME involvement	Excessive exposure to large corporates	28	22.0
Three important drivers of SME involvement	Excessive exposure to retail customer sector	40	31.5
Three important drivers of SME involvement	Possibility to seek out SMEs through existing relations with large clients (e.g., reverse factoring, leasing)	54	42.5
Kind of involvement with SMEs	The bank primarily offers deposits and cash management products	40	31.5
Kind of involvement with SMEs	The bank primarily offers loan products	15	11.8
Kind of involvement with SMEs	The bank offers both deposits and loan products	31	24.4
Kind of involvement with SMEs	The bank offers deposits, loans, and off-balance-sheet commitments (bid bonds, performance bonds)	41	32.3

Table 7.6 Additional geospatial indicators used in the analysis

Category	N	Minimum	Maximum	Mean	SD
Following bank guidelines	127	2.00	5.00	4.11	0.43
Using measures to monitor SME activities	127	1.00	5.00	4.22	0.51
Impact of factors on duration of partnership	127	2.56	5.00	4.00	0.46

Table 7.7 Geospatial model of SME lending intensity

Variable	B	Std. error	Beta	t	Sig.
(Constant)	−0.065	0.236		−0.276	0.783
Bank classification	0.651	0.114	0.385	5.731	0.000
In Ouagadougou	0.271	0.167	0.241	1.618	0.108
In Bobo-Dioulasso	0.675	0.131	0.370	5.159	0.000
In total in Burkina Faso	−0.034	0.135	−0.034	−0.254	0.800

Note. $F(4, 122) = 67.522$, $p < .01$, R-squared = .689

borrower. The most consequential institutions are often those able to combine reach with routines. That is why the geospatial result is so important. It points away from a simplistic story of banker caution and toward a stronger claim about the institutional production of credit knowledge.

There is also a practical implication for regional banking strategy. Branch networks are often evaluated primarily in terms of cost efficiency, deposit mobilization, or brand presence. The findings of this chapter suggest that, for SME finance, branches should also be understood as information assets. They matter because they lower the cost of producing credible local knowledge. In a shared banking space such as WAMU, where many institutions pursue scale and centralization, that lesson is especially important: Proximity remains economically valuable not in spite of modernization, but because it complements it.

7.4 Information Asymmetry

The second empirical block turns to information asymmetry. Here, the objective is to capture how lenders perceive the informational environment surrounding SME appraisal: the quality of borrower information, the role of relationship characteristics, and the weight of contextual conditions that make assessment easier or harder.

Respondents evaluated the importance of firm characteristics, owner characteristics, relationship-specific features, and market or infrastructural conditions in credit assessment. The consistently high scores reinforce a simple point: For lenders, opacity is an operational constraint rather than a purely theoretical concept (Table 7.8).

The survey also identified which information channels banks regard as most reliable. Internal databases, credit bureaus, rating agencies, and both formal and informal relationships all appear in the evidence, though they do not (Tables 7.9 and 7.10). This distribution matters because it reveals the informational architecture through which banks seek to reduce uncertainty before approving a loan.

In the regression results, only the variable capturing the effect of cost factors on SME loan contract terms emerges as a significant predictor. Its negative sign indicates that when these frictions become more constraining, SME lending intensity declines (Table 7.11).

The statistically significant coefficient sits inside a model with limited explanatory power. The appropriate interpretation is therefore restrained: Information asymmetry matters, but its effect is thinner and less institutionally decisive than the organizational-geographic variables identified earlier.

This is also why information reform cannot be reduced to a call for "more data" in the abstract. The issue is not only volume, but credibility, usability, and institutional acceptance. SMEs may already generate fragments of evidence—sales records, payment histories, inventory patterns, and supplier relationships—without those fragments becoming decision-grade information inside a bank. Information asymmetry persists when evidence exists but cannot travel convincingly through the lending process.

The weaker explanatory power of the information-asymmetry model does not mean that informational problems are unimportant. Rather, it suggests that their effects are more diffuse and often operate through contract structure rather than

Table 7.8 Information conditions in SME credit assessment

Category	N	Min	Max	Mean	SD
Firm characteristics	127	2.63	5.00	4.35	0.36
Owners' characteristics	127	2.83	4.83	3.89	0.39
Firms' relationship characteristics	127	2.50	5.00	4.12	0.44
Market infrastructure factors	127	2.57	4.86	4.19	0.32
Screening of SME applications	127	2.57	5.00	3.53	0.47
High transaction cost	127	2.50	5.00	4.39	0.44
Assess SME creditworthiness	127	2.50	5.00	3.98	0.53
Important documentation for SME requests	127	2.60	5.00	4.44	0.42
Impact of cost factors on SME loan contract terms	127	2.17	5.00	4.33	0.60
Importance of factors on credit allocation	127	2.50	5.00	4.36	0.48
Importance of decision to decline	127	2.60	5.00	4.45	0.46

Table 7.9 Reported sources of reliable borrower information

Source	Response	Frequency	Percent
Internal database	Yes	121	95.3
Internal database	No	2	1.6
Internal database	Indifference	4	3.1
Credit bureaus or similar central base	Yes	109	85.8
Credit bureaus or similar central base	No	8	6.3
Credit bureaus or similar central base	Indifference	10	7.9
Credit rating agency	Yes	99	78.0
Credit rating agency	No	5	3.9
Credit rating agency	Indifference	23	18.1
Private information providers	Yes	62	48.8
Private information providers	No	25	19.7
Private information providers	Indifference	40	31.5
Associations	Yes	40	31.5
Associations	No	44	34.6
Associations	Indifference	43	33.9
Formal/informal desk with other banks	Yes	47	37.0
Formal/informal desk with other banks	No	37	29.1
Formal/informal desk with other banks	Indifference	43	33.9

through an all-or-nothing lending decision. A bank may still lend to a smaller firm while shortening maturity, increasing collateral demands, or adjusting pricing to compensate for uncertainty. In that sense, information asymmetry frequently changes the terms of credit before it changes the existence of credit. This helps explain why one coefficient can be meaningful inside a model whose total explanatory power remains modest.

A second reason for interpretive caution is that informational frictions are often embedded in organizational variables rather than fully separable from them. Better branch presence, stronger internal databases, and more coherent approval chains all

Table 7.10 Perceived relevance of rating and information systems

Category	Level	Frequency	Percent
Data availability	Low	24	18.9
Data availability	Medium	37	29.1
Data availability	High	66	52.0
Reliability of data	Low	23	18.1
Reliability of data	Medium	38	29.9
Reliability of data	High	66	52.0
Quality of data	Low	22	17.3
Quality of data	Medium	40	31.5
Quality of data	High	65	51.2
Timeliness of data	Low	33	26.0
Timeliness of data	Medium	44	34.6
Timeliness of data	High	50	39.4
Rating system measurement	Low	11	8.7
Rating system measurement	Medium	63	49.6
Rating system measurement	High	53	41.7

Table 7.11 Information-asymmetry model of SME lending intensity

Variable	B	Std. error	Beta	t	Sig.
(Constant)	2.465	2.038		1.210	0.229
Firm characteristics	0.098	0.439	0.030	0.222	0.825
Owners' characteristics	0.214	0.326	0.071	0.655	0.513
Firms' relationship characteristics	−0.152	0.316	−0.056	−0.482	0.631
Market infrastructure factors	−0.155	0.427	−0.042	−0.363	0.718
Screening of SME applications	0.021	0.240	0.008	0.088	0.930
High transaction cost	0.074	0.327	0.028	0.227	0.821
Assess SME creditworthiness	−0.082	0.228	−0.036	−0.359	0.720
Important documentation for SME requests	0.073	0.300	0.026	0.242	0.809
Impact of cost factors on SME loan contract terms	−0.614	0.255	−0.310	−2.408	0.018
Importance of factors on credit allocation	0.601	0.317	0.241	1.897	0.060
Importance of decision to decline	0.028	0.254	0.011	0.109	0.913

Note. $F(11, 115) = .754$, $p = .684$, R-squared = .067

influence how asymmetry is managed. Some of the work of information may therefore already be captured by the organizational-geographic block. That possibility reinforces the main lesson of the chapter: The financing gap is shaped not by isolated variables, but by institutions that organize the production and use of borrower knowledge.

7.5 Demographic Characteristics

The third empirical block tests whether observable staff characteristics help explain SME lending intensity. The survey captured role, gender, education, tenure, and perceptions of the relative importance of competencies and emotional intelligence in SME-related work (Table 7.12).

The occupational composition of the sample is sufficiently diverse to encompass several points in the lending chain, including risk managers, credit managers, senior executives, and officers responsible for small-business services. The sample is also predominantly male and strongly concentrated at the university level, which is useful descriptively but not, in itself, strongly predictive.

Respondents generally rated professional competence above emotional intelligence as a practical requirement of SME lending (Table 7.13). Yet the regression evidence shows that these observable staff characteristics explain very little of the variation in SME lending intensity: None of the coefficients is significant, and the model-level explanatory power remains weak.

The null demographic result is one of the most important findings in the book because it redirects the conversation about reform (Table 7.14). If the staff profile does not explain much of the observed variation, then efforts to broaden SME finance should not be built primarily on the search for different personalities or on the assumption that a more sympathetic loan officer will solve the problem. Training still matters, and professional competence matters greatly. But the evidence suggests that the larger constraint lies in systems, procedures, and the quality of information available to those who must decide.

At the same time, the null result should not be overstated. It does not imply that officers are irrelevant. Officers remain the practical interface between institutional

Table 7.12 Professional profile of lending staff in the sample

Category	Item	Frequency	Percent
Position	CEO/MD/deputy MD	20	15.7
Position	Small business services manager	19	15.0
Position	Relationship manager	14	11.0
Position	Credit manager	23	18.1
Position	Risk manager	25	19.7
Position	Supervisor	12	9.4
Position	Credit analyst	14	11.0
Experience with SME loan requests	0–5 years	15	11.8
Experience with SME loan requests	6–10 years	39	30.7
Experience with SME loan requests	10–15 years	53	41.7
Experience with SME loan requests	Above 15 years	20	15.7
Highest education	High school diploma	10	7.9
Highest education	Bachelor's degree	34	26.8
Highest education	Master's degree	79	62.2
Highest education	DBA/Ph.D.	4	3.1

Table 7.13 Reported importance of competencies and emotional intelligence

Category	N	Min	Max	Mean	SD
Competencies	127	1.00	5.00	4.08	0.53
Emotional intelligence	127	2.00	5.00	3.84	0.59

Table 7.14 Demographic model of SME lending intensity

Variable	B	Std. error	Beta	t	Sig.
(Constant)	3.703	1.057		3.504	0.001
Position	0.045	0.060	0.073	0.750	0.455
Years of experience with SME loans	−0.036	0.135	−0.027	−0.264	0.792
Highest education	0.020	0.165	0.011	0.120	0.904
Competencies	0.114	0.229	0.051	0.499	0.619
Emotional intelligence	−0.357	0.198	−0.177	−1.798	0.075

Note. Statistical output adapted from the author's doctoral research. $F(5, 121) = .809$, $p = .546$, R-squared = .032. The demographic model does not support the claim that observable officer characteristics explain much of the variation in SME lending intensity

rules and real borrowers. It shows that observable personal characteristics are a weak basis for explaining cross-institutional patterns in SME lending intensity. The book's preferred explanation, therefore, remains organizational: Staff matter, but they matter most through the structures within which they work and the evidence those structures permit them to use.

7.6 Bank Perception of SMEs

The final empirical block considers how banks perceive SMEs. The relevant items capture views about risk, trust, financing obstacles, and the broader place of SMEs within the bank's lending environment (Table 7.15).

The regression results show that only the perception of obstacles to SME lending is statistically significant. Perception, therefore, matters, but not as a comprehensive explanatory framework (Table 7.16).

The broader pattern reinforces the book's main claim: Perceptions influence decisions, but they do so inside organizational structures and under informational constraints that shape what those perceptions can become in practice.

The practical significance of this finding is that perceptions are most likely to loosen when institutions gain better classification tools. Banks tend to perceive fewer insurmountable obstacles when borrower information is cleaner, when branch knowledge is more usable, and when approval chains can absorb contextual evidence without sacrificing control. In that sense, perception is not the starting point of reform. It is often one of its downstream outcomes.

The perception results point in a similar direction. Obstacles matter more than abstract representations of SMEs as a category. In practice, this means that banks are shaped less by sweeping generalizations about whether SMEs are "good" or

Table 7.15 Bank-level and officer-level perceptions of SMEs

Category	N	Minimum	Maximum	Mean	SD
Perception on SME market	127	2.00	4.00	3.17	0.37
Drivers of SME involvement	127	1.86	4.71	3.46	0.49
Common standards for SME loaning	127	3.00	4.80	3.96	0.27
Obstacles in lending SMEs	127	1.92	4.23	3.44	0.39
Opinion on information given by SMEs	127	1.00	3.00	1.67	0.45
Categorization of common impediments	127	1.29	3.00	2.53	0.38
Importance of analysis factors of SMEs	127	1.75	3.00	2.62	0.32

Table 7.16 Perception model of SME lending intensity

Variable	B	Std. error	Beta	t	Sig.
(Constant)	3.785	2.067		1.831	0.070
Perception on SME market	0.091	0.294	0.028	0.308	0.759
Drivers of SME involvement	−0.262	0.229	−0.108	−1.143	0.256
Common standards for SME loaning	−0.593	0.428	−0.135	−1.384	0.169
Obstacles in lending SMEs	0.649	0.295	0.214	2.202	0.030
Opinion on information given by SMEs	0.193	0.241	0.073	0.804	0.423
Categorization of common impediments	−0.025	0.290	−0.008	−0.085	0.933
Importance of analysis factors of SMEs	−0.147	0.350	−0.040	−0.419	0.676

Note. Statistical output adapted from the author's doctoral research. $F(7, 119) = 1.083$, $p = .379$, R-squared = .060. In the bank-perception model, only obstacles in lending SMEs are significant ($B = 0.649$, $p = 0.030$), and the model explains 6.0% of the variance

"bad" borrowers than by specific beliefs about why they are difficult to lend to—weak records, thin collateral, legal uncertainty, or monitoring cost. Perception is therefore selective and problem-focused. It influences decision-making by directing attention to bottlenecks rather than by functioning as a total worldview.

That is precisely why perception should be interpreted as endogenous to institutions. Banks do not form their views in a vacuum. Their perceptions are shaped by portfolio experience, systems quality, local market knowledge, and recent defaults. Where institutions improve their ability to interpret smaller borrowers, perceptions may become less restrictive because ambiguity itself is reduced. Reform should therefore aim not only at changing attitudes, but at changing the informational conditions that generate those attitudes in the first place.

7.7 Regional Lessons for WAMU

The final step is to clearly distinguish between what the Burkina Faso evidence directly supports and what it helps illuminate at the regional level. Figure 7.2 distinguishes mechanisms likely to travel across WAMU from outcomes more likely to vary across national markets.

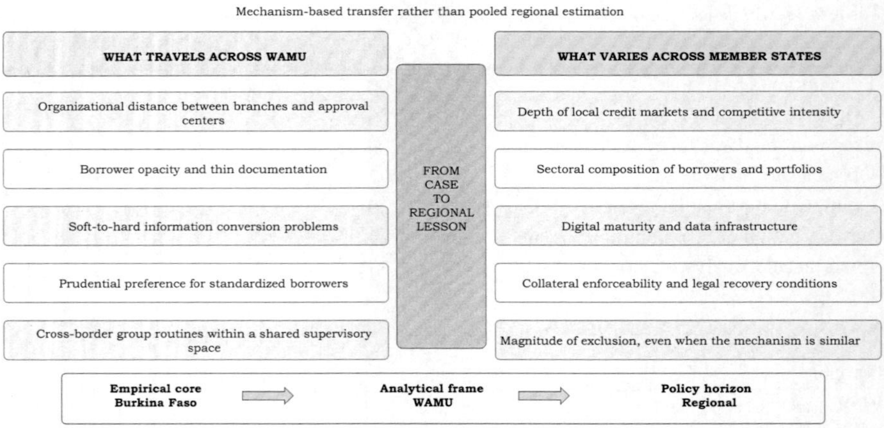

Fig. 7.2 From Burkina Faso findings to WAMU lessons: what travels and what varies. Source: Author's conceptual synthesis based on Sect. 7.7

This distinction is essential to the book's regional argument. Shared monetary and supervisory structures make many lending mechanisms portable, but they do not erase variation in banking depth, competition, digital maturity, or legal enforcement. The figure, therefore, clarifies the book's concluding claim: Burkina Faso provides the empirical core, while WAMU provides the wider space in which the institutional lessons acquire broader relevance.

Three lessons travel most plausibly from Burkina Faso to the wider WAMU space. First, organization and branch geography matter more than broad appeals to banker psychology. Wherever SME finance depends on repeated contact and soft information, branch reach and approval architecture are likely to shape credit availability.

Second, information frictions remain central even when their measured statistical footprint is thinner than that of organizational variables. Across WAMU, many SMEs operate with uneven accounting quality and incomplete digital traces. The pressure these place on screening costs is not unique to Burkina Faso.

Third, the weak explanatory power of officer demographics should caution practitioners against overpersonalizing the credit gap. The more promising reform agenda lies in data systems, bank structure, branch incentives, and the design of lending technologies.

These are regional lessons, not regional coefficients. They do not assume that every WAMU market will display identical magnitudes or rankings. They argue instead that the mechanisms identified in Burkina Faso travel plausibly across a shared monetary and supervisory space.

A fourth lesson concerns sequencing. In many policy debates, the first instinct is to expand dedicated funds or guarantee mechanisms. Those can be useful, but the evidence here suggests they will have limited effect if the underlying problem of borrower legibility is not addressed simultaneously. Regional reform, therefore, needs to proceed on two tracks: expanding risk-sharing capacity where appropriate and improving the informational and organizational conditions that enable banks to use that capacity productively.

What travels most confidently from Burkina Faso to the wider Union is the mechanism, not the coefficient. The evidence suggests that wherever banks operate under common prudential discipline, with cross-border ownership and a need to standardize decision routines, SME finance will depend heavily on the ability to connect branch knowledge to central approval structures. That is a regional lesson because those institutional tensions are widely shared across WAMU, even when national banking depth or borrower profiles differ.

A second lesson concerns what may vary. Markets with denser digital footprints, stronger credit registries, or more competitive banking structures may manage some frictions more effectively than Burkina Faso. Others may remain even more dependent on relationship lending and local knowledge. The book, therefore, resists a one-size-fits-all regionalization. It argues instead for a structured portability of explanation: the mechanisms travel, but their intensity and exact combination can still vary meaningfully across member states.

A third lesson is practical. For banks, the agenda is to treat branch presence, data systems, and approval design as complements rather than substitutes. For regulators, the agenda is to support the infrastructures that make SME borrowers more legible—credit information systems, collateral frameworks, accounting formalization, and interoperable data. For development finance institutions, the agenda is not simply to increase lines of credit, but to improve the institutional conditions under which smaller firms can be prudently evaluated. Those are regional lessons in the strongest sense: They do not depend on claiming that every country has already been statistically measured in the same way.

Reference

Sory, K. A. (2021). *Risk aversion behaviors in the bank-SMEs relationship: Predictors of credit in Burkina Faso* [Doctoral dissertation, Franklin Hudson International School of Management].

Chapter 8
From Burkina Faso to WAMU: What Travels, What Varies

The argument of this book begins with a national case and ends with a regional lesson. Its evidence comes from Burkina Faso. Its wider significance lies in what that evidence reveals about the institutional financing of small and medium-sized enterprises (SMEs) within the West African Monetary Union (WAMU). The central conclusion is that SME credit scarcity is not best explained as a vague culture of banker caution. It is produced more concretely by the way banks organize proximity, gather information, make decisions, and manage uncertainty. Smaller firms remain underfinanced not only because they are risky, but because they are often difficult to render legible within the routines of formal banking.

That conclusion matters because it changes the diagnosis of the problem. The strongest findings of the study point to bank organization and branch geography, not to the demographic profile of lending staff. Information frictions and perceived obstacles matter, but less strongly and less consistently than the broader organizational architecture through which banks encounter SMEs. The practical implication is clear. The financing gap cannot be closed simply by appealing to goodwill or by training officers to be less conservative in the abstract. It must be addressed through the systems that convert local knowledge into decision-quality information.

Seen from Burkina Faso, the SME credit problem is therefore an institutional problem before it is a psychological one. Banks screen, document, classify, and approve. Each of those stages can widen or narrow the set of firms that become financeable. Where branch networks are too thin, where internal data are weak, where soft information is gathered but cannot travel upward, and where documentary requirements are calibrated mainly to larger firms, prudence will tend to exclude many viable smaller borrowers. The missing middle persists when smaller firms matter economically but remain administratively expensive to know.

At the same time, the book has insisted on an important methodological boundary. The empirical evidence presented here was collected in Burkina Faso, specifically through bank records and surveys conducted in the country's main banking centers. For that reason, the findings cannot be presented as pooled statistical proof

K. A. Sory, *Banking the Missing Middle*, Research Series on Responsible Enterprise Ecosystems, https://doi.org/10.1007/978-3-032-34582-0_8

for all WAMU member states. To do so would collapse the distinction between evidence and extrapolation. The argument of the book is stronger than a casual extrapolation, but narrower than a region-wide econometric claim.

What, then, travels from Burkina Faso to WAMU? Four elements travel with confidence. The first is the institutional setting. WAMU is not a loose geographical expression; it is a monetary and banking space structured by common authority, common currency, and common supervision. The second is the presence of cross-border banking groups whose internal practices, portfolio logics, and risk governance often operate across several member states. The third is the recurrence of the same practical financing obstacles: weak borrower documentation, incomplete accounting records, collateral constraints, costly screening, and tension between branch-level relationship knowledge and head-office approval requirements. The fourth is the policy relevance of these obstacles for a region where SMEs are central to employment and domestic commerce, yet remain structurally disadvantaged in formal credit markets.

These shared features justify a regional reading of the evidence from Burkina Faso, but not a mechanical one. What varies across WAMU is the magnitude and market expression of the problem. Financial depth differs by country. Credit concentration differs. The sectoral composition of formal enterprise differs. Competition among banks differs. The adoption of digital financial tools differs. Legal enforcement, the practical use of collateral, public guarantee mechanisms, security conditions, and the pace of financial formalization also differ. All these factors can shape how strongly the mechanisms identified in this book operate in any given national market.

The right regional conclusion is therefore neither maximalist nor timid. It is not maximalist because it does not claim that all eight member states produce the same quantitative outcomes. It is not timid because it recognizes that common institutions make common mechanisms plausible. The book's regional claim can be stated precisely: Burkina Faso provides the empirical core for identifying bank-side mechanisms that are likely to recur across WAMU, even though their intensity, interaction, and policy salience may vary from one member state to another.

This formulation also clarifies the place of professional experience in the argument. Long executive practice in SME finance across Burkina Faso and Côte d'Ivoire, together with exposure to linked operations in Mali, Togo, and Benin, reinforces the plausibility of regional lessons. It does so, however, as interpretive and practical knowledge, not as a substitute for formal empirical testing. This distinction is important. Practitioner experience can help identify recurring patterns, validate institutional realism, and sharpen the relevance of policy recommendations. But it should not be mistaken for a statistical design. By keeping those forms of knowledge distinct, the book remains both regionally engaged and methodologically disciplined.

Once that distinction is accepted, the practical agenda becomes clearer. The first priority is informational infrastructure. Banks need better ways to collect, store, and escalate borrower information, especially when SMEs cannot be adequately assessed using standardized financial statements alone. Better credit information systems, more reliable accounting documentation, clearer borrower files, and stronger internal databases can lower the cost of understanding smaller firms. In many cases, the problem is not the total absence of information, but the difficulty of making the available information usable for formal approval.

The second priority is organizational design. The evidence suggests that the presence of branches matters because proximity is an informational asset. The policy lesson is not crude decentralization, nor blind faith in head-office control. It is a better integration. Branches often possess the local knowledge needed to interpret SMEs, while headquarters often control risk standards, pricing discipline, and final approval. A more effective system is one in which locally gathered soft information is translated into formats that are credible enough to matter at the center. The failure to build that bridge is one of the hidden mechanisms that keep viable firms outside formal finance.

The third priority is lending technology. WAMU banking systems cannot assume that all firms will become financeable through the same transaction-based model. Hard information is indispensable, but many smaller firms remain economically active while administratively thin. In such cases, relationship lending remains necessary. The challenge is to structure it well: to rely on local knowledge without collapsing into arbitrary discretion and to preserve prudence without reducing all creditworthiness to standardized documentation. Better SME finance requires banks to combine hard information where possible with disciplined use of soft information where necessary.

The fourth priority is borrower capability. The book has emphasized bank-side mechanisms, but the policy horizon cannot ignore the firm. SMEs need stronger bookkeeping, clearer financial reporting, a better understanding of credit processes, and more consistent loan application preparation. The financing gap is not closed only by urging banks to change; it is also narrowed when firms become easier to evaluate. The central point, however, is that this is not merely an entrepreneurial education problem. It is a joint institutional problem in which banks, regulators, business support organizations, and public policy all play a role.

For regulators and development practitioners, the regional lesson is equally important. If WAMU wants deeper and more productive SME finance, it must focus on the institutions that enable prudential inclusion. That includes credit bureaus and reporting systems, accounting and formalization practices, legal predictability in contract enforcement, risk-sharing instruments that reduce the cost of lending to smaller borrowers, and supervisory approaches that recognize the specific informational challenges of SME portfolios without diluting standards. Inclusion and prudence are not opposites. The real task is to make prudence more intelligent.

This book also points toward a future research agenda consistent with its own limits. The most obvious next step is comparative multicountry work within WAMU. A regionally designed study could test directly which of the mechanisms identified here remain stable across member states and which are more context-specific. Such research could compare branch structures, SME definitions, information-sharing regimes, legal enforcement, and lending technologies across several national markets while remaining inside the same monetary and supervisory union. That would be the natural quantitative extension of the present book.

A second direction would examine SME-side heterogeneity more closely. Not all smaller firms are informationally opaque in the same way, and not all sectors present the same monitoring challenge. Future work could distinguish among formal and semiformal firms, among younger and older enterprises, and among sectors whose cash flows are easier or harder to verify. A third direction would study the organizational life of approval itself: how local knowledge is written up, how committees read it, when it is discounted, and how different banks balance hard and soft information in practice.

Even without that future research, the present argument has practical force. Burkina Faso shows, in concentrated form, the deeper problem of financing the missing middle in a shared West African banking space. The key issue is not that SMEs are invisible to public policy discourse. On the contrary, they are constantly celebrated. The key issue is that many remain only partially visible to the institutions that allocate formal credit. Until that problem of legibility is addressed, exhortations to support entrepreneurship will continue to outrun the banking systems on which productive growth depends.

The final lesson of the book can therefore be stated simply. Burkina Faso is the empirical core. WAMU is the analytical horizon. The book's conclusions should travel regionally at the level of mechanisms, institutional lessons, and policy design—not as unqualified statistical generalizations. That is not a weakness. It is the condition of methodological seriousness. By keeping the boundaries of evidence clear while still taking the regional banking space seriously, the book seeks to offer a contribution that is at once more modest, more credible, and more useful.

In the end, widening SME access to finance in WAMU will not come from choosing between discipline and development. It will come from designing banking systems in which discipline can recognize productive firms earlier, understand them better, and finance them on terms proportionate to their real risk rather than to their documentary thinness alone. The task is not to eliminate caution. It is to build institutions capable of lending more intelligently across the missing middle.

8.1 The Future of the Missing Middle: From Credit Rationing to Intelligent Credit Infrastructure

The future of SME finance in WAMU will depend less on exhorting banks to lend more and more on building an intelligent credit infrastructure. Such an infrastructure would combine stronger borrower documentation, better credit information systems, appropriate financing instruments, branch-level knowledge, digital transaction data, guarantee mechanisms, and prudentially governed artificial intelligence (AI) tools. Its purpose would not be to weaken risk management. Its purpose would be to improve the quality of risk interpretation.

The central lesson of the book can therefore be stated simply. The missing middle persists where economically important firms cannot be translated into creditworthy, monitorable, and decision-quality information. Better credit infrastructure does not mean abandoning prudence. It means organizing prudence more intelligently.

This has implications for all actors. Banks must improve their ability to integrate hard and soft information. Specialized financial institutions must deepen instruments such as leasing, factoring, guarantees, equipment finance, and risk-capital partnerships. SME managers must become active producers of bankable information. Regulators must encourage innovation while protecting stability, transparency, and fairness. Development finance institutions must support the credit infrastructure, not only the volume of lending.

Burkina Faso is the empirical core of this book, but the logic extends to the WAMU region, which shares monetary, supervisory, and banking structures. The challenge is not identical across countries, but the underlying mechanisms are: information gaps, organizational distance, documentation weaknesses, collateral constraints, and the difficulty of translating local knowledge into formal credit decisions.

The path forward is therefore not only more credit. It is a better credit architecture. Banking the missing middle means building institutions, products, data systems, and decision processes capable of seeing viable SMEs before they become large enough to be obvious.

Seen from this perspective, the regional promise of SME finance is not abstract. WAMU already possesses much of the institutional architecture that reform requires: a shared monetary authority, expanding digital infrastructure, prudential supervision, increasingly capable domestic banking groups, and a policy agenda more attentive than before to productive inclusion. The remaining task is to connect these assets more directly to the everyday realities of smaller firms. The missing middle will narrow only when banks, regulators, and enterprise-support institutions treat legibility, proximity, and disciplined risk-taking as complements rather than competing objectives.

As this book comes to a close, it is important to move beyond a mere synthesis of the main findings and to highlight the broader value it provides to its key stakeholders.

8.2 Final Synthesis: Takeaway Value and Contributions

The analysis developed throughout this work shows that SME finance in the West African Monetary Union cannot be understood solely through the cost of credit or the level of interest rates. Rather, it is a multidimensional issue shaped by risk, distance, information, lending technologies, institutional capacity, and the wider dynamics of productive transformation.

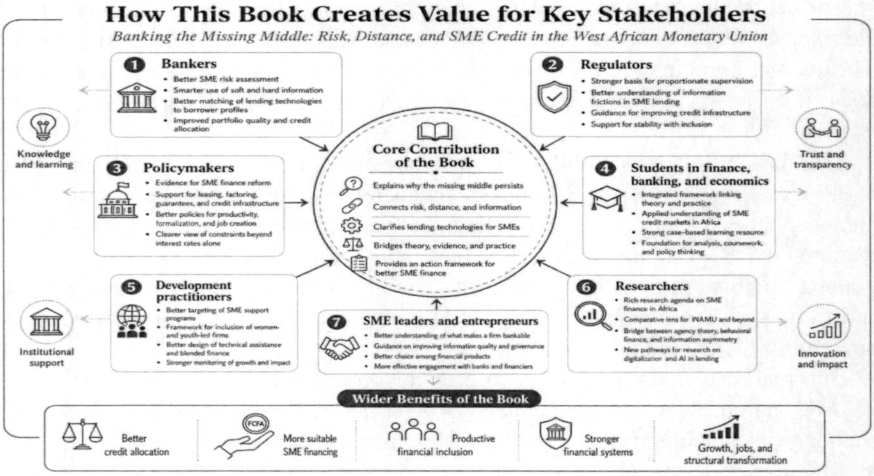

Fig. 8.1 How this book creates value for key stakeholders

From this perspective, the value of the book lies in its ability to connect issues that are often examined separately: bank lending decisions, financial regulation, public policy, productive inclusion, digital transformation, academic research, and the practical needs of SME owners and managers. The framework proposed in this manuscript, therefore, provides an integrated understanding of the "missing middle" in finance, showing how a better grasp of information frictions and risk-management mechanisms can improve credit allocation, strengthen financial stability, and support more inclusive growth.

As Fig. 8.1 makes clear, the contribution of this book lies not only in explaining why the SME "missing middle" persists but also in offering a common analytical framework that links risk, distance, and information, clarifies lending technologies, bridges theory and evidence, and points toward a more practical architecture of SME finance.

The seven stakeholder groups surrounding that core contribution—bankers, regulators, policymakers, students, development practitioners, researchers, and SME leaders—show that the same argument generates distinct yet connected forms of value across the financial ecosystem, while the inward arrows indicate that this contribution can be interpreted and applied differently by each audience without losing its coherence.

The wider significance of the book is therefore not confined to scholarship alone. As the side labels suggest, its effects extend across knowledge and learning, institutional support, trust and transparency, and innovation and impact; and, as the bottom panel indicates, these effects matter because they translate into better credit allocation, more suitable SME financing, more productive financial inclusion, stronger financial systems, and, ultimately, growth, job creation, and structural transformation. In that sense, the central lesson of this book is both simple and demanding: The problem of the missing middle will not be resolved by weaker prudence, but by more intelligent prudence—prudence capable of making economically important but institutionally difficult-to-read firms visible, assessable, and financeable within the banking systems of the West African Monetary Union.

To ultimately conclude, the central lesson of this book is that banking the missing middle is not a matter of lowering standards but of improving the institutions through which standards are applied. The problem is not that SMEs lack economic relevance; rather, too many remain insufficiently legible within the routines of formal finance.

Where banks can connect branch knowledge to central approval, combine soft and hard information, deploy lending technologies suited to borrower realities, and operate within regulatory and policy frameworks that strengthen credit infrastructure rather than merely expand liquidity, the domain of prudently financeable enterprise can widen significantly. In that sense, the contribution of this book extends beyond a national case and beyond a scholarly debate. It offers a common framework for bankers, regulators, policymakers, development practitioners, students, researchers, and SME leaders alike: a framework for understanding that better SME finance is not achieved by weakening prudence, but by making prudence more intelligent, more informed, and more institutionally capable.

If that shift is taken seriously across the West African Monetary Union, the reward will not be merely more lending, but better credit allocation, more productive financial inclusion, stronger financial systems, and a more credible path toward growth, employment, and structural transformation.

Appendix A: Supplementary Diagnostics and Figures

This appendix gathers the empirical diagnostics that underpin the regressions reported in the main text. It reproduces the variance inflation factor tables and the normal P-P plots used to assess the adequacy of regression models for geospatial relationships, information asymmetry, demographic variables, and banks' perceptions of small and medium-sized enterprises (SMEs).

Variance Inflation Factors

The appendix tables and figures reproduce technical diagnostics in revised format from the author's doctoral research so that the statistical backbone of the analysis remains visible without reproducing the full apparatus of the dissertation (Tables A.1–A.4).

Table A.1 Collinearity diagnostics for the geospatial model

Variable	Tolerance	VIF
Bank classification	0.565	1.771
In Ouagadougou	0.115	8.693
In Bobo-Dioulasso	0.495	2.021
In total in Burkina Faso	0.145	6.900

K. A. Sory, *Banking the Missing Middle*, Research Series on Responsible Enterprise Ecosystems, https://doi.org/10.1007/978-3-032-34582-0

Table A.2 Collinearity diagnostics for the information-asymmetry model

Variable	Tolerance	VIF
Firm characteristics	0.444	2.253
Owners characteristics	0.691	1.446
Firms' relationship characteristics	0.593	1.687
Market infrastructure factors	0.598	1.672
Screening of SME applications	0.880	1.136
High transaction cost	0.543	1.843
Assess SMEs creditworthiness	0.787	1.270
Important documentation for SME requests	0.710	1.409
Impact of cost factors on SMEs loan contract terms	0.490	2.040
Importance of factors on credit allocation	0.501	1.997
Importance of decision to decline	0.833	1.201

Table A.3 Collinearity diagnostics for the demographic model

Variable	Tolerance	VIF
Position	0.842	1.188
Years of experience with SME loans	0.778	1.285
Highest education	0.887	1.127
Competencies	0.765	1.308
Emotional intelligence	0.829	1.206

Table A.4 Collinearity diagnostics for the perception model

Variable	Tolerance	VIF
Perception on SME market	0.935	1.070
Drivers of SME involvement	0.876	1.141
Common standards for SME loaning	0.828	1.208
Obstacles in lending SMEs	0.835	1.198
Opinion on information given by SMEs	0.946	1.057
Categorization of common impediments	0.905	1.105
Importance of analysis factors of SMEs	0.889	1.125

Diagnostic Figures

Figures A.1–A.4 present the normal P–P plots used to assess the regression models for geospatial relationships, information asymmetry, staff demographics, and bank perceptions of SMEs, respectively.

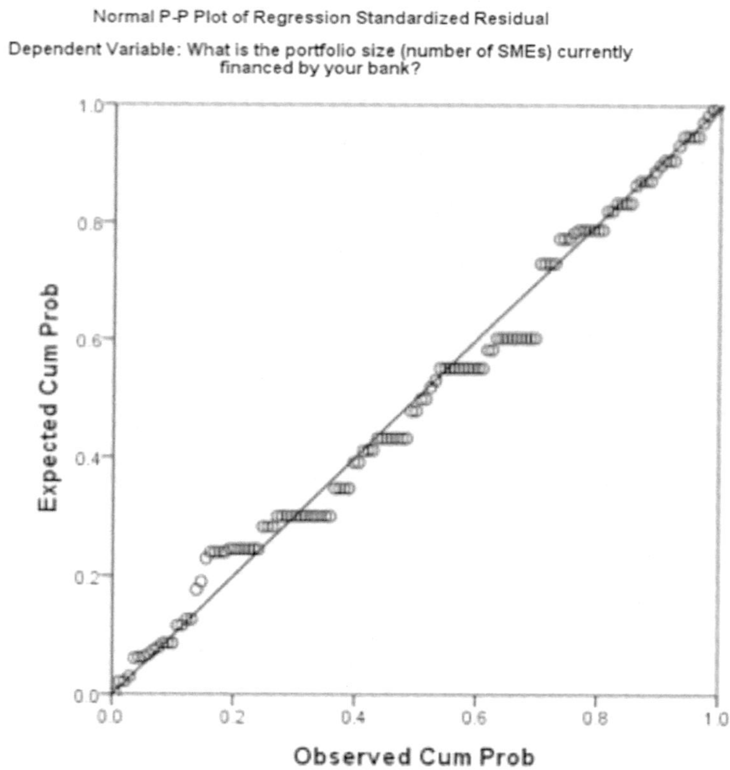

Fig. A.1 Normal P-P plot of regression for geospatial relationship variables

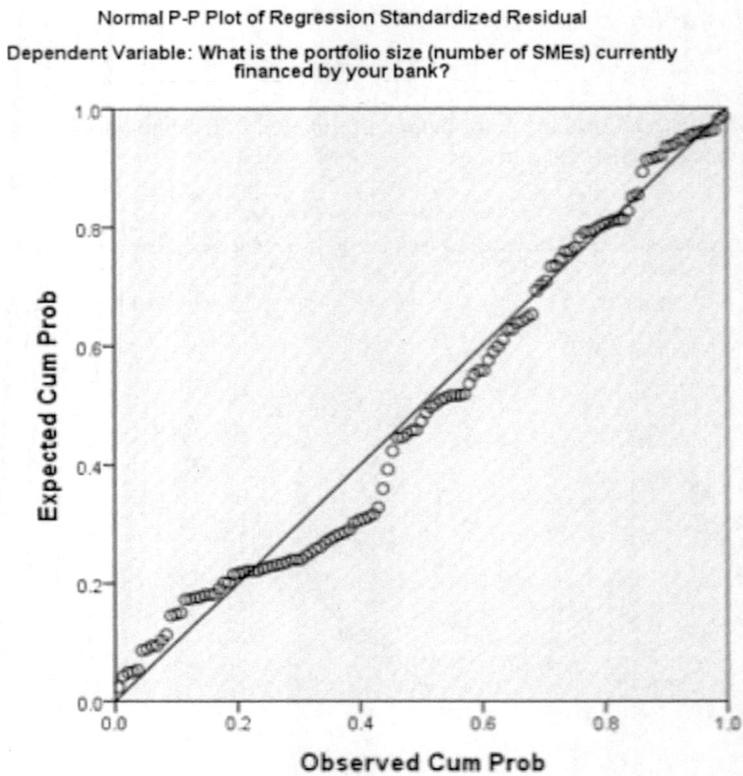

Fig. A.2 Normal P-P plot of regression for information asymmetry variables

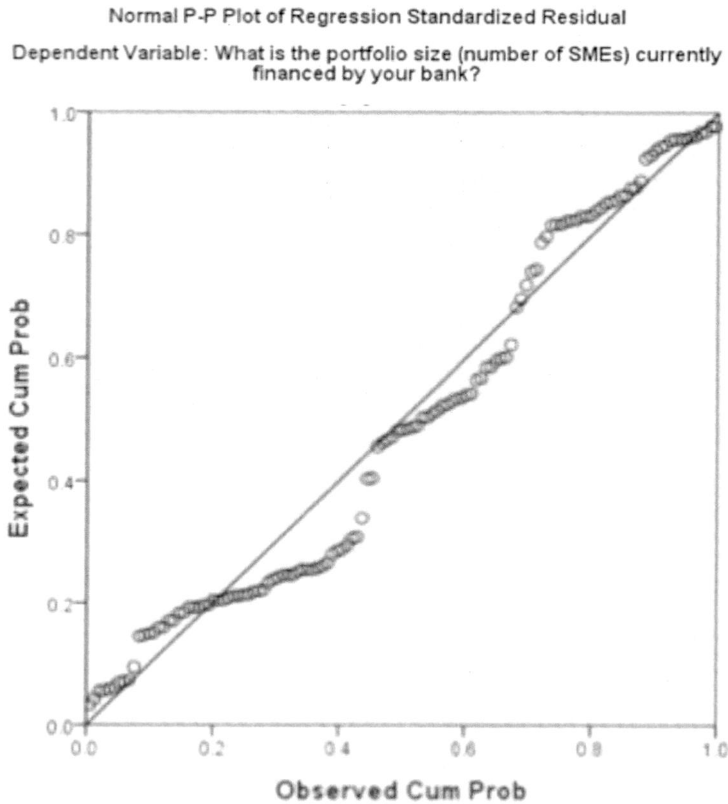

Fig. A.3 Normal P-P plot of regression for demographic variables

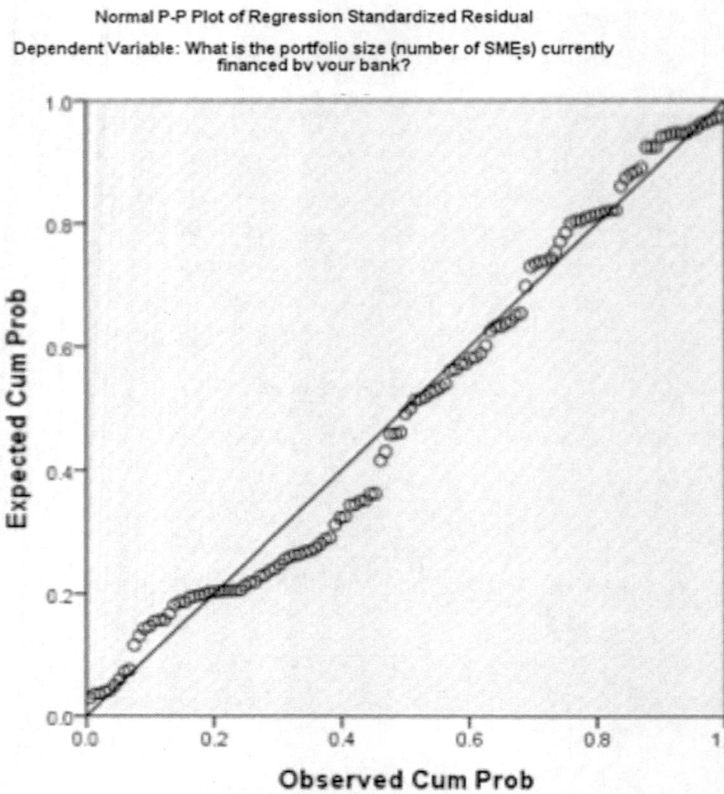

Fig. A.4 Normal P-P plot of regression for bank perception of small and medium enterprises

Appendix B: SME Product Selection Logic

Figure B.1 summarizes the product-selection logic linking SME financing needs, required information, product fit, risk controls, and expected effects.

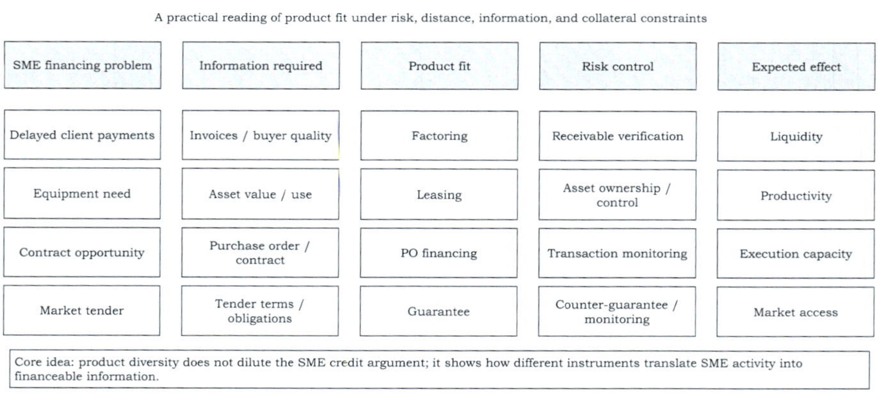

Fig. B.1 SME product selection logic under risk, distance, information, and collateral constraints. Source: Author's conceptual synthesis.

K. A. Sory, *Banking the Missing Middle*, Research Series on Responsible Enterprise Ecosystems, https://doi.org/10.1007/978-3-032-34582-0

Kolibri 360 GmbH
Ferdinand-Jühlke-Straße 7
99095 Erfurt, Deutschland
produktsicherheit@kolibri360.de